Private Lives, Public Deaths

Private Lives, Public Deaths

Antigone and the Invention of Individuality

Jonathan Strauss

FORDHAM UNIVERSITY PRESS

NEW YORK   2013

Frontispiece: Funerary stele, Attic, late fifth century B.C.E. National Archaeological Museum, Athens.

Library of Congress Cataloging-in-Publication Data

Strauss, Jonathan.
  Private lives, public deaths : Antigone and the invention of individuality / Jonathan Strauss.
    pages cm.
  Includes bibliographical references and index.
  ISBN 978-0-8232-5132-2 (cloth : alk. paper) — ISBN 978-0-8232-5133-9 (pbk. : alk. paper)
  1. Sophocles. Antigone. 2. Greek drama (Tragedy)—History and criticism. I. Title.
  PA4413.A7S78 2013
  882'.01—dc23

                                            2012049118

Printed in the United States of America

15 14 13 5 4 3 2 1

First edition

For Jeanne

CONTENTS

ACKNOWLEDGMENTS

This book would not exist without the help of many people who have engaged it at various stages of its coming into being. Mitchell Greenberg, in particular, has been an inspiration and a faithful friend for this, as for the other books that I have written. Without his persistent encouragement and fine intelligence, I might have abandoned this project long ago. Colleagues in Miami University's Department of Classics, notably Steve Nimis, Denise McCoskey, and Peter Rose, have given generously of their time and provided invaluable feedback on earlier versions, helping to orient a non-specialist in the arcana of their discipline. Piero Pucci shared important bibliographical recommendations and more general advice. Dimitris Vardoulakis, Gabriela Basterra, and an anonymous reader for Fordham University Press offered astute and detailed readings of the manuscript and provided recommendations that strengthened it significantly. Jacques De Groote, of Roger Violet in Paris, Marilyn Katz of Wesleyan University, and curators at the National Archaeological Museum of Athens helped me with information about Attic funerary monuments and iconography. Many other colleagues and friends have lent aid, insight, and advice at various crucial moments, especially Bruno Chaout, Tim Melley, Jim Creech, Emily Zakin, Elisabeth Hodges, Sven-Erik Rose, and Claire Goldstein. And I am grateful to Helen Tartar, Eric Newman, Teresa Jesionowski, and Derek Gottlieb at Fordham University Press—their intelligence, judgment, and support have made this book possible. An Assigned Research Leave from Miami University allowed me access to the resources of the Bibliothèque Nationale de France while giving me the time to concentrate and write.

In deference to nonspecialists, all untranslated Greek texts have been transliterated into roman characters, even in quotations where they originally appear in Greek characters. Transliteration leads to heated debates, but in practice I have tried to balance faithfulness to the original Greek with ease of reading.

Private Lives, Public Deaths

Introduction: Tragedy, the City, and Its Dead

Sophocles's tragedy *Antigone* represents an immense effort to imagine the origins and limits of the political state. Law sets against law in the play, while a tenuous new order is won at huge sacrifice from their confrontation. For whom the city and by what right authority over it? the chorus ponders as the protagonists struggle to impose their image of the social order, create its very fabric, and explain its legitimacy. One can think of the action as a savage, blood-soaked version of a courtroom drama, similar in that respect to the other Attic tragedies, which centered overwhelmingly on judgments, and whose oldest extant cycle, Aeschylus's *Oresteia*, culminates in the trial of Orestes and the establishment of a new justice in Athens. These are plays about the punishment of crimes, but with the peculiarity that the law finds itself as much in the dock as the criminal supposedly under its purview. Indeed, the very meaning of criminality raises problems, for even the definition of a judicable individual—what a person is and how to delimit his or her responsibility before the law—comes into question. With its arguments and trials, tragic drama condensed the turbulence of a period caught in the throes of self-invention down to a series of dialogues among a handful of characters. By its very nature, as Nicole Loraux put it, Greek tragedy contained "an opposition between two discourses, an *agōn logōn*," but one could go further and say that Greek tragedy *is* the space of such an *agōn logōn*, that it is the contestatory verbal place in which the city could take shape as a conscious self-creation.[1]

The reading of *Antigone* that makes up this book will treat it as a struggle to understand the shape, limits, and meaning of the city at one of its defining moments, a reflection on the rise of the state from the viewpoint of a privileged representative and at a time when the polis was just emerging from its birth phase. The memories of its invention lingered on, wrapped in the mysterious form of myth, while the task of justifying—of conceptualizing, rationalizing, and *legalizing*—that invention now fell to the population and its leaders. Fifth- and fourth-century Athens was, as Loraux put it, "a cultural period when all reality still found its model in the *polis*."[2] That change of outlook did not come without a cost, and the one who paid the price of this new reality was a figure who, paradoxically, did not really yet exist. The security and identity of the city depended on the mastery of the individual person, and it achieved this mastery through death both in theoretical terms (through the subjugation of private will to the general will) and in practical terms (by a soldier's really being killed in war). Similarly, in the writings of philosophers from the same period, the notional or rational was understood to subsume the material, which in turn amounted to a rejection of the particular in favor of the universal. Across key discourses, the individual was thus condemned to sublimation in a larger truth and a higher good, from which an ethics and law were derived. But something remained after the death of the individual, and that remnant was, in one form or another, a corpse. It remained as the sign of the unique and material in the person. As such, the dead body played the role of an alien force constitutionally hostile to the city, but it also served as an unconscious reminder of the city's mythical origin, the other that needed to be excluded but that could never be fully removed. The corpse was associated with the archaic order, with familial miasmas, the old gods, and the Eumenides of Aeschylus's *Oresteia*. Because of its connection to the family, it was also linked to women, who served as guardians of kinship and the past.

The corpse was thus the remnant of a person who, I have said, did not otherwise exist, and this paradox forms the crux around which all the following readings will turn. It is this aspect of the play that makes it important even now, nearly two and a half millennia after it was written. For *Antigone*, I will argue, attempted to define an individual person within a language and a cultural moment that did not have clear ideas of what such a being was or what its value could be. Those notions, insofar as they existed, derived largely from the idea of mortality, so that to a surprising degree an individual in ancient Greece was defined and given worth by his or her death. In what follows, I will try to show how Sophocles's tragedy attempts—and suggestively fails—to define that person otherwise, which is to say, through his or her life rather than through death. I will also argue that the meaning of tragedy lies in that failure, while its significance to modern readers derives, substantially, from the way in which the genre (1) nonetheless indicates a possible value of the unique individual person and (2) reveals the difficulty of recognizing that person. Accordingly, Sophocles's play remains meaningful to us now because it shows the facticity, fragility, and importance of individual subjectivity, its status not as a given but as a still unfinished project. For although much of what Sophocles was struggling to formulate has become second nature to us, I would argue that European thought has been marked by its persistent difficulty in imagining a living individual. There has been a strange resistance to the very idea of such a person, as if human thought, indeed humanity itself, formally and constitutionally negated the plenitude of its own experiences—as if at every moment we must deny not only our baser instincts and the crass profusion of animal existence, but our life itself. Even Heidegger's attempt in the mid-twentieth century to move beyond the transcendentalism of metaphysics and to embed human meaning in experience structured the individual *Dasein* around the absolute finitude of its death.[3] To the extent that this difficulty still marks our own time, what Sophocles was attempting to imagine still escapes our understanding. *Antigone* is, in this sense, a text not from the past but from our future.

One way to appreciate the work undertaken in *Antigone* is to treat it as part of a larger event by replacing it within its original historical and cultural context. Significantly, the play was written at a crucial moment not only in the history of the state but also, it seems increasingly clear, in the history of death. The two, I argue, go together. The archaeological evidence about Attic burial practices is scant, and only one major cemetery—the Cerameicus outside Athens—has been excavated using modern methods.[4] Such as it exists, however, that archaeological record attests to a link between the rise of poleis and changes in the treatment of the dead. Tracing shifts in Attic practices of inhumation, the historian Ian Morris has argued that burial patterns reflected social differences and relative status among the living. More significant, according to him, formal burial was at times restricted to a smaller percentage of the population, and this restriction reflected periods of social stress, when uncertainty about rank and the organization of the community created a need to enforce hierarchical distinctions. These periods of tension could be long, for Morris observes that "exclusion from formal burial was practised in Attica from c. 1050 to 750 and 700 B.C. to the late sixth century."[5] Conversely, in his estimation, the brief moment during the second half of the eighth century when burial spread to a larger portion of the population mirrored both a pan-Hellenic trend and the invention of the polis.[6] In other words, as the rule of the state extended from a few notables to the citizenry as a whole, so too did the privilege of inhumation.

Although this "social revolution" of the dead seems to have met with a repressive backlash among the upper classes at the end of the eighth century, when the burial group again contracted, another expansion of funerary privileges appears to have occurred abruptly around 510 B.C.E.[7] This change would have coincided almost exactly with the end of the Peisistrid tyranny, for in late 507 or early 508 B.C.E., Cleisthenes came to power, reestablished democracy, and drafted a new constitution.[8] Then, from about 500 to 430 B.C.E.—or from the end of the Persian to the beginning of the Peloponnesian wars—there is a break in the archaeological evidence.[9] Various indicators attest that this was a time of restraint in Attic burials. Tombs from before and after were generally much more ornate and costly than those remaining from the first seventy years of the fifth century. The impetus for this shift seems to have come from governing bodies in Athens, for newly enacted sumptuary laws limited the cost and ostentation of private funerals and burials, which were increasingly replaced by public memorials, such as the *epitaphioi logoi* and the Demosian Sema.[10] Overall, the evidence suggests that the period beginning with Cleisthenes's reforms represents a broadening of funerary practices to a larger segment of the population and their increasingly political, rather than familial nature. Now, Aeschylus's birth is roughly contemporary with Cleisthenes's rise to power, and so the tragedies were produced during a span of time marked by a flowering of both political and funerary democracy.[11] And as the rituals of death changed in nature and meaning, they would have come to symbolize the political structure of the new city.

Indeed, they would have come to define the limits of the city itself, as another, concomitant development suggests, for the deceased were now excluded from the spaces inhabited by their survivors. The years up until about 700 B.C.E. saw a gradual movement to isolate the adult dead into areas specifically set apart for them, but these zones were often situated within the settlements themselves. Children—and in some cases women killed in childbirth—were commonly buried among or even below houses.[12]

Around the end of the eighth century, however, this tolerance for the dead within the precincts of the living seems to have disappeared, and burials were pushed outside the limits of the town. In Thorikos, adults were still being inhumed "within a few metres" of dwellings, but otherwise the general trend at this point was toward an "almost complete cessation of burial within or between areas of settlement."[13] If, by Morris's account, "classical notions of the impurity of the dead seem to have been a late development," they appear, nonetheless, to have been decisively adopted by the turn of the seventh century.[14] This means not only that the advent of the polis dates from roughly the same moment as the brief, original expansion of the formal burial group in Attica, but also that it coincides with the removal of the dead from within city limits. As the city became a political entity, in other words, it simultaneously defined itself physically as a space free from graves.

This moment predated the birth of Aeschylus by about two hundred years, but during his youth he would have witnessed a renewed democratization of formal inhumations and a return, therefore, to the practices that accompanied the creation of the city-state. It is difficult to determine if that return brought with it a memory of the old moment when the corpse was chased away and the polis began or what associations this second revolution of the dead would have had for those who lived through it and its aftermath. But whether they recall that distant past or—what is more likely—reach down to some pre-original impulse connecting the two, the tragedies strongly argue for a link between the birth of the city and the expulsion of the dead, for they stage the struggle to overcome a more archaic, prepolitical social order, which was intimately connected to the deceased. They seem to bear witness to this memory, to betray a fascination with it, to be haunted by its guilt. It may have been over two centuries since adults were buried within a few steps of the familial house or children inhumed beneath its floor, but their presence lingered in the family gods and in what Hegel called the "ironic" faithfulness of women to individual memories. In this sense, the walls that ringed the city held off not only the armed assaults of other states, they also delimited the boundaries of the living and the dead. They stood, moreover, as an ongoing memorial to that originary political act: the expulsion of the corpse.[15]

Antigone, it is often argued, condenses a broad historical situation into an intense, personal confrontation, but this notion of a "personal confrontation" can be misleading. The ancient Greeks seem to have been fundamentally different from us, and by modern standards they were also different from themselves—or, indeed, selfless. One's "self-identity is no more an immediate given than the unity of the ego," Jacques Brunschwig has observed. "The relation to oneself [*l'être pour soi*] has its own history."[16] The return to the Greeks is a return, in this sense, to the earliest moments of that history, to the time when the "I" was emerging from prehistory into the objectivity and collectivity of writing. Hermann Fränkel has argued that in the Homeric period, individuals lacked any reflexive awareness of their own being as a finite, unified entity and experienced their existence instead as an unbounded field of forces, similar, in that regard, to the "living multiples" that Alain Badiou sees as the precursors and ground of contemporary subjective consistency.[17] In an attempt to comprehend the conceptual gap that separates the ancient experience of identity from more modern theorizations and practices of selfhood, scholars have recently focused on issues of subjectivity and self-consciousness in Greek thought. The general opinion, as outlined by Jean-Pierre Vernant, agrees that the founding dictum of modern subjectivity, Descartes's "*cogito ergo sum*, 'I think therefore I am,' has no meaning for a Greek."[18] For James Redfield, the epic hero "is in his own eyes nothing but the mirror that others hold up to him," while Brunschwig understands that "mirroring" to extend as far as the works and acts of individuals, such that one can "follow through Greek thought the traces of a sort of paradoxical *cogito* that could be formulated in the following terms: I see myself (in my works or in some other projection of myself . . .), therefore I am. I am where I see myself: I *am* that projection of myself that I see."[19] Taking this objectification to mean an embeddedness in the external world, Gilbert Romeyer Dherbey argues that while "divine thought thinks of the self alone, human thought thinks of oneself and things, or rather of oneself in relation to things. The soul is not what it will be in Descartes, a *mens pura et abstracta*, or even in Plotinus, where it is revealed by 'removing everything.'"[20] In Martin Heidegger's words, "Among the Greeks there were no personalities yet."[21] But if the notion and experience of subjectivity would have been utterly foreign to the ancient Greeks, the issue of intelligible human individuality was nonetheless of primary importance to their tragedians and to the Sophocles of *Antigone* in particular. In the very way that it confronts different models of personhood along the mobile lines of conflict that cross through its characters as much as between them, his play as a whole embodies something similar to the "open field" of possibilities and forces that Fränkel describes. In this respect, the play itself is a person, open to the powerful stresses of an identity under construction. It is, I will argue, a powerful, if groping and incomplete, act of subjectification, written against the backdrop of fundamental changes in the significance of death.

Reading *Antigone* from this perspective is an exploration of the historical and aesthetic facticity of the individual subject and its dynamic, confrontational relation to the city.[22] But it is also an engagement, I have said, with issues of ongoing importance to us now. I will try to show in theoretical terms why the play is still significant, but the timeliness of Sophocles's drama is also attested by the number and quality of readings that have recently been devoted to it. Indeed, given this history of criticism, it may seem strange to add yet another analysis, but what I am undertaking in the following pages is fundamentally different from previous approaches, although, in many cases, it builds directly on them. I focus on certain key points in the play and its context, especially the individual and its relation to the ideas of death and life, arguing that Sophocles's tragedy condenses a traumatic moment in the elaboration of individual self-identity. Now, many recent treatments of *Antigone*, and some of the most interesting, take the category of the individual as strangely unproblematic or uncritically impose anachronistic models on it. This is notably the case in George Steiner's reading of the relation between death and subjectivity, but the problem affects many other writers as well, both in their handling of the play itself and in their treatments of subsequent philosophical analyses.[23] Some of the most important of these philosophical approaches—especially Hegel's and Herman Fränkel's—treat individuation as a product of human mortality, as does Jacques Lacan, in his own, highly influential psychoanalytic reading of *Antigone*. They are not entirely wrong, and indeed, as we shall see, the classical Greek notion of the person was born out of death. But my reading seeks to identify the ways in which Sophocles's play stages an attempt to imagine the subject otherwise and to ground it in the plenitude and complexity of living experience. Tragedy, I will argue, is a labor not *of* but *against* death, it is the expression of a longing for a meaningful individual life, and it is the attempt to understand what that life would be.

I thus describe ideas and attitudes that were in flux, emerging and developing over an extended period. These ideas and attitudes often originated as unconscious motivations or aspirations that only subsequently reached conscious or clearer expression. Indeed, my whole argument about tragedy understands it as an attempt to bring such unconscious or poorly formulated concerns into expression, so I will often frame the "living individual" more as an identifiable absence than as a positive entity. In this respect, *Antigone* participates in and helps shape a larger history. At first, I will argue, the individual is recognized only in death, but even there only problematically, since he disappears into the abstractions of death or the state. Then, he emerges somewhat more clearly, in the form, for instance, of a legally responsible individual, accountable for his own acts rather than for those of his ancestors. And then, one finds intimations that this formation of individuality omits something—something like life—without its being possible to articulate what that missing element is. These steps overlap and include much back- and sidetracking, but they delineate a general history of the individual in this particular period. Insofar as an individual and life can exist not only as the ability to recognize and articulate them but also as the inarticulate desire for their existence, tragedy represents a crucial moment in their invention. And it should not be surprising that the language of emotions plays such an important role in that invention, for these new concepts, these new entities, express themselves initially more through longing than through reason. This is, after all, the language of tragedy.

In the wake of Luce Irigaray's 1974 *Speculum of the Other Woman*, Sophocles's *Antigone* became the subject of vigorous and sustained analysis among feminist and gender theorists, and this work has continued up into the present. Philosophers such as Judith Butler, Tina Chanter, and Kelly Oliver have devoted important studies to the play, and in almost all cases, these readings pass through Hegel—as do Derrida's and many others.[24] Even Lacan, who dismisses the value of Hegel's work on *Antigone*, ends up reproducing its most significant and original moves.[25] This is so true that in order to engage Sophocles within our contemporary context, one cannot avoid reading him through Hegel, but these recents texts generally stop *at* Hegel, as if his were the definitive—indeed, the original—version of the play. At times, it is true, some of these authors, such as Kelly Oliver and Patricia Mills, support their critiques of Hegel by comparing his interpretations with Sophocles's original text, thereby gesturing, if only cautiously, to an earlier history.[26] Classicists, however, are often at a loss to find a transhistorical meaning in *Antigone*, and Sarah Pomeroy, for one, cautions against just such sorts of moves.[27] Others have tried to incorporate modern theoretical approaches into their work. Simon Goldhill has been exemplary, in this respect, advancing interpretations of tragedies such as the *Oresteia* that build on poststructuralist insights.[28] Rush Rehm uses Freud and Georges Bataille, whereas Piero Pucci, in his reading of *Oedipus Rex*, draws on deconstruction.[29] For my own part, I have attempted to link the pre-Hegelian readings of *Antigone* with the post-Hegelian ones in order to bring some of the philosophical work done recently on the play to bear on its original cultural context. I have wanted to place these contemporary approaches to the text by nonclassicists in dialogue with the issues and conflicts roiling this exceptional moment in Western—indeed, human—history. This book thus represents an attempt to read backwards, through Hegel and readings of Hegel, to the historical, political, and epistemological world that gave birth to this particular tragedy, a world that is, I argue, both refracted and invented in it. And this *is* an important moment: Categories of human experience such as life, death, individual identity, and love are all in painful but exciting crisis at this time, I argue, and those crises are staged in tragedies such as *Antigone*. My approach, which seeks to work through rather than simply avoid anachronism, may be met with skepticism by some classicists. I hope that they will instead consider some of the interpretive advantages that this study offers and that they will view it as an access to new fields that might enrich their own work.

The value of Hegel's claims will be "tested" against the work of the Hellenists, and their work will, in turn, be given depth and continued urgency by Hegel and his followers. For the sake of economy and out of respect for readers from other disciplines, I have largely relied on Vernant and Loraux to represent classical studies in the body of the text. Those who would like more detail, and classicists in particular, are encouraged to consult the endnotes. Vernant and Loraux will prove to be particularly helpful not merely because of their stature within their field—especially in relation to the questions of individuality that will concern us here—but also because, without mentioning Hegel directly, many of their most striking insights bear close resemblance to ideas already formulated more abtractly in Hegel's *Phenomenology of Spirit*.[30] The dialogue between these two disciplines, in other words, already seems to have started, and often all that remains is to make it more explicit. Vernant offered the seductive narrative of a passage from myth to law in the tragedies, a historical process from which one can deduce the emergence of one sort of subjectivity from another. But Hegel presented another, somewhat more complex scenario, in which two standards, myth and law (or family and city), are equally valid and yield, in their mutual exhaustion, to a deeper insight: that neither position is sufficient and that the truth lies, instead, in their communality, which he called the ethical as such. By recognizing the validity of both Vernant's and Hegel's incompatible positions, one is forced to view the tragedy of *Antigone* not as a historical event but as an ahistorical or protohistorical one. *Antigone*, that is to say, is not a stage that is passed through. And similarly, the advent of the individual subject is not a finished process or trauma, but an ongoing labor. The play is, therefore, not an event *in* history, but the event *of* history: of the city, the subject, and meaningful time themselves, their becoming possible.[31] Heidegger wrote, "The *polis* is the site of history."[32] One could add: Tragedy is the site of the polis.

Before turning to the play itself, I should take a moment to preview the principal documents that I will be working with, both Hegel's and Sophocles's, since each forms part of a larger textual network with its own complicated history. As he hurried to meet a publisher's deadline for finishing the *Phenomenology of Spirit*, Hegel could see and hear the world changing around him, for Napoleon's armies had surrounded and begun bombarding Jena, where the philosopher was living.[33] On October 13, 1806, the last day for him to send the manuscript, French troops entered the city. Hegel was torn between anxieties about the future of his book and enthusiasm about the world-historical events that seemed to have sprung from its pages to engulf him. "I saw the Emperor—this world-soul—riding out of the city on reconnaissance," he wrote in a letter to a friend. "It is indeed a wonderful sensation to see such an individual, who, concentrated here at a single point, astride a horse, reaches out over the world and masters it."[34] And in the preface to the *Phenomenology*, he reflected that "it is not difficult to see that ours is a birth-time and a period of transition to a new period. Spirit has broken with the world it has hitherto inhabited and imagined, and is of a mind to submerge it in the past, and in the labour of its own transformation."[35] An old world was disappearing, re-created in the ferment of war that encircled his city. He was writing as fast as his pen would move, apparently more frightened of his publisher than of the French armies. And in the document that he was drafting, his history of thinking matter, a text so abstract that scarcely a name or precise example troubles its eternal introspection, he devoted a lengthy passage to the analysis of a single play, using it to summarize an entire epoch. On two occasions he even cited it, a rare, perhaps unique event in the text. This is his *Antigone*. The drama of a besieged city that rises up again in a besieged city.

Hegel's analyses warrant attention because among all the readings of *Antigone* they develop the issues of conflicting social orders, personhood, and gender in greatest depth—although that depth is created, in large part, by the philosophical materials in which they are buried. They are also the only readings of the tragedy to situate it within a general world-historical program of, well, Hegelian proportions and to understand it, within that context, as the supreme expression of a crucial cultural moment. One may disagree with Hegel's interpretation, but one must at least give him credit for taking the play seriously—perhaps too seriously, but that can only be established by reading and refuting his interpretation. Now, it is quite possible that to understand Hegel's take on *Antigone* is to understand the history of subjectivity not so much in ancient Greece as in post-Enlightenment Europe, but to the extent that we are the inheritors of that Europe and to the extent that we remain Hegelian (and that would include anti- or post-Hegelian), such an understanding represents both an important self-perception and the attempt to overcome its constraints. The central, the crucial, the defining limits of that self-perception are probably those of the self itself, the fact that we can even talk of self-perception as such.[36] More, perhaps, than the Marxist distinctions between economic base forces and their secondary manifestations in "superstructure," more than the advance of Enlightenment reason or other modern categories of experience and knowledge, it is the problem of subjectivity that has forced contemporary European cultures to take stock of themselves as historical, delimited entities, since the apperceptive individual is not merely the essential unit of their societies but also the model for their organization.[37]

The French Revolution, in particular, inaugurated a new and characteristically modern form of statehood not so much in its institutions or even theories as in its determination to create a legitimate means for the state to construct itself, that is, to express itself purely to itself in a mode of its own autonomous choosing. The successive constituent assemblies, which convened popularly elected representatives to establish the appropriate procedures of self-representation for the nation, bear witness to the circular structure—and ambitions—of this new, explicitly self-positing entity.

Among its consequences, this reflexivity makes the self capable of identifying others as others in a way that could not previously have occurred, for with self-perceptive subjectivity comes an other specific to it, and the two parties are bound together in the very distance of their exile from each other. Among these others are the Greeks themselves, who did not have a self as post-Cartesian Europeans would understand it. The attempt to reconstruct the experience of those ancients in their difference from us is itself, in other words, a consequence of post-Cartesian subjectivity. The preeminent guide to that subjectivity is Hegel.[38] He is, consequently, key not only to understanding how the Greeks were different from us but also to understanding why that difference matters to us. And that, rather than the unparalleled depth or scope of his interpretations, is the principal reason one should take his analysis of *Antigone* so seriously.

Before setting into our reading of *Antigone*, it will be useful to survey the larger argument that I will be advancing in the following pages. As has been remarked by Hegel, Vernant, and others, *Antigone* stages a tension between two different formulations of individuality, one more archaic and mythical, the other more modern and political. The following chapter ("Two Orders of Individuality") shows how that basic antinomy simplifies tensions in the play, which themselves expressed a cultural moment in which the notion of individuality—and the means for conceiving it—were elusive and often contradictory. Beginning with a description of the civic importance of tragedies that includes a reading of Aeschylus's *Eumenides*, the chapter situates Hegel's readings of *Antigone* within that historical context and then focuses on Sophocles's play itself.

In Chapter 2, "The Citizen." I look at the figure of the citizen, who was one of the key models for attributing value to an individual in fifth-century Athens. The conceptual emergence of the citizen was specific to the city celebrated—and constructed—in the tragedies, and it marked a break with older, more incoherent forms of individuality based on myth and family. But the value of the citizen as individual was, paradoxically, his nonindividuality, which was expressed through his death in service to the city. My discussion of this point contextualizes *Antigone* through readings of Hegel, Plato's *Republic*, Aristotle's *Rhetoric*, and the *epitaphioi logoi*, or public eulogies held annually in Athens for soldiers fallen in battle. Despite their overwhelmingly negative tone, the latter texts, in particular, indicated a vague but stillborn notion of a valuable individual life.

The valuable living individual did not exist in clear conceptual terms within the historical context in which *Antigone* was written, but he nonetheless made his possibility felt as an absence. This absence revealed itself as an object of desire and as sign of a loss. Although subsequent sections will discuss desire, Chapter 3, "Loss Embodied," focuses on the sign of loss and sees in the corpse an important figure for conceptualizing a missing individual. Polyneices's dead body, which plays a central role in *Antigone*, is thus read as an instrument for understanding and appreciating the specificities and contingencies of individual life. This is an inherently frustrating attempt, since the corpse itself is defined by the lack of life. I will concentrate here on Hegel's readings of burial rites in *Antigone*, since he offers the richest and most far-reaching conceptualizations of death in the play.

As Chapter 3 showed, the dead body represented both the value of the individual and an indeterminate state between life and death. As such, I will argue in Chapter 4, "States of Exclusion," it was excluded from the city and echoed other categories that did not fit comfortably into the conceptual structures of the state: the criminal, the ostracized, the abject. The paradox of these elements is that although they must be excluded from the polis they are also necessary to its identity and cannot therefore be eradicated from it. In this respect, the corpse represents an aporia at the heart of the city and a reminder of its mysterious origins. Through her allegiance to the body of her dead brother, Antigone thus grapples with the original paradox of the state while indicating the possibility for a different but still gendered notion of the political—one based on feminine love. The readings in this section draw on several texts by Plato, including *Alcibiades I*, *Parmenides*, *Crito*, and the *Laws*.

By examining both the notion of *philia* in fifth-century Greece and Antigone's fascination with her own death, I am able in Chapter 5, "Inventing Life," to refine our understanding of the ways in which Sophocles's play struggles to identify the value of a living individual. The key to this value, hinted at but never entirely expressed in *Antigone*, would lie in the affection felt for a person in his or her uniqueness. Desire—and especially feminine desire—would thus express that value, but within the play the importance of interpersonal desire can be validated only through the death of the heroine herself. Once again, the significance of an individual life can be asserted only through its extinction. My reading contextualizes Sophocles's play through reference to Aeschylus's *Seven against*

Thebes and Euripides's *Suppliant Women*. It also includes an extended analysis of Hegel's notion of war in relation to tragic representations of the city.

In respect to the individual, the Greek culture that emerges from these readings is thus strangely death-loving, and the tragedy of the period would consist in its failed attempt to value love when it is oriented toward a living individual. Although Chapter 5 identified the importance of a repressed erotic desire in *Antigone*, Chapter 6, "Mourning, Loving, Longing," argues that a similar desire played a crucial role in the conceptualization of the city's relation to the individual in fifth- and fourth-century Athens. To elaborate on this, I will draw on passages from Plato's *Republic*, the Oedipus myth, and a reading of a fourth-century funerary stele from the Cerameicus cemetery. This is placed in a larger historical perspective through comparisons with the story of Alcyone and Ceyx from Ovid's *Metamorphoses*.

The book concludes by arguing for the continuing importance of *Antigone* and by reading it in relation to twentieth- and twenty-first-century theorists such as Jacques Lacan, Luce Irigaray, Tina Chanter, and Lisa Walsh. Tragedy, according to Hegel and Lacan, is the impossibility for the self to recognize itself as anything other than dead. But in *Antigone*, we nonetheless see an attempt to affirm the value of female desire in identifying living individuals.

The analysis of *Antigone* undertaken in Chapter 7, "Exit Tragedy," shifts attention from the pair Creon-Antigone, which is traditionally placed at the center of the play, to the couple formed by Haemon and Antigone. While Creon's rhetoric of statehood asserts that women are interchangeable, Haemon, through his behavior, treats Antigone as irreplaceable, thus consciously and directly contradicting his father. By choosing a wife and remaining faithful to that choice, he rejects Creon's subordination of individual inclination to the larger identity politics of the city. He also differs, in this respect, from Antigone herself. Within the economy of the play, then, Haemon chooses Antigone because of who she is, and in that sense he individuates her. At the same time, he chooses her because of who *he* is, and thus his choice also individuates him. He is consequently the character who indicates most powerfully the possibility of creating a living individual through interpersonal choice, through an erotics and philia of reciprocal self-identification.

As a reference in those moments when dates or narrative structures start to blur, two appendices follow the body of the text. One offers a chronological outline of relevant events occurring in ancient Greece during and around the fifth century, and the other summarizes the three extant plays that Sophocles devoted to Antigone's family.

Two Orders of Individuality

Fifth-century Greek tragedies were not merely entertainments. For the playwrights and their audiences, these dramas were important civic events. Christian Meier has gone so far as to argue that Greek democracy was dependent on these plays, in part because they filled the role of a state apparatus that was otherwise missing in classical Athens and other cities.[1] His claim is not as extravagant as it might seem. Tragedy's political function is evidenced by the organization of the festival of Dionysos itself, which mixed displays of *imperium*, such as the delivery of tribute money from subjugated states, with the dramatic contests themselves.[2] At the center of these contests, the dramaturge's creations straddled both worlds, with political issues flowing back and forth between the stage and the state, as when Sophocles took up Pericles's building policies in his *Antigone* or Demosthenes approvingly quoted Creon's speech on the polis in one of his own orations.[3] Beyond his activities as playwright, Sophocles held important public offices, serving as treasurer of the Delian confederacy in 443–442 B.C.E. and *strategos* in 441.[4] But the relations between city and stage functioned on a deeper, more complex level as well, which I will examine over the course of the following chapters. Meier has pointed to this other connection by describing tragedy as a confrontation between myth and rationality that bound citizens together.[5] As an inherently rational structure, according to him, the political system of isonomy was concerned not only with issues of justice and injustice but also with the irrational chaos from which the state had emerged.[6] Tragedies, we shall see, played on this double concern, staging the origins of justice and the emergence of the polis. In this way they offered a justification of the city by demonstrating the justice of its laws—or the justice of its justice—and for that reason more than any other, I would argue, they were treated not as diversions but as civic responsibilities. To attend their performances, judge them, and award an annual prize to the best was to ponder the meaning of the city and to rededicate oneself publicly to its cause.

At the same time, those performances and the tragedies themselves included a substantial and necessary element of mystery, not simply because they evolved historically from older, ritualistic practices whose divine and incantatory elements never entirely vanished, but also because the attempt to justify justice itself must reach back to some nonjudicial, nonpolitical, and indeed irrational substrate that was inexplicable within the norms of the state. Heidegger made a similar observation about the inception of history as it is memorialized in *Antigone* when he wrote that "the genuineness and greatness of historical knowing lie in understanding the character of this inception as a mystery."[7] Tragedies were, in this sense, an endless attempt to assimilate the strangeness of the city's origins, the arbitrariness of its legal foundations, and the relativity of its meaning. This attempt was endless because the origin to be assimilated was constitutionally alien to the city, and so in practice the function of tragic art lay somewhere between working through and melancholia: It entailed the process of incorporating and making sense of an original loss, which was, at the same time, memorialized by the continuing existence of the city itself and perpetuated in the interminable mourning represented by the tragedies themselves.

Aeschylus's *Oresteia* represents these relations between the city, its justice, and its alien origins especially forcefully, and for that reason it deserves some scrutiny. First produced in 458 B.C.E., the *Oresteia* is the earliest of the tragic trilogies that have been handed down more or less intact to the present, and it expresses concerns about the origins of the civic order with a particular directness. The action of the final play, *Eumenides*, centers on the passage from one system of justice to another and culminates in the representation of what it imagines to be the first jury trial.[8] Pursued by the Erinyes, or Furies, for the murder of his mother, Orestes seeks refuge in Delphi at the oracle of Apollo, who originally commanded him to kill Clytemnestra and promised to protect him in the aftermath. The god of light then whisks his charge off to Athens, where he asks his sister Athena, the patron goddess of the city, to adjudicate the dispute between the Erinyes, who demand that justice be served by Orestes's death, and the killer himself, who acknowledges that he has committed the deed but argues that he is innocent of the crime. Athena agrees to preside over the case, appoints a jury, and instructs the opponents to call witnesses and lay out their positions. The Erinyes assert that Orestes has killed his own kin and must be held to account. Were such a crime to go unpunished, they contend, order would give way to anarchy. "Now is the end of all things wrought by new ordinances," they predict, "if the wrongful cause of this slayer of his mother is to triumph. Straightway will his deed reconcile all men to licence" (ll. 490–95).[9] In constrast, Orestes's argument is threefold: He has not so much murdered his mother as avenged his father, whom Clytemnestra had earlier killed; he was acting under the orders of a god; and he has undergone the necessary purification rites for crimes of blood. With Athena casting the tie-breaking ballot in favor of the defendant, Orestes is declared innocent— but the play is only three-quarters finished at this point, and in the long remaining section, Athena persuades the embittered Erinyes not to turn their anger toward Athens but to become instead its honored guardians. This final, drawn-out resolution is much more than a coda to the main action of the play, and for contemporary audiences it was probably more important than the mythic elements that precede it, for it represents the reconciliation between two apparently incompatible but equally legitimate forms of justice. The play itself is explicit about what is at stake in the events it describes. Athena insists repeatedly on the originary status of the trial over which she presides, observing that it is "the first trial ever held for bloodshed" (l. 682)[10] and that in holding it she has chosen to "stablish . . . a tribunal to endure for all time" (ll. 483–84).[11] The Furies themselves also recognize the foundational importance of the event, as when they speak of the catastrophes that might be unleashed by the "new ordinances (*neōn thesmiōn*)" (ll. 490–91).[12] What is on trial, then, is not so much Orestes as the new system of justice that Athena has devised, and the final quarter of the play thus depicts the reconciliation of that system with the principles of vengeance that had earlier prevailed: It is the legitimation of the new through the acquiescence of the old. The rights and power of the Furies are not denied or cast from the city but are, instead, integrated into it. Under the name of the Eumenides—"the benevolent goddesses" whom the Furies have agreed to become—an archaic justice is incorporated into the new, but that incorporation remains an uneasy one, as subsequent tragedies will make clear. For that reason, it is worth tracing some of the distinctions between the two orders that confront each other in this play.

A central issue in dispute is the definition of kinship, or the nature and limits of the family. Twice in the play, the Furies dismiss Orestes's argument that Clytemnestra was also guilty of murdering her own kin, in the person of Agamemnon, on the grounds that husband and wife do not share the same blood (ll. 212 and 605). Since they are not blood-relations, according to the dark goddesses, the law of vengeance that governs crimes within families does not apply to spouses. Apollo counters their argument on two heads. First, according to him, the bond of marriage is at least as strong as those of kinship because it is underwritten by the guarantees (*pistōmata*) of Zeus and Hera (ll. 213–14). For this reason the wedding contract is even "mightier than an oath [*orkou 'sti meizōn*] and Justice is its guardian" (ll. 217–18).¹³ Apollo's notion of justice (*dikē*) is thus established not on the basis of procreation and inheritance but through a divine guarantee that gives force to the marriage vows. The latter differ from blood ties, more-over, in that they are voluntary, for both parties to the marriage must, at least formally, give their consent. The relations of blood, in contrast, are involuntary, for one cannot choose the persons to whom one is sibling, child, or even parent. Although in dissimulated form, a vague notion of subjective agency thus divides the newer law from the archaic in this discus-sion of kinship, and the same theme is picked up elsewhere in the play, as when Orestes accepts that he has killed his mother but objects that he is not guilty of a crime. "I slew her," he acknowledges before the court. "Of this I make no denial" (l. 588).¹⁴ But even in recognizing his act, he adduces mitigating circumstances to argue that his matricide was not a crime, since in committing it he was only obeying the command of Apollo. The Furies, for their part, had already rejected this argument, asking Athena, "Where is there a spur so keen as to compel to murder of a mother?" (l. 427).¹⁵ For Orestes, crime is determined, at least in part, by intention. For the Furies, however, there can be no excuses, and the deed alone suffices to condemn Orestes, since it stands with a certain irrevocable criminal objectivity: By simply having occurred, the act attests to some sort of guilt, regardless of the intentions or circumstances of its perpetrator. The Furies bear witness, in this sense, not only to crimes but also to certain inflexible notions of being and time in relation to justice: One can never retract from an event the fact of its having happened, and this ontological insistence demands some symmetrical punishment in the future. It is this passage from the ontological permanence of the act's having occurred to the requirement of legal retribution that Apollo and the play as a whole put into question, and the rule of ethics and justice is thus separated from the laws of being.

In pitting its protagonists against each other on the issue of free will, however, Aeschylus's play does not merely stage some arbitrary fantasy about the origins of justice or the pure invention of its author's imagination. Instead, it reaches back into an earlier and not entirely finished period in which the notion of subjective will had not been clearly defined and could not, therefore, be used as a measure of guilt. As Vernant put it, "As is well known, in ancient Greece there was no true vocabulary to cover willing [*vouloir*]."[16] The pronouncement is a little stark. Aristotle devoted an entire book of the *Nicomachean Ethics* to a discussion of voluntary and involuntary acts, and even in *Eumenides*, the Furies themselves acknowledge the importance of freedom from restraint in just behavior, as when they assert that "whoso of his own free will and without constraint is righteous [*ekōn d'anagkas ater dikaiosōn*], he shall not fail of happiness" (ll. 550–51).[17] For the classical period and after, the validity of Vernant's assessment depends on how one interprets his use of the word "true [*véritable*]," but for the archaic era there is little need for such hesitations and qualifications. As James Redfield has observed,

> In certain cases, Homer's language lacks equivalents to express a good
> number of ethical terms that are essential to us: "duty," "conscience," "sin,"
> "temptation," "will." The concept of "virtue" seems to be entirely absent:
> the *arete* of Homer, widely but mistakenly translated as "virtue," does not
> express conformity with some moral law but instead the quality of a certain
> kind of man . . . who dominates others by his speech and acts. . . . Good
> will does not suffice: people are judged on the evidence based on what Arthur
> Adkins has called a "results ethic." While our stories deal with conflicts
> between vice and virtue, Homer's deal with the confrontation between
> strong and weak.[18]

The language of moral responsibility is thus absent, according to Redfield, from the Homeric world and with it, then, all of those psychological states that would separate accidentality from intention or incident from crime, such that the criminal, like the hero, is the one who did the deed regardless of his desires. Similarly, Marie Delcourt remarks that in the archaic mythopoetic tradition that provided the materials for Sophocles's *Oedipus Rex*, "it is not criminal intention but the fact of the murder that pollutes" and that, as a consequence, even if the death of Oedipus's father, Laius, had been an accident, its status as a crime would have been unchanged.[19] Still, as we shall see later, it is precisely this notion of intentionality that the heroes and heroines of Sophocles's Theban cycle will call upon to declare their innocence, marking and remarking a turning point in the notions of individuality and criminality. And so, the Furies, in their intransigent morality, represent an archaic justice that corresponds to an earlier notion of subjective responsibility, a responsibility that is, in turn, attested to in the Homeric texts and in the mythopoetic foundations of the legends about the Labdacids. They personify, in this sense, older concepts of justice and selfhood that still bear on Athens in the classical period, that linger in its stagings of the foundational myths of the city, and that continue to generate enough anxiousness that they must be worked through and exorcised in the civic rituals of the Dionysia. The second argument that Apollo adduces to disculpate Orestes of matricide reveals just as much about the forces bearing on the city and the law as the theories of intentionality marshaled by the defense, but it is much stranger, at least to modern ears. Matricide, according to the god, is not a crime against the family, because mothers and their children are not related by blood. If Orestes's doubts about his blood-kinship to his mother fill the Furies with indignation (ll. 606–7), they are left literally speechless by Apollo's explanation of why mother and offspring are, despite appearances, unrelated. "The mother of what is called her child is not its parent," he contends, "but only the nurse of the newly implanted germ" (ll. 658–59).[20] Theories about sexual generation aroused intense debate in ancient Greece, and this particular opinion enjoyed widespread currency, appearing in other tragedies and in the works of both Plato and Aristotle.[21] Unlike the argument about the relative strengths of matrimonial and filial bonds, what is at stake here is not the value of blood relations, since Apollo recognizes one between fathers and their children. In question, instead, are the role of women in the family and their ability to create relations. All blood-kinship, according to the god, must pass through the father, and so women can only be related to existing or previous generations, never to future ones. They are, in this respect, relegated to the past, of which they, like the Furies, will become guardians. And if Athena casts the deciding vote in favor of Orestes, it is not, according to her, so much because she is convinced by the logic of the arguments as from her inherent sympathy for all that is masculine. "This my vote," she proclaims; "I shall add to Orestes' side. For mother have I none that gave me birth, and in all things, save wedlock, I am for the male with all my soul, and am entirely on the father's side" (ll. 735–38).[22] The final judgment is not, therefore, merely against the Furies; it is also against women, who in that same gesture are consigned to a past for which they become figures.[23] Aeschylus's *Eumenides* thus attests to several significant issues in the tragic vision of the state: the origins of the city as a legal entity, the uneasy reconciliation between two forms of justice, the separation between an old order and a new one, the assimilation of the archaic with the female, and the retention of the superseded laws in the netherworld. These issues, moreover, correspond to transformations in the experience of subjectivity as attested to by other documents and traditions, such as the Homeric texts and the mythopoetic materials underlying Sophocles's Theban cycle.

The tragedies of fifth-century Athens are, as I have said, a working-through of these issues, a process that Vernant has described as an "effort to elaborate [*travail d'élaboration*]," thereby emphasizing the futurity of the labor undertaken by the dramas.[24] In formulating the situation in these terms, he put his finger on what is perhaps the fundamental anxiety of tragedy and its true, ongoing, but always dissimulated, crisis: To the extent that it must be ritualistically confirmed in tragedy, the state does not yet legitimately exist, and so its public performances are not merely a reminder of a repressed origin, but also, and more importantly, the creation of that origin. Tragedies do not, therefore, memorialize in the passive sense of representing something preexisting, but rather represent the invention of a city yet to come and whose justification is guaranteed, in part, by the fantasy that the polis does in fact exist and that its birth happened in a mythic past.

For Vernant, that mythic past usually took the form of a concrete, historical conflict between two incompatible formulations of the social order and culminated in the rejection of an older, prepolitical order organized according to *gene*, or familial lines.[25] In his words:

> The legends of the heroes are connected with royal lineages, noble *gene* that in terms of values, social practices, forms of religion, and types of human behavior, represent for the city-state the very things that it has had to condemn and reject and against which it has had to fight in order to establish itself. At the same time, however, they are what it developed from, and it remains integrally linked with them. The tragic turning point thus occurs when a gap develops at the heart of the social experience. It is wide enough for the oppositions between legal and political thought on the one hand and the

mythical and heroic traditions on the other to stand out quite clearly. Yet it is narrow enough for the conflict in values still to be a painful one and for the clash to continue to take place.[26]

The "tragic moment" thus enacts the tension between two opposing social orders by representing it, on the one hand, through an event in the past; the contemporaneity of that opposition, emerges, on the other hand, in the pain that the audience feels in those representations, which is itself an indication that the confrontation remains unresolved. More important, however, questions about the legitimacy of the polis and the justification of its laws are transferred from the atemporal and insoluble confrontation of the city with the irrational itself to a historical—and thereby temporalized, finalized, terminable—conflict between two conceptions of the state. By its very structure, however, the true object of tragic art—the justification of the city—remains insolubly mysterious. Its time is not that of history but of endless ritual reenactments such as the tragic competitions themselves, the time out of time in which the gods live and in which we are, briefly, drawn to them. But to reach the specificity of that more genuine, more important, and more mysterious origin, one needs to work through the concrete mythic fantasies that at once dissimulate and reveal it.

As Vernant reminds us, within the older, mythological image of the social, guilt was understood to be a transmissible pollution, a *"souillure"* or *miasma* that spread through families and could be handed down hereditarily.[27] It was, he argues, out of and against this archaic order that the tragic polis defined itself, such that Athens was organized as a purging of the *miasma*. More important, however, Vernant's reading construes the origin of the political as a transformation of the concept and experience of the human individual. In crucial ways, especially his insistence on tragedy's role in both documenting and fostering the emergence of a new kind of subjectivity, Vernant's interpretation of the plays builds on Hegel's analysis of *Antigone*, so if we want to read—that is, *critically* read—the political function of tragedies from Vernant's perspective, we must try to understand the philosopher's position. This is a somewhat complicated undertaking, since Hegel's relation to the play evolved over the span of his life, and in order to appreciate its impact on subsequent generations—and indeed, its interpretative value in relation to tragic Athens—one has to look over the successive articulations of his thinking, from the early fragment "Jedes Volk . . . ," which was written during his period in Berne (1793–96), through the treatment in *The Phenomenology of Spirit*, published in 1807, to the *Philosophy of Right* of 1821, and the lectures on the philosophy of religion given near the end of his life, in 1827.[28] Despite significant variations, the four versions are linked by an overall constancy of approach, which is most fully developed in the *Phenomenology*. All four repeat certain details, such as the term "Kollision," which is used to describe the play's central *agōn logōn*, or struggle between conflicting discourses. And the different versions agree that the latter can be situated in the confrontation between two opposing sets of laws, one human, the other divine. In his more detailed handlings of the play, Hegel came to view this dispute explicitly as an ethical issue and identified the two irreconcilable positions involved in it as a familial order of justice pitted against a more generalized collective identity. As he put it in the *Phenomenology*, the community, on the one hand, "*is, moves,* and *maintains* itself by consuming and absorbing into itself the separatism of the Penates, or the separation into independent families presided over by womankind, and by keeping them dissolved in the fluid continuity of its own nature,"[29] while the family, on the other, instantiates the "rebellious principle of pure individuality."[30] These two antagonistic ethical positions were personified, in turn, by Antigone and Creon, with Oedipus's daughter representing the familial bonds over which women preside and his brother-in-law figuring the larger, masculine collectivity of the state, which attempts to break down and dominate the family.

While Vernant agrees with Hegel's reading in identifying an opposition between family and state at the crux of the tragic, the two interpretations do not fit together seamlessly. When it comes to situating the tragic *agōn logōn* as a moment within a larger historical trajectory, the two authors treat the play very differently. For Hegel, both of the antagonistic positions carry equal weight, and it is only their partiality that creates the conflict between them.[31] The impasse will not be resolved, therefore, by agreeing with either Antigone or Creon, but by recognizing both of them to be incomplete visions of a larger field, which is the ethical itself. As Hegel describes the situation in the *Lectures on the Philosophy of Religion*:

> The resolution of the collision is when the ethical powers that are in collision (due to their one-sidedness) themselves renounce the one-sidedness of independent validity; and the way that this renunciation of one-sidedness appears is that the individuals who have committed themselves to the realization of the singular, one-sided ethical power perish. For example,

in *Antigone* the love of family, the holy, the inner, what is also called the law of the lower deities because it belongs to sentiment, comes into collision with the right of the state. Creon is not a tyrant, but rather the champion of something that is also an ethical power. Creon is not in the wrong; he maintains that the law of the state, the authority of the government, must be preserved and punishment meted out for its violation. Each of these two sides actualizes only one of the two, has only one side as its content. That is the one-sidedness, and the meaning of eternal justice is that both are in the wrong because they are one-sided, but both are also in the right. In the unclouded course of ethical life, both are acknowledged; here each has its validity, but one counterbalanced by the other's validity. . . . This is the clarity of insight and of artistic presentation that Greece reached at its highest stage of culture; but there still remains something unresolved, to be sure, in that the higher element does not emerge as the infinitely spiritual power; there remains an unhealed sorrow here because an individual perishes. The higher reconciliation would consist in the subject's disposition of one-sidedness being overcome, in its dawning consciousness that it is in the wrong, and its divesting itself of its unrighteousness in its own heart. But to recognize its guilt and one-sidedness, and to divest itself of it, does not come naturally in this domain. This higher [reconciliation] would make external punishment and natural death superfluous.[32]

Despite the somewhat off-putting nature of Hegel's prose, I find something strangely thrilling about this passage, with its enthuasiam for the Greeks—even in their failure and unhealed sorrow—and its fantastic promise, from a philosopher in the last years of his life, that natural death could be superfluous. This is not the Hegel who put death and terror to work as the negative force of history, the Hegel of Alexandre Kojève's 1930s lectures or his continuators.[33] Perhaps if the tone is different here, that is in part because these are lecture notes taken by students, who might have left some impress of their youth on them, but still the voice is rapid, repetitive, and, by Hegelian standards, almost light, as if the words were being worked at still, rather than simply delivered in their predetermined exactitude. One does not feel here the decades of labor, reaching back to the Berne period, that have worried at this passage. But this quickness of tone does not prevent Hegel from summarizing an entire epoch, and perhaps the most moving to his eyes, in a single, intimate feeling of loss, the "unhealed sorrow . . . because an individual perishes." With that individual consigned to an unnecessary death, to death in the real rather than as the power of determinate negation, an entire worldview displays to posterity a fatal blindness it could not recognize in itself.[34] The play vibrates with the suffering of these limits, as do Hegel's words, for the departed dead is tragic Athens itself. The city could just recognize and give plastic shape to this painful irreconciliation, but it could not see its way through to a resolution that did not cost the life of its characters. Like Hegel's Antigone, the citizens themselves could say, "Because we suffer we acknowledge that we have erred," but, like her again, not know the meaning of that error or how to read the sign that was their pain.[35]

For Vernant, in contrast, history clearly chose sides, although the distribution of the roles among the dramatis personae is less clear than for Hegel. In Vernant's reading, and it conforms to a widespread contemporary view of the fifth century, the law of the family gave way to a more abstract order of justice under the authority of the state. In Hegel's terms, Vernant's history of the Greeks would see them moving from Antigone to Creon, but Vernant also differs from Hegel in that he sees each tragic figure already internalizing the larger conflict between two orders "so that the tension that we have noted between past and present, between the world of myth and that of the city, is to be found again within each protagonist."[36] At the beginning of Aeschylus's *Seven against Thebes*, for instance, "Eteocles corresponds to a particular psychological model, that of the *homo politicus*, as conceived by the Greeks of the fifth century," but as the play unfolds another, more ancient aspect of the character emerges, and the "destructive frenzy that grips the leader of Thebes is none other than the *miasma* that is never purified, the Erinyes of the race."[37] Although he thus shifts the historical conflict from the interactions among characters to the inconsistencies within their individual psychologies, Vernant nonetheless recognizes that tragedy depends on disputes between individuals: "For each protagonist, locked into his own particular world, the vocabulary that is used remains for the most part opaque. For him it has one, and only one, meaning. This one-sidedness comes into violent collision with another."[38] And as an example of this oppositional unilateralism, Vernant cites *Antigone*:

> The conflict between Antigone and Creon reflects a similar antinomy. It is
> not an opposition between pure religion, represented by the girl, and total
> irreligion, represented by Creon, or between a religious spirit and a political
> one. Rather it is between two different types of religious feeling: One is a
> family religion, purely private and confined to the small circle of close relatives,
> the *philoi*, centered on the domestic hearth and the cult of the dead; the other

is a public religion in which the tutelary gods of the city eventually become confused [*se confondre*] with the supreme values of the state.[39]

Consequently, according to Vernant, the "the term *nomos* [i.e., law] as used by Antigone means the opposite to what Creon, in all confidence, calls *nomos*."[40] It is as if there were a centripetal pull to this play that draws Vernant back to a model of tragic conflict he had earlier attempted to modify. The characters, whom he previously had internalize the social tensions of a period, again embody opposing ethical orders, and the Hegelian distribution of roles reasserts itself once more: The virgin stands on the side of the family and the gods of the netherworld, "close to women and foreign to politics," while Creon personifies a fusional political mass capable of dissolving ("confondre") other transcendental authorities into itself.[41] For Vernant, in short, the characters inwardly mirror a conflict that divides them outwardly from others. Although each one, like Eteocles, may be subject to divergent forces partially beyond control, one of these forces will dominate when the character is confronted by the one-sided positions of others in the play. In this way, the fault lines of contention, the *agōn logōn* of the drama, cross over and among other divisions, such as those that separate person from person and individual from community. It is, in part, I would argue, this confusion of codes that makes the play at once so familiar and so strange to later readers. The conventions of intelligible drama assert themselves in character and conflict, and yet they do not appear quite where we remember or expect them to be.

These categorical shifts and inconsistencies show themselves in the play of resemblance and difference among readings of *Antigone*, and nowhere is this more apparent than in treatments of individuality. This, I would argue, is at once the thorniest and most important aspect of the play, and Vernant has analyzed some of the historical context for these questions. He and other recent authors have described the waning genetic order that still asserts itself in fifth-century tragedies as a force contrary to both the state and the individual. Unlike Hegel, who saw the civic law trying to absorb the family into itself, Vernant finds *gene* that are utterly incompatible with the political, that must be excluded altogether from the city and held outside its walls in "another world rejected by that of the *polis*."[42] This extramural zone is thus the place of the ancient lineages, the ones susceptible to a pollution that passes among their members and their generations, a filth that, like a virus, contaminates those who share blood or other intimate fluids, so that punishment falls on the family as a whole. The Cylonides paid for the crime of Cylon, the Alcmeonides for that of Megacles.[43] Theirs is a law in which guilt precedes the guilty, standing independent and ready, in which the criminal exists more as a by-product of the crime than as its author. The guilty deed, as Hegel understood it in the *Phenomenology*, would be utterly alien to the social world created by the old families described by Vernant. For Hegel, the act surprises because it cannot be undone, disavowed, or disowned, and its inalienable ownership reveals her crime to the perpetrator.[44] But, under the ancient laws of pollution Vernant describes, there is no individual ownership through action, that is, through the objective materialization of an ethical order in the deed. Eteocles, for example, inherits guilt without doing anything guilty.[45] His father, Oedipus, finds tragic resolution when he sees what he has done, when he discovers the crime he committed in ignorance and recognizes himself as its perpetrator; but for the son such resolution lies out of reach, since he has done nothing, has no act in which to see his agency objectified (and even his father, as we shall see, ends up questioning his own responsibility in *Oedipus at Colonus*).[46] Eteocles's own deed is only that of being born, and even there he is not the doer but the done.

Guilt thus saturates the child's life and spreads beyond, condemning him to atonement through death, but to a death that, in this respect at least, is not even his own, since it offers only partial payment for a larger debt. His demise cannot stitch together the victim and the agent as a single person who endures over time through the continuity of individual responsibility. Instead, it comes to him like the sacrificial knife to the offering: The victim bears away the fault of another's act, to which it can be attached only externally, through the happenstance of birth or selection by an alien force. And so, when Eteocles the statesman gives way to murderous rage at his brother Polyneices, it is, according to Vernant, the old crime that takes possession of him and with it the old order that did not recognize the state he leads. "The madness of Eteocles is present in him," Vernant writes, "but that does not prevent it also appearing as extraneous and exterior to him. It is identified with the malignant power of defilement that, once engendered by ancient crimes, is transmitted from one generation to the next right down the Labdacid line."[47] This furor, this *miasma*, is a "sort of non-individualized, divine force that acts upon the heart of human life, most often in a destructive way."[48] As expressed in the miasma of familial guilt, the archaic structures of the *gene* described by Vernant serve to block the emergence of a certain legally responsible individual, one who would be determined by his or her agency in relation to a criminal act and by the necessity that he or she alone atone for it.

Other scholars have offered, however, a somewhat contradictory description of the individual's status in prepolitical Greece and have argued that the individual, cherished and recognized by the earlier familial structures, yielded, under pressure from the new democratic state of the fifth century, to the more impersonal figure of the citizen. This would seem to be especially evident in changing attitudes concerning funerary monuments and laments. Bonnie Honig, in particular, has cited "the clash between Homeric/elite and democratic mourning practices" in *Antigone* to argue that "the former (represented by Antigone) memorialize the unique individuality of the dead, focus on the family's loss and bereavement and call for vengeance," while the "latter (represented by Creon) memorialize the dead's contribution to the immortal polis and emphasize . . . the replaceability of those lost."[49] For Honig, the tragic moment would thus represent a historical period in which the individual was lost, dissolved into the impersonality of the state. "Antigone," Honig writes, "memorializes the family's dead in Homeric terms (in terms of the dead's individuality, the loss to the surviving family, and the need to avenge it), exhibiting fidelity to natal over marital family, clan over polis."[50] Conversely, "Creon metonymizes democracy substantively. His ban on lamentation and his repeated emphasis on the harms of individuality represent the fifth-century democratic view."[51]

As evidence for the archaic family's individualizing tendency, Honig adduces private mourning practices, and especially the dirges they included, noting in particular their emphasis on the plight of the bereaved and their characteristic calls for vengeance to atone for the loss of a kinsman.[52] Her interpretation bears scrutiny, since it is based on analyses of ancient practices and would appear to belie my own argument that the individual lost to the polis is "paradoxical," because it did not previously exist. There are problems with her approach, however. First, Honig's principal source for this part of her analysis is Gail Holst-Warhaft, who argued that the emergent Greek polis replaced private female laments with public mourning as part of a larger appropriation of women's power over life and death. Holst-Warhaft described the threefold aspect of that power, as expressed by dirges: By calling for revenge, those dirges could lead to potentially interminable cycles of violence; by focusing on the loss of the dead rather than what the state gained by that loss, they made it harder for the city to field an army; and by asserting a proprietary relation between female mourners and the dead, they helped consolidate biopolitical power in the hands of women, who already controlled the giving of life.[53] There is, however, little about individuation in her study. The loss that the survivors express in the prepolitical laments is largely utilitarian, concerning, for instance, security in old age or the protection of women, and it has little to do with the personal value of the dead as an inherently irreplaceable individual.[54] The dirges in Homeric epic do little, moreover, to alter this general impression, with Holst-Warhaft noting how Hecuba's grief over her son Hector treats the dead hero "impersonally."[55] Second, the call for vengeance seems an odd way to recognize the irreplaceable individuality of the dead. On the contrary, it serves to establish an equivalence between individuals, a fungible currency of loss, in which one death equals—and thus atones for—another.[56] This requirement of "a death for a death" would seem to place the archaic family within the "economy of substitution" that Honig associates, instead, with the new democratic order.[57] Indeed, the formulaic qualities of these dirges tended, as a whole, to minimize any individualizing force in them. And, as Margaret Alexiou has observed, the threnodies of the lyric poets did not individuate either. They were, if anything, even more polished and impersonal than the *goos* of women mourners.[58]

This is not to say that the prepolitical laments did not represent genuine suffering or that they did not attempt to articulate the individuality of the lost. What I am arguing, instead, is that these dirges evidence certain difficulties in identifying such an individual, and that it is, as a whole, reductive to see the conflict between the archaic families and the emergent democracy as a struggle between individuality and impersonality. In its official mourning practices, the democratic Athens of the fifth century did, indeed, subordinate the individual to the state, as we shall see in the next chapter, but at the same time it gave birth to a legally responsible individual, unimaginable within the earlier familial structures of guilt. Both the family and the democratic polis were thus capable of creating and dissolving individuals in their own, characteristic ways. Each approach illuminated the shortcomings of the other, but, as *Antigone* demonstrates, it was not clear whether the two could be reconciled.

My analysis would seem, however, to be at odds both with *Antigone* and Hegel's reading of the play. Helene Foley, for instance, has described the relation between Creon and his niece as a confrontation between community and individuality. Foley stresses the young heroine's resolute isolation from others and notes that Creon, in contrast, tends to speak in generalizations, thereby leveling uniqueness and particularity.[59] Antigone, she further observes, attempts to include emotions and specificity in the notions of the ethical and the legal, which are at the heart of the play, while Creon shuns expressions of affect and other signs of individualism.[60] Even Creon's tendency to explain people's motivations by their supposed venality reinforces this apparent dichotomy between the two principal protagonists: Whereas Antigone acts alone and out of love for a single person, Creon attributes her—and other characters'—actions to their desire for money.[61] Through its very fungibility, money represents the negation of particularity: It is an abstract value that allows the exchange of individual items by establishing a general equivalency among them.[62] In a similar vein, Luce Irigaray sees in Creon the "abstract universality" of the particular "I," the representation of a uniquely masculine ability to negativize one's own singularity into a universal.[63]

In the *Phenomenology of Spirit*, Hegel ostensibly took an approach similar to Foley's, Irigaray's, and Honig's, referring to the family, which he associated with Antigone, as "the rebellious principle of pure individuality."[64] This would seem to thrust his interpretation into direct contradiction with Vernant's, but one needs to pay careful attention to the complexities of Hegel's conception of an individual, the meaning of which shifts somewhat confusingly over the course of his argument.[65] In the first half of that argument, he uses "individual" to designate a unified group of people such as the family itself.[66] In the second half, however, the term's meaning slips abruptly toward its more modern use and comes to designate a singular human consciousness or person.[67] It is, in fact, this very slippage that constitutes, for Hegel, the crisis at the heart of the play's action, for as he puts it:

> The way in which the antithesis is constituted in this ethical realm is such that self-consciousness has not yet received its due as a particular individuality. There it has the value, on the one hand, merely of the universal will, and on the other, of consanguinity. *This* particular individual counts only as a shadowy unreality. As yet, no deed has been committed; but the deed is the *actual self.*[68]

In the earlier cultural organization, the bonds of the family had been balanced against the universal will of the state, while a sort of harmony prevailed between their respective forces and notions of law.[69] But in that world, the individual as a single person did not exist and entered into consideration only as the ghost of something yet to come. The rupture between that older world and the newer one that would replace it, the deed that disrupted the fragile harmony between family and state, was, as Hegel puts it, the advent of the actual self. The "collision" and crisis at the core of the play, the deed, is not really, by Hegel's account, Antigone's decision to cover her brother's body, but something more abstract and conceptual: the particular individual. This, for Hegel, is the deed, the event, the drama.

As we shall see, however, the "shadowy unreality" of the particular individual is never entirely resolved into a real and living human existence in Hegel's reading—and this shadow life, this phantasmatic and fantastic (pre-) existence, is part of what makes the individual so interestingly problematic to us in this historical and aesthetic moment. Not yet present as an actor or reality, it will continue, nonetheless, to haunt, lifelessly, the cultural universe Hegel saw embodied in *Antigone*. In the first half of his argument, Hegel writes that "in the essence we are considering here, individuality has the meaning of *self-consciousness* in general, not of a particular, contingent consciousness," and in the second half he writes that "the ethical individuality is directly and intrinsically one with this his universal aspect, exists in it alone."[70] Throughout, the philosopher warned repeatedly against confusing "individuality" with any particular person, so that when he spoke of the family as "the rebellious principle of pure individuality," he used the term "pure" to mean considered as an abstract universal.[71] One might be tempted to imagine that paradoxically universal individual as a category, that is, the individual as such or in one of its relational manifestations—as "the brother" say—but as his argument progresses, it becomes clear that Hegel has another, less intuitive sense of the abstract in mind.[72] In characteristic fashion, he conceives of it as the intervention of pure being in the existence of a particular person. This intervention occurs when the individual, "after a long succession of separate disconnected experiences, concentrates himself into a single completed shape and has raised himself out of the unrest of the accidents of life into the calm of simple universality. . . . This universality which the individual *as such* attains is *pure being, death*."[73] A pure individual is, in other words, a dead one, and although death has a range of meanings in Hegel, he is using the term here in its most literal and conventional sense, as the end of natural life. The deceased is a specific entity rather than a category, yet he or she no longer exists in any but a conceptual or abstract way, in other words as "this particular individual who belongs to the Family, but is taken as a *universal* being freed from his sensuous, i.e. individual, reality."[74] At death, a sensuous individuality converts into a pure individuality. That is to say that somehow, through the intervention of the family, the transient and contingent existence of the individual is transformed into his invariable essence or truth.

Some lines later, Hegel will clarify what he means by this: In the familial religion of the underworld, the dead has become "the Eumenides of the *departed* spirit: . . . negativity in the form of individuality. Absolute Being is, in the latter form, indeed the *self* and *present*, since other than present the self cannot *be*. But the individual self is *this* self which has separated from itself the universality which Fate is. True, it is a shade, a superseded particular self, and thus a universal self."[75] In other words, while still alive, Antigone's brother, for instance, is a particular, sensuous individual, whose uniqueness derives in fact from his embeddedness in the world of time, accidents, and vagaries, but once he has died he becomes a thought or a memory, objectified into autonomous existence as the Eumenides, who cling to the imperturbable ontology of the past. In death, however, the particularities of his historical existence yield to his essence as a finished and perfected individual. But that individuality is threatened by the generality of death, since, as the Greek eulogists liked to recall, everyone dies. It is therefore only by withholding himself from the impersonality of such abstract categories as Fate or death that he attains individuality, but since that withholding cannot be accomplished by the dead person himself it must be effected by his survivors. A reverence for the ancestral dead thus hovers over the household gods, or what Hegel anachronistically calls the Penates, binding the family together and individualizing it in face of a larger, more indistinct mass of humanity. In this way, the family persists by thrusting its roots ever farther into the past and ever deeper into the pure being of its own nonexistence. As the guardian of the household and its archaic ethical life, moreover, woman is attached to the underworldly gods through the bonds of death. The individuality that Antigone represents for Hegel is thus the piously preserved memory of the departed and not the living person who has disappeared.

Vernant observed a similar relation between individuality and death among the Greeks, finding in it one of the underlying principles shaping their experience of life: "To exist 'individually' for a Greek," he wrote, "means becoming and remaining 'memorable': one escapes anonymity, forgetting, and erasure—and therefore death—through death itself, a death that, by giving you access to glorifying songs, makes you more present to the community."[76] It is memory that individuates, and memory relies, in turn, on the completion of death. Within the archaic community that is giving way, in the tragic plays, to the pressure of a new order, the individual can be identified only as a product of his demise, which poetry further subtlizes and confirms. The immateriality of death thus finds its place, the field of its elaboration, in the purity of language, which consequently becomes a form of afterlife.[77] In his own way, Vernant thus corroborated Hegel's insight that for the Greeks individuality was available only in death and only through the intervention of others who preserved the memory of the deceased. The two differed, however, in how they identified the techniques by which that memory was attached to the once living person. For Vernant, memorialization came through language and was connected to the lost by the latter's own actions, by his efforts while still alive to "make himself memorable." For Hegel, as we shall see, the linkage between individuality and the dead depended instead on ritual acts involving the corpse of the deceased, acts in which the latter played only a passive role.

In the old order of the *gene*, individuality derived from death, while *miasma*, the autonomous guilt haunting a crime, spread among the living. Fifth-century tragedy, according to both Hegel and Vernant, marked a break with that world, asserting in its place new and still unfocused protocols for defining a single person. But the emergence of this new figure was symptomatic of a larger disturbance: Broader lines of pressure were slipping, and the paradigms that separate such fundamentals as the person from the mass and the meaningful from the meaningless were changing. Vernant argued that in distinction to such cultures as ancient India, where individuality was attained through the renunciation of social bonds, in Greece, the individual was recognizable only as a function of society itself.[78] Or, as Hegel stated in the *Phenomenology*, "because it is only as a citizen that he is actual and substantial, the individual, so far as he is not a citizen but belongs to the Family, is only an unreal impotent shadow."[79] So, although Antigone and the family ostensibly represented a force of individualization, it was an insufficient one. For the tragic Greeks of Hegel and Vernant, there was consequently no intelligible, living person beyond the structures of the city. And as it pressed the logic of the old lineages beyond its walls, the polis forced out too, into the zone of incomprehensibility and nonsense, the archaic and ghostly notion of individuality that derived from them.

The tragedies, including *Antigone*, thus enacted a paradoxical temporality, in which the past remained yet to come, for, by memorializing the mythic origins of the state, they returned to its prehistory, to the heroic and familial figures that needed to be mastered and then excluded in order for that state to exist. That return represented an attempt to justify the legitimacy of the city and the rightness of its laws through a reconciliation with those whom the city had excluded as irredeemably hostile to it: the Eumenides, the family, women, the hero. It was the attempt to include somehow in the structures of the state those entities that were constitutionally alien to it. And so, to the extent that the city could only truly exist once it had justified itself, it was caught in an interminable birth. Conversely, however, the prime embodiment of the excluded, the individual, also existed in a paradoxical temporality, for although the state, as we shall see in the next chapter, strove to suppress the autonomous individual, that figure is hard to discern within the prepolitical cultures of ancient Greece. Indeed, he or she may at first have existed only in that very suppression.

TWO

The Citizen

The tragedies, then, mark the rise of a new sort of person, one defined not by his or her place within a familial structure but in relation to a larger notion of civic justice. Abstract as it may seem, this shift echoed changes in the legal system that accompanied the rise of the polis. In the Homeric period, or around the ninth century, it was the head of a household, or *oikos*, who enjoyed absolute authority over those in his extended family, including the right to punish them with death.[1] By many indicators, the *oikos* prevailed during this time as an autonomous entity over the individual, often in ways, such as the laws of inheritance, that would persist even beyond the fifth century.[2] In this prepolitical state, as Trevor Saunders has observed, a

> regular and established system of law backed up by a systematic infliction
> of punishment after due process of law is nowhere to be seen. To be sure,
> law did exist in some sense: it was certainly not written, but consisted of
> customary conduct reinforced partly by the *dikhai* ("judgments") and *themistes*
> ("layings-down"), delivered by the kings or others, and partly by direct
> communal action.[3]

One point in Saunders's observations merits our particular attention, and this is the reference to the *dikai* that characterized the older order.[4] In Plato, *dikē* tends to mean a private legal action, as opposed to *graphē*, which has been defined as "*an indictment* in a public prosecution, *a criminal prosecution* undertaken by the state."[5] The word *graphē* itself comes from the verb *graphō*, and has the more primary sense of that which is represented by means of a likeness or by writing. Not only are the *dikai* associated with an older, more fluid and familial way of delivering justice, they are remembered in the political period as a more private sort of legality that stands against the public laws. These latter, as their very name indicates, are in turn linked to the notion of writing and likeness. Theirs, then, is the realm of the trait, the character, the distinguishing mark, the law itself as an intelligible, defined world: *Graptos*, it is spelled out in letters, but also distinguishable, visible, even. And conversely, when Antigone denies Creon's authority as head of state to adjudicate the disposition of her brother's corpse, she does so in the name of unwritten codes: "It was not Zeus who made this proclamation," she argues, "nor was it Justice (*Dikē*) who lives with the gods below that established such laws [*nomous*] among men, nor did I think your proclamations strong enough to have power to overrule, mortal as they were, the unwritten [*agrapta*] and unfailing ordinances [*nomima*] of the gods."[6] Antigone's laws are those of the ancient world, and they echo still in the word *dikē* to remind the language of an earlier, unmarked, even invisible justice.[7] They are also the laws that the young Hegel called, "a sacred law . . . set down without letters . . . invisible [*ein göttliches Gebot . . . in keinem Buchstaben gegeben . . . unsichtbar*]."[8]

In opposition to these vague but powerful rules of the ancients, there arose a new sense of the law and with it a new concept of personhood. Beyond the city lay the zone of the miasma, the "pollution" and the "unindividualized" that were connected with the unwritten *dikē* of the family.[9] In place of and against that poorly differentiated filth, the tragic authors evoked another concept of the person, one defined graphically through an individual's accountability for his or her own actions.[10] During the fifth century—the century of the tragedians—the Athenians had, as Gustave Glotz remarked, "purged the public laws of their traditional injustices," by subordinating them to "the principle that governed private law, that of personal responsibility."[11] Glotz was writing in the nineteenth century, but his observations still seem valid, and by the time that Plato wrote the *Republic*, in the first half of the fourth century, this new figure of legal individuality had become firmly established, and the archaic image of guilt as miasma had almost entirely yielded to a notion of individual responsibility.[12] Although Plato does not raise the issues of intention and free will in the final paragraphs of the *Republic*, which are given over to a demonstration of the immortality of the soul and a description of the punishments and rewards that await it in the afterlife, and although his concept of individuality is accordingly vague, it is nonetheless the individual and not the family or its miasmas that is targeted in his vision of cosmic justice. After death, the just and the unjust, according to the philosopher, receive what is due them, the former enjoying the fruits of the blessed while the latter redeems his or her misdeeds through punishments.[13] "For all the wrongs they had ever done to anyone and all whom they had severally wronged they had paid the penalty in turn," he writes of the souls in Hades.[14] It is not inherited guilt that is in question here, but rather the doings of each person during the span of life allotted to him or her, and that person's every act is meticulously counted and judged. The individual is defined with an almost mathematical precision in this fantasy of the underworld, and as Catherine Joubaud has commented:

> Although he makes use of traditional elements of Greek thought, it is no longer a question for Plato of sanctions to punish an "ancestral crime that calls down belated retribution upon an innocent descendant nonetheless stained by an ancient pollution." . . . Although satisfying to the extent that punishment certainly exists and the principle of justice is respected, such a conception is no longer acceptable, for it is not the guilty party himself who is punished for his crime, but another. It is now necessary for the soul of the guilty man to pay his debt, whatever form that may take. Both evil and good have internal or intimate consequences that will always out.[15]

There is, as Joubaud puts it, an "intimate" causality at work in this new idea of guilt, for the crime carries within it ineluctable consequences destined to manifest themselves inside the person of the perpetrator himself or herself. With her use of the terms "innocent descendant" and "guilty party," however, Joubaud obscures the more fundamental distinction at the heart of tragic drama. To call the descendant innocent in the old order of justice is anachronistic: According to the pertinent definitions, he or she was guilty. It is only with the end of that archaic world, or within the definitions of another, opposing order, that the son can appear, in retrospect, to have been blameless. Under the previous system of punishment, moreover, the difference between "the guilty party" and "another" would not have been perceived in the same way as it is in Plato. It is not that the old law perversely punished another than the criminal. Rather, it did not see that other as other. The creation of a judicial system, in contrast, brings with it the ability to separate the child from the criminal and, more generally, to distinguish within a single family various individuals by their differing relations to a single crime. With this new sense of criminality, in short, there comes a new perception of what an individual is.

According to the Platonic system, crime stems from agency, punishment is an answer to that crime, and individual personhood hangs between the call and response of the deed and its atonement. This is subjectivity as the thread that links agency to responsibility.[16] Under this law, one is most one's own self, or ownmost, to borrow a term from Heidegger, in owning the action, and one becomes conscious of that self by owning up to the deed. In opposition to the abstract individuality of the dead mythic hero, there emerges another individuality that is identifiable through its persistent internal relation to a previous agency—and where internal means within a single soul. But here again, the determination of a single soul was not unproblematic in the prepolitical world. Death, as we have seen, did not *in itself* bestow individuality. On the contrary, the mythic imagination tended to view the afterlife as a largely undifferentiated state, a horrifying "formless magma" where words lost their meaning and identities disappeared.[17] Death, in this fantasy, is "unspeakable" and "unintelligible," a nonplace "no word can reach without losing all meaning: a world of night ruled by the inaudible, at once silence and din."[18] It was *against* this mass of the indistinguishable dead that the archaic hero won his individuality. Were he not memorable, he too would vanish among the shadows of the deceased, would really die. That was the underworld that Plato left behind, for even as the soul suffered for its crimes in the visionary end to the *Republic*, it achieved a self-recognizable individuality that it never previously could have attained. Its punishment was an expression of the soul's own agency, and the fact that the crime could not be redeemed by another, that the debt of guilt was untransferable, determined the inviolable limits of that soul. In this respect, the archaic hero stood between two conceptions of death, for even though it was contested, the idea that the soul retained its individuality even after death nonetheless gained a widespread acceptance, attested by the Eleusian mysteries, Orphic rites, Aristophanes, and Pindar, among others.[19] Plato's underworld thus represents a larger historical change not only in the notion of death but also in the idea of the individual.

In life as in death, the state gave rise to an identifiable individual, and in so doing it pushed what had previously been an intelligible, if largely unarticulated order—the familial and mythic—toward the realm of meaningless indifferentiation. The language of the old world had become a garbled murmuring of fastidious distinctions in which the family dissolved, as a whole, into what Vernant called the "formless magma" of its meaningless death, into the vagueness of its miasma. And whether or not he actually stank of his own rotting flesh, like Sophocles's character Philoctetes, the tragic hero embodied that putrescence of the past. He was unclean, polluted by his guilt, his very memory a magnificent obscenity. Under pressure from the civic, the family, as a whole, began to lose its ability to articulate a recognizable person or to bestow sense. It would seem that Creon, as representative of the *gegrammenoi*, or written laws of the state, had prevailed, historically at least, over his niece and the dark, unrecorded mutterings of the dead. And so Hegel was wrong, perhaps, to assert that neither side could win, that the truth of those conflicting positions lay not in the one or the other, but in the ethical itself, the broad field that sustained them in their difference. And yet the victory of light and of the gods who walk the upper world was not, for all that, an unalloyed triumph of life. Instead, the individual who was born of this conflict often vanished into the abstractions that conceived him. For the citizen celebrated by the polis was less a specific person than an example of the state itself, the momentary incarnation of its will.

This disappearance is clearly attested in the Athenian *epitaphioi logoi*, the public eulogies for dead soldiers that were delivered in the Cerameicus cemetery just outside Athens. According to Plato, these eulogies were given every year, but only a handful have survived, and the authenticity of even these is disputed.[20] From the evidence that remains, however, we know that these speeches constituted a highly conservative genre that tended to perpetuate both older standards and the preestablished forms for expressing them. Principal among the features characterizing the eulogies is a displacement of praise from any specific dead to a more general glorification of the city and its values. Since the fallen soldiers are held to be glorious because they died for a noble cause and that cause is Athens, the unique importance of the state is developed at length by the orators. The Athenians are consistently portrayed as standing out among other peoples for their commitment to justice, and the funerary speeches regularly illustrate this commitment by recounting the city's intervention in the war between Oedipus's sons. In this sense, the orations are civic commentaries on the source material for *Antigone*.

As Demosthenes said of the early citizens: "In addition to these and many other noble deeds they refused to suffer the lawful rites of the departed to be treated with despite when Creon forbade the burial of 'the seven against Thebes.'"²¹ It seems to be no more than a passing remark, but that is perhaps because the topos had become so well established in the annual ceremonies, and indeed in the popular conception of the state, that there was no need to go into further details when Demosthenes delivered his speech, in 338 B.C.E. Some fifty years earlier, however, Lysias had recounted the incident in greater depth, reappropriating, in his own turn, some of the same concerns that had figured another fifty years before in *Antigone*—such as the defilement of sanctuaries—and explaining the rationale behind the Athenians' decision to take sides against Thebes.

> They marched against them: no previous quarrel subsisted between them and the Cadmeans, nor did they wish to gratify the Argives who were yet living; but thinking it right that those who had died in the war should receive the customary treatment, they risked combat with one of the parties in the interest of both, that on the one side they should cease from grossly outraging the gods by their trespass against the dead, and that on the other they should not hasten away to their own land frustrated of an ancestral honor, cut off from Hellenic custom, and disappointed in a common hope.²²

The justice and value of the Athenians is demonstrated in their decision to fight not for themselves or for the surviving inhabitants of Argos, but for a principle, and that principle is literally embodied in the cadavers to which the Thebans have refused burial. The goodness of the combatants thus lies in their disinterest, and this disinterest is guaranteed by the fact that they fight for those who are already fallen. Now, the willingness to sacrifice oneself for the deceased, or rather for the *rights* of the deceased, is to subordinate the living to the dead. This, according to the tradition represented by Lysias, is justice. The fair treatment of the fallen is thus part of the heritage and distinctive nature of Athenians, who are, as the *epitaphioi logoi* tirelessly remind their listeners, the only true Greeks. The dead are thus glorified and the city justified in their selfless concern for the valiant but powerless. The mention of the Seven against Thebes has, moreover, a self-referential quality within the funeral orations, for it brings the attention of the audience back to the event of the speech itself and to the commemorative ceremony in the Cerameicus. The message is apparently that unlike the Thebans, the Athenians were just in their treatment of the dead and indeed still are, as is evidenced by the ceremony and the speech. And so the eulogies reject Creon and affiliate the citizens of Athens with the figure of Antigone. They are, in this sense, readings of Sophocles's play—they are readings, moreover, that pass judgment on the actions of the characters and seem to choose a side. Through the *epitaphioi logoi*, *Antigone* had, in other words, entered the official Athenian discourse of self-determination, becoming a key topos in the identity and uniqueness of Athens.

But this ostensible affiliation with Antigone is undercut throughout the *epitaphioi logoi*, for as a whole they recuperate an earlier system of memorialization, moving it from the realm of the household to the public sphere. Like the Furies at the end of Aeschylus's *Eumenides*, the role of the family is both preserved and superseded in these speeches, which systematically acknowledged the sacrifice and pain of the surviving relatives while subordinating them to the needs of the state. Plato explicitly described this passage from one register to another in his own funeral oration, from the *Menexenus*, when he wrote: "Nor does the City ever omit to pay honour to the dead heroes themselves, seeing that she herself year by year performs publicly, on behalf of all, those customary rites which are privately performed for each."[23] In his interpretation of the ceremonies, moreover, the polis appropriates for itself the roles of various relatives, at once subsuming their archaic claims to the dead into a broader community and transforming the rituals of individuation into the business of the state. "And thus, in simple fact," Plato observed of the city, "she stands towards the fallen in the position of son and heir, towards the sons in that of father, and towards the parents of the dead in that of guardian, thus exercising towards all all manner of care throughout all time."[24] But, as other elements in the funerary tradition show, Athens is not merely a replacement for the bonds of kinship: Despite the seeming anteriority of the family unit over the public community, another logic weaving through the *epitaphioi logoi* indicates, conversely, that the city is the true model for familial relations and the principle that underlies them. The funerary discourses uniformly distinguish between Athenians and all other peoples on the basis of the former's autochthonous origins. These passages, which normally come toward the beginning of the speeches, trace the specificity and legitimacy of the Athenian population to the fact that it springs from the local earth itself, and the authors insist on the notion of maternity to make this point. The Athenians, declared Lysias, "were born of the soil, and possessed in one and the same country their mother and their fatherland."[25] For Demosthenes, "this land is the mother [*mētera*] of our ancestors," and so while the inhabitants of other cities "are comparable to adopted [*espoiētois*] children," the Athenian dead "are citizens of their native land by right of legitimate birth."²⁶ According to these narratives, in other words, only the Athenians are the children of a true mother and so they alone are the rightful citizens of their fatherland. This argument would seem literally to ground citizenship in a biological relation between mothers and their offspring, but in fact it works more to the opposite end, serving instead to discredit maternity. According to the *epitaphioi logoi*, true motherhood is expressed in the state, which subsumes into itself familial bonds; woman, on the other hand, "is but the imitation of the earth."²⁷ Biological mothers are thus only copies of something more profound, and as Aeschylus's *Eumenides* makes clear, they cannot even establish blood relations.

In fact, the language Aeschylus used to describe the dubious link between individual mothers and their children in *Eumenides* foreshadows the words Demosthenes chooses to connect other cities and their geographic setting. In his eulogy, the non-Athenian is an *espoiētos* or adopted child, and in *Eumenides* every human mother "is not the mother of its so-called child but rather a nurse swollen with the newly implanted seed [*ouk esti mētēr hē keklēmenou teknou tokeus, trophos de kumatos neosporou*]."²⁸ In their fantasies about the origins of the state, both Aeschylus's tragedy and the *epitaphioi logoi* thus deny the importance of maternity by transferring women's procreative powers to the city and its male ideals. For the authors of the public eulogies, moreover, this transfer was linked to the subsumption of familial bonds within the institutions and values of the state. The need to repeat the narrative and reasoning of this transfer in the tragedies and annually over the bodies of the dead, this hammering away at the same theme for nearly two hundred years, suggests, however, that somewhere within the state something resisted this creation story. This resistance made itself felt in moments of piety toward the dead, as if the treatment of their remains was necessarily linked to unease about the legitimacy of the city.

The dead who are eulogized by the civic orators are different from the dead that family members mourn, for they are by necessity impersonal. The goodness of their deeds derives from their altruism, their nobility from the sacrifice they made of themselves on behalf of the city, and so they are, in a crucial way, without a self to mourn. If they are memorable among all men, if they are not consigned, like others, to the indifferentiation of the dead, it is, paradoxically, because they have chosen to live and die without an individual identity. "Bartering little for much, a brief time for all eternity," the fallen, according to Demosthenes, "leave behind them an ageless fame," and Lysias observed that "our ancestors, without stopping to calculate the hazards of war, but holding that a glorious death leaves behind it a deathless account of deeds well done, had no fear" before the prospect of battle.[29] And yet they do, clearly, gauge the risk, and in their careful reasoning are led to the inevitable conclusion that in death alone will they win the greatest rewards. This is not reckless enthusiasm that the orators are describing but the coldest of calculations, indeed almost a commercial transaction. Unromantic as this rationality might appear to us, it is crucial to the notion of valor being described here, for the warrior's act is worthy of praise only by virtue of the decision that motivates it—a far cry from the logic of the Furies, who saw in the deed, regardless of its motivations, a crime. "Of all virtue," Demosthenes argues, "the beginning is understanding and the fulfilment is courage; by the one it is judged what ought to be done and by the other this is carried to success."[30] The heroic action, therefore, "is a demonstration of sound judgment joined with public spirit."[31] The act of judgment is crucial to the value of a warrior's deed—and death—and that judgment must be sound, which is to say, reasonable rather than simply personal. It must, moreover, be subordinated to the public cause, and so the notion of personal impulse is ruled out in attributing virtue to the fallen. This same idea reappears more explicitly in Lysias, who wrote of the war dead: "They proved their worth as men, neither sparing their limbs nor cherishing their lives when valor called, and had more reverence for their city's laws than fear of their perils in face of the enemy."[32] The dead who are being commemorated in these eulogies are, in short, absent from them as individuals, for they have sacrificed their lives to the abstract principles of virtue, justice, and the laws. Even the potentially individuating act of judgment by which they accede to valor and secure the right to immortality is based on a coldly impersonal act of reasoning. The person is subordinated to the justice of the city much as the family is subordinated to its institutions. Almost nowhere in these speeches does the image of a living individual rise up, no sign of a commendable or even memorable particularity, no distinction except the paradoxical lack of distinctiveness, no sign that the dead should be remembered for anything but their willingness to die in the cause of reason itself. One of the consequences of this concept of virtue is that life itself seems to be excluded from it, as if the living had no legitimate place among the citizens. "Among good men," Demosthenes pronounced at the beginning of his oration, as if it were the axiom on which was founded the nature of the city, "the enjoyment of the pleasures that go with living are scorned."[33]

In the orators' descriptions of the families themselves, however, one finds a pale flicker of living individuality, but even there it is difficult to separate affection from self-interest, and such genuine love as emerges in these passages is described as something inherently alien to the city. Demosthenes, as usual, is expeditious in his treatment of the theme, observing rapidly that "it is a grievous thing for fathers and mothers to be deprived of their children and in their old age to lack the care of those who are nearest and dearest to them."[34] The pain of loss seems to derive only from the material hardship that will befall the parents, who find themselves suddenly destitute in their infirmity. If Demosthenes had some other notion of suffering in mind, some grief over the disappearance of a person simply for who they are, that idea is passed over in silence in his and all the other existing *epitaphioi logoi*, as if it were an attachment that had no place within the language of the state. Lysias had offered a similar notion of familial grief in his own eulogy, starting, like Demosthenes, with references to the sorrow that relatives feel when deprived of the affection of the dead, but then developing the theme in more pragmatic terms: "For what woe could be more incurable," he asked, "than to bring forth and rear and bury one's own children, and then in old age to be disabled in body and, having lost every hope, to find oneself friendless and resourceless? to have the very cause of former envy turned now to a matter of pity?"[35] The lost son is a resource, a force, a protection against humiliation, but not an object of simple, disinterested love. Indeed, the eulogies constantly reinforce the monopoly of the state over selflessness, making of it a civic virtue that distinguishes not only the fallen from the survivors but also the city from the family. And so it is that almost nowhere in the funeral speeches does one find the vaguest hint of the love that will appear so simply and clearly in the early modern era, the "because it was he; because it was I [*par ce que c'estoit luy; par ce que c'estoit moy*]," with which Montaigne explained his friendship with Etienne de La Boétie.[36]

The one, faint glimmer of such a sentiment comes later in Lysias's description of the grief the relatives feel, but even here one wonders if that glimpse is not just a projection of more modern sensibilities. He proposes that the state take over the responsibilities of the dead towards the surviving members, but he points to some pain that the city, for all of its benevolence and resources, cannot assuage. "For what woe could be more incurable," he asked, "than to bring forth and rear and bury one's own children . . . ? For whom could we be expected to honor in preference to those who lie here? Whom among the living should we more justly hold in high regard than their relations, who were on an equality with us all in reaping the fruits of their valor, but now that they are dead bear alone the kinsmen's part in their misfortune?"[37] The city can protect and honor the orphans and the parents, but they are nonetheless prey to an incurable evil, a suffering that the state cannot reach or palliate, and since the material resources of the city are not wanting, it is some other pain that is in question here. Death strikes only the family, according to the orator, and the irreparable suffering that it causes is uniquely the family's. The family members alone feel a pain that has nothing to do with material concerns or social standing. And because it is incurable, their pain indicates that the deceased is irreplaceable and therefore unique. But in describing that pain as unique to the family, in observing that it is not the city that feels such a loss, Lysias defines the missing individual—and the love that is attached to him—as something inherently and constitutionally outside of the city.[38] Thus the great divide that crosses through Hegel's interpretation of *Antigone* reappears in the official discourse of the state: On the side of the family lies affective individuation, on the side of the community, rational and virtuous impersonality.

From the viewpoint of the city, the individual was valued only in his death, but in the eulogies that same death was the property of the state itself, which became the goal and meaning of mortality. Even by the last quarter of the fourth century, public funerals would still commemorate the slain not so much for their specialness as for their personal insignificance, demonstrating that the citizen acquired identity by coalescing with the polity, indeed, by sacrificing himself as an individual to it. Nor was this attitude reserved entirely for public funerary discourse. It found expression in highly different areas of thought, echoing still in Aristotle's *Rhetoric*, where the philosopher stated that

> those actions are noble for which the reward is simply honour, or honour more than money. So are those in which a man aims at something desirable for someone else's sake; actions good absolutely, such as those a man does for his country without thinking of himself. . . . Noble also are those actions whose advantage may be enjoyed after death, as opposed to those whose advantage is

enjoyed during one's lifetime; for the latter are more likely to be for one's own sake only.[39]

The dead, for Aristotle, were disinterested. They had no self for selfishness. Their acts lived on independently of them until, as Nicole Loraux put it, the just could disappear into their deeds.[40] The dead, in this sense, set the standard for altruism, and even those who in their lives did good, did so in imitation of their death, for they acted as if they were in their own absence. Still, something had obviously emerged in the period that separated the prepolitical from the *Rhetoric*, for Aristotle's notion of the ethical depended on its separation from the interests of the individual. The isolated person, whose identification was so problematic in the older eras, did not merely appear in this passage; he must now be contained, his actions channeled toward others, his desires denied him, his value alienated from him into a community from which he, specifically, was absent. This need for containment reflected a movement that took place over the course of the fifth and fourth centuries, what Loraux has called a "hypertrophy" of the individual, for the tragic period was marked by a crisis in the relation between individual and community, a crisis that played itself out not only in the theater of Dionysos but also in the cemetery and in other, more intimate aspects of life.[41] An older tradition still consecrated the dead by heralding their disappearance as a sublimation of the personal into the political, speaking out through the voices of Herodotus, Pericles, Demosthenes, Lysias, and Hyperides. At the same time, however, another tendency gained strength, in which the pathos of individual suffering found expression, as in the stelae erected at tombs and even, if much more obliquely and fleetingly, in the public discourses pronounced over the deceased.[42] The personality of the dead, as we shall see in the following chapter, began to appear in the feelings that their absence evoked in those who had loved them. From this mourning arose the fragile notion of meaningful individual life.

The state created a new, autonomous, and legally responsible individual—but only as an abstraction. Nicole Loraux has summarized the state-sponsored subjectivity represented by the *epitaphioi logoi* in the following blunt terms: "So we can now understand the importance of the praise offered by the city: the dead had no other life than that of Athens."[43] Aside from this depersonalization of the citizen, which was indeed crucial to the idea of citizenship in the tragic century, I have tried to emphasize several other key traits in the eulogies: their appropriation of the familial rites of the dead, their exclusion of women from the phantasmatics of legitimacy, their relation to the tragedies in respect to the state and its origins, and the association of the family with the vague but powerful notion of affective individuation in life. For this is what is achingly absent from the discussion so far: the concept of a living individual. As we will find in the next chapter, that absence makes itself felt indirectly through the remainder of its loss, in the material remnant that survives death. This means that the citizen is the loss of an individual *who may never previously have existed*, since the individual of the family is not, as we have seen, entirely an individual either. The loss, in this circumstance, precedes the lost, but it is, as we shall see, a crucial step in the formulation of a living individual. In tragedy, death precedes life, which is known only negatively, as that which is missing.

THREE

Loss Embodied

In *Antigone*, different modes of individuation confront each other through a dispute over the treatment of a corpse, and the choice of this particular object does not seem to have been pure happenstance. Of the seven plays by Sophocles that remain, three revolve around the disposition and burial of the dead: *Ajax*, *Oedipus at Colonus*, and *Antigone*. Euripides's *Suppliant Women* returns to the same theme, again in relation to the war on Thebes.[1] In *Antigone*, Polyneices's remains are the disputed matter of the *agōn logōn*, and as such they form the terrain on which the various agencies struggle for dominance, the unresolved disaster around which they compete. To understand the significance of the differing notions of justice that conflict in the play, one would consequently have to understand the nature of what divides them. One must ask, in other words, what a corpse is. Analytically, one can say that it is dead and some kind of a human body, but even if we bracket the already discussed complexities of "death," the second term remains problematic. The Cartesian mind-body dichotomy, fruit of a self-reflexive model of subjectivity whose divided legacy Hegel will work tirelessly to reconcile, would have been understood in very different terms among the Greeks. Indeed, as imagined by scholars such as James Redfield or Bruno Snell, the Homeric Greeks lived much like Merleau-Ponty's "embodied subject," who joins itself to others "in a sort of blind recognition that precedes the definition and intellectual elaboration of meaning"—with the important distinction that the ancient Greek probably did not relate primarily to others that way, but instead and above all to himself or herself.[2] A dead body was, in short, a complicated thing, and once again we must abandon our most basic preconceptions in order to appreciate the work that is undertaken in Sophocles's play.

George Steiner has tried to explain the importance of corpses in *Antigone*, focusing especially on the way in which images of the abused dead haunt its action and dialogues. Consistent with his general strategy of reading the play through other readings of it, Steiner brings out the horror of the unburied cadaver in the reactions of earlier authors. In Robert Garnier's sixteenth-century translation, for instance, "We hear in *inhumanité*, as Garnier will have heard, the verb 'to bury': *inhumer*. Deeper still, and radical to both, lies the necessary kinship of the 'humane' and of the 'earthly,' of *humanitas* and *humus*. To deny earth to the dead is to negate their humanity and one's own."³ If for Garnier the question of inhumation already puts humanity itself at stake, the implications of neglecting the dead were even more profound for other readers. Steiner turns to a much later French author, whose writings, marked by the atrocities of the first world war, saw in the failure to bury a much greater crime: "For Romain Rolland, as for Sophocles' Teiresias, but on a far vaster scale, the nakedness of the dead between the barbed wires meant an outrage not only against humanity, but against the cosmic order."⁴ This, in turn, echoes Steiner's reading of Hölderlin: "There can be no more cataclysmic *Umkehr* and inversion of values than the exposure of the stinking dead on the earth's sunlit surface and the relegation of the living to the lightless underground of death."⁵ Catastrophe, crime against humanity and the cosmic order themselves— injustice against the corpse would seem to be worse than violence against the living, and to some extent Steiner gropes to justify, or at least comprehend, the horrified outrage that such abuse elicits. His explanation of the *Umkehr*, or reversal, is perhaps the most developed of these attempts. He argues that this represents violence of a cosmic order because Creon

> has turned life into living death, and death into desecrated organic survivance. Antigone is to "live dead" below the earth; Polyneices is to be "dead alive" above. The wheel of being has been turned obscenely full circle. Greek perception as a whole, and that of Sophocles more especially—witness the great monologue to the sunlight in *Ajax*—intimately associated light and life. To be alive is to see and to be seen by the sun; the days of the dead are unlit. Creon has done final violence to this equation. Alive, Antigone is thrust into blackness; dead, Polyneices is left to rot and to reek in the light of the sun. Teiresias suggests to us the twofold, subtly equivalent, nature of the outrage. For if the sun is sacred, so is the dark of Hades. Creon has polluted both the light and the dark, both the day and the night.⁶

The corpse befouls the very "wheel of being" itself by exposing day to night and crossing the ontological divide that separates the living from the dead. This is pollution in the sense that the structuralist anthropologist Mary Douglas gave to the term: a confusion of categories, the breakdown of those distinctions that allow sense to be generated and exchanged within a social order.[7] This argument raises, however, certain provocative questions, for it is unclear why this particular transgression of the classificatory system should generate such cataclysmic results, whereas others might have less serious consequences. Would carousing by day and working by night, for instance, have been so cosmically "obscene"? What, moreover, is the significance of the foul smell that Steiner remarks on? Does the corpse reek because it violates the order of meaning, or does it violate that order because of its loathsome odor, which would derive, for its own part, from a more fundamental aversion, perhaps biologically determined, to putrefaction— or what Steiner elsewhere calls "the primal dread of decomposition . . . central to the play"?[8] In speaking of such a "primal dread," Steiner seems unable to choose between the structuralist approach he had earlier adopted and a more positivist one. The unburied corpse is a cataclysm; it is the center of the play; but his two explanations of its extraordinary force do not sit easily together.

Strain like this at the heart of such a magisterial reading as Steiner's suggests significant trouble in the original text itself and, indeed, in the whole history of its reception, which he traces. Steiner's interpretation becomes particularly problematic—and consequently promising—in his handling of how Hegel theorizes Polyneices's corpse. First of all, Hegel treats the question as part of an analysis of the universal individual, that is to say, the individual who is honored by the family. As has already been seen, this individual attains universality through death, but Steiner's understanding of the function of death in this passage is quite different from the one I worked out earlier, and his approach bears some scrutiny, especially since it reveals the ways in which more contemporary ideas of mortality can anachronistically torque readings of both Hegel and, to a greater degree, Sophocles. As Steiner writes, "Within the family, the commanding agencies of consciousness are those of relationship to individualized particularity. It is the specific persona which is conceived as totality. To it is assigned a weight of presentness denied to the 'generalized individuality' of the citizen in the perspective of the state. Death, as it were, 'specifies this specificity' in the highest degree. It is the extreme accomplishment of the unique (as in the Kierkegaardian-Heideggerian postulate of one's *own* death, inalienable to any other)."[9] Quite aside from the fallacious argument that death is uniquely untransferable, what is troubling here is the conflation of Heidegger with Hegel and, more seriously, of Heidegger with Sophocles.[10] Now, Hegel does not see death as bestowing individuality on the family member, but rather a paradoxical universality. On this he is quite clear: "This universality which the individual *as such* attains is *pure being, death*."[11] In fact, death's universality threatens to dissolve the particularity of the individual, and it is against this menace of impersonality that the surviving family members must take action. At death, according to Hegel, the bond holding self-consciousness and matter together is broken, and

> individuality passes over into this *abstract* negativity, which, being *in its
> own self* without consolation and reconciliation, must receive them
> [i.e., the two sundered aspects of its consciousness] essentially through
> a *real* and *external act*. Blood-relationship supplements, then, the
> abstract natural process by adding to it the movement of consciousness,
> interrupting the work of Nature and rescuing the blood-relation from
> destruction.[12]

To understand how burial rites—for that is the "movement of conscious-ness" in question here—can intervene between the dead and death, between individual existence and its absolute destruction, one must look more closely at how Hegel uses the different terms of this passage. He gives two princi-pal reasons to explain why death is a violence against individuality that must be repaired by the living, and that there are exactly two derives from his view of death as the splitting or "diremption" of a pair of elements that had previously been joined in the living person: on the one hand, the abstract force of self-consciousness and, on the other, the material person or body.[13] First, the abstract consciousness of the individual is freed from the particu-larity of his actual, physical existence and threatens to vanish into the pure impersonality of death, the nonexistence that befalls all alike and therefore indifferentiates them. Second, the body starts, for its part, to lose its hold on individuality, because the death that befalls it, whether or not it culminates some knowing action on the part of the deceased, is fundamentally a natural event, involving the mere physical existence of the person. For Hegel, natu-ral means unconsciousness, which is to say, the inhuman world of rocks, plants, animals (and women) that expresses universal spirit but remains incapable of rising to awareness of it.[14] Against this, he sets a higher order of individuality, which is the autonomy of human consciousness. For natural death to have human meaning, it must therefore be attached, by way of a conscious act, to the autonomous individual who suffers it.[15] The natural, bodily event of death must, in short, be made conscious for it to be individual.[16] The deceased himself cannot do this, so the duty falls upon the family, and in the funeral rites it dedicates to the dead, the family wills the death that befell their member. This is not the same as wanting that loss, but instead means removing its accidental aspect. Through the "supplement" of these rites, death becomes a conscious piece of work, owned and subjectivized. By recognizing, if only in act, the need for this supplement, these rites mark, too, the fragility of the link that binds a subject to its demise. We will encounter a version of this fragility in Antigone's refusal to let her sister "share" her death. Far from specifying the specificity of a person, as Steiner puts it, death itself must be specified. This is not at all the untransferable, the inalienable finality that Heidegger sees separating the individual *Dasein* from the rest of humanity and imposing on it the infinite isolation of its authentic being. Instead, for the Hegel of this passage— as for Sophocles—the individuality of death is not an absolute but a construct.[17]

For Steiner, the fear attending neglect of these rites translates "the primal dread of decomposition, of violation by dogs and birds of prey, central to the play," a dread that the "esoteric concreteness of Hegel's vision reanimates, as does almost no other commentary on *Antigone*."[18] In something of the same way that he treats death as an absolute, Steiner also seems to see in decomposition a primordial, almost axiomatic object of horror. But if we are to understand this fear that is central to the play, we must push farther and ask why the unburied corpse is so dreadful. And Hegel is particularly helpful in this regard, since he does not merely "reanimate" the horror of the rotting dead, but also, and more important, attempts to dissipate that fear by understanding it and by making it an object of reason. As he puts it:

> The dead individual, by having liberated his *being* from his *action* or his negative unity, is an empty singular, merely a passive being-for-another, at the mercy of every lower irrational individuality and the forces of abstract material elements, all of which are now more powerful than himself: the former on account of the life they possess, the latter on account of their

negative nature. The Family keeps away from the dead this dishonouring
of him by unconscious appetites and abstract entities, and puts its own action
in their place, and weds the blood-relation to the bosom of the earth, to the
elemental imperishable individuality. The Family thereby makes him a
member of a community which prevails over and holds under control the
forces of particular material elements and the lower forms of life, which
sought to unloose themselves against him and to destroy him.[19]

Against the now entirely passive individual are arrayed both "every lower
irrational individuality," or beasts, and "the forces of abstract material
elements," or the processes of putrefaction and decay. As agents of nature,
animals are irrational, which is to say, incapable of recognizing their relation to absolute Spirit, while material dissolution is abstract in the sense
that it cannot attain to form-giving consciousness. In burying its dead, the
family protects their individuality from the predations of these lower
elements. But these elements do not exist as utterly external to the individual or in a realm entirely separated from subjectivity, for they also
embody, in objectified form, the unconscious appetitive drives of human
beings. In this sense, Hegel's analysis grapples with one of the great problems of post-Enlightenment philosophy: how to draw the line between
thought and nature, or between the autonomous individual and the great
forces of the material world. If Kant saw an insuperable divide between
things in themselves and our understanding of them, if Fichte abandoned
the thing in itself altogether to posit a world of pure ideality, Hegel argued,
instead, for a communality of substance between nature and consciousness,
a communality in which human beings, at the moment of their highest historical attainment, embody the self-awareness of the world. But although it
reconciles us to a nature from which we had formerly been exiled, this continuity of substance also means that we are not entirely safe from natural
forces, even in the intimacy of our own being. And here that danger takes a
specific, grotesque form in the exposed cadaver, for this passage reminds us
that we are animals and material organisms too. That is why we can fall
under their power, can lust and long and moulder. The corpse offers up, in
this sense, a one-sided image of ourselves, a figure of all that is beastly and
material within us and that we must struggle against at every moment. In its
passive abjection, the corpse thus represents forces that we must constantly
fear and dominate throughout our lives if we are to be human and if we are
to be individuals.

Although, for Hegel, the individual separates into a material, or unconscious, principle on the one hand and "the calm of simple universality" on
the other, the two aspects remain joined in the corpse. In becoming a
memory, in joining the Eumenides, the deceased has passed into the purity
of thought, but that thought can still be endangered by what befalls its
material remains. The departed, in short, tarries somehow with his cadaver,
still invested in it. Were this not the case, the funeral rites would have no
meaning, for their task, according to Hegel, consists precisely in maintain-
ing this link between the individuality of a now absolutely vulnerable body
and the immaterial person it represents. Or more precisely, through their
treatment of the corpse, the rites assure that the deceased retains his or her
personhood. The very fact that such an action is necessary indicates that the
dead risk disappearing, dissolving into the sheer impersonality of "mere
being." The dead, in other words, can still die. This possibility of dying
again or more than dying reverberates on various registers throughout
the play. Tiresias, for example, voices it when he asks Creon, "What is the
bravery of killing a man over again?" and so does Creon himself, when
he later receives a messenger bearing news of his wife's suicide: "Alas, you
have killed a dead man a second time!" he cries. "What new message of my
wife's death, alas, alas, lies upon me, bringing destruction after death?"[20]
Even Antigone's question to Creon: "Would you now do more than seize
and slay me?" echoes this concern.[21] Her words, as Steiner contends, could
simply betray fear of the physical suffering that seems implicit in the "dreadful death" with which Creon has just threatened her. But they more likely
address his decision to have Ismene share her fate, since in what follows
Antigone makes no mention of bodily pain but does vigorously refuse to
share punishment with her sister, culminating her argument with the line:
"My death will be enough!" In this latter sense, the real threat from Creon
is that he will take her death away from her, that he will do more than kill
her, or somehow kill her again, that is, kill in retrospect the person she had
become in crafting her own, solitary mortality.[22] Within the larger context
of the play—with its central fixation on funeral rites and violence against
the dead, with its corpse-strewn setting and the references by Creon and
Tiresias to double-killing—Antigone's fear of a fate worse than death seems
part of a more general concern that the fragility of selfhood extends beyond
the moment of demise, that it is not enough to die well, but that one must
also successfully stay dead.

Hellenists have devoted significant attention to the Greek obsession with the "beautiful corpse" and the general treatment of the slain, while recent readings of *Antigone* have focused on the idea of life in death that seems to run through it.[23] Robert Garland has observed that Greek funerary practices seemed to imply some remnant of sensitivity and consciousness among the dead, and Rush Rehm has remarked of Antigone herself, "She is like a traveler who never arrives, caught in the liminal state between living maiden and dead bride."[24] Judith Butler has interpreted that "liminality" between two states as an expression of nonnormative sexuality, trapped between societal interdictions and its need for expression.[25] For Lacan, it represents the condition of humanity caught between living experiences and the language that negates them.[26] In Chapter 7, I spend some time analyzing these different approaches, but here I want to push the analysis in a different direction. By arguing throughout his mature works for a continuity between the natural and spiritual worlds, Hegel places his reading of *Antigone* in a larger context that would not have been conceptually possible before him and that allows his readers to understand Polyneices's funeral rites not merely as a means to secure the deceased's identity but also as a way to figure anxieties about the living. The unsatisfied and vulnerable dead are fantasies that the survivors produce, and they are fantasies of a fragile subjectivity on the verge of death again, laid open to the predations of lower forces. Or, to put it differently, if the dead can die, it means that they are still alive; and if their identity depends on the treatment of the corpse, it means, too, that they are still invested in it, that they remain embodied. The deceased are pathetic, in an etymological sense, because they suffer and can only suffer. And in this suffering, they offer images of a frightening subjectivity, of a consciousness among its own mouldering remains.[27] Although Hegel imagines the consciousness of the corpse to come from outside of it, from the kinfolk who, through their mourning and funerary rituals, resolve the opposition between their beloved and an inherently alien death, the great, strange force of his argument is to help us see that this pathetic subject is not simply a projection of our own self-awareness into a state of absolute powerlessness, but also gives image to an identity that is different from ours (and by us, I mean those who can write and read words like these), one that is neither clearly defined as an individual nor entirely separable from the corpse it inhabits. Over what he calls the Penates looms this personification of the lower orders, of consciousness among the rotting flesh, among the rocks and dirt and animals. This is the dark face of the Eumenides, perhaps better designated here under their less friendly name of Erinyes. This is also the fantasy that must necessarily haunt the mourners as they consecrate the body of the dead, for the "supplement" they offer could not work if it did not attach death to the consciousness of the deceased, if it did not feign, in all sincerity, to please and sacralize the wishes of the dead. Were the rites to correspond to the wishes of anyone but the dead, if those wishes were recognized, for instance, as projections from the living onto the deceased, they could not be effective, for insofar as he is living the individual is inherently alien from his death, while insofar as he is nonexistent he is unavailable for reconciliation with his death. And so, the mourners must maintain the fantasy that the dead is still present *in his death*, that it is his conscious desire *as dead* that is respected in the funeral rites. And because these rites are directed toward his corpse, because they are impossible without it, it is the physical remains of the dead that localize and give shape to the fantasy of his consciousness in death. This is not what Hegel says, and he would probably react with indignation to the idea that his notion of funerary rites depends on an unstated fantasy that the dead body retains some sort of awareness and suffers its fate, but without such a fantasy the dead disappear into the anonymity of their nonexistence. It is this fact that is attested to, moreover, in Hegel's specific reference to the presence of the corpse in the funerary rituals and in the intense suffering that the fate of Polyneices's mortal remains have produced in Antigone, *Antigone*, and the Western literary tradition.

The play, moreover, works through this vision of the sentient corpse in the great symmetry of crime and punishment that underlies its plot. The penance for burying the dead is to be buried alive, and as Polyneices must rot uncovered, so is Antigone sentenced to live entombed. She takes with her to the grave her desires, her fears, and even her sense of a possible guilt, but most important, she carries with her the consciousness that she is alive in death. She will still suffer the urgings of her body, its longings for the nuptial couch. She will still feel the uneasy spur of conscience, worrying that her punishment has met approval from the very gods that she had meant to serve. And she will know herself in the powerlessness of a death imposed on her living being. There is, as we've seen Steiner remark, some profound violence in this confusion of opposites. Creon, as he wrote, "has turned life into living death, and death into desecrated organic survivance. . . . [He] has polluted both the light and the dark, both the day and the night."[28] Hegel's reading refocuses the nature of this transgression. In his interpretation, the violence of Creon's acts is directed not so much against the cosmic order as against the internal structures of the human individual who perceives that order—what is expressed in the nakedness of Polyneices's corpse and Antigone's living entombment is the animal, almost mineral, unconscious underlying the self. And as expressions, both acts represent a consciousness of the unconscious in humanity.

Antigone betrays her anxiety about this unconscious consciousness through her words, quoted in part by Hegel: "If this is approved among the gods, I should forgive them for what I have suffered, since I have done wrong; but if they are the wrongdoers, may they not suffer worse evils than those they are unjustly inflicting upon me."[29] The last two lines give voice to a cosmic fear, the apprehension that the world itself may be unjust, but those are the very lines that Hegel omits.[30] He concentrates instead on the first two, in which Antigone worries that she has misunderstood the order of being. This she can forgive, for in such a turn of events the world as a whole remains fair, and in this way the supposition that she has done wrong in her intended piety draws the issue of guilt down to her own person, her own perception of justice. She allows the possibility that one can misread the meaning of the gods and the order of being that they represent. Even according to Antigone herself, the just punishment for this misconstrual is a living death. Or, to force the issue: This misconstrual is itself already a living death. To misunderstand that the laws of the city Creon promulgates are those of the gods as well is to misunderstand what a person is, the limits of one's being and its place in the fabric of sense. If the punishment is just, Antigone will be, already always will have been, the corpse-consciousness sinking into the earth, torn by the teeth of dogs, littering, criminal and incoherent, the space outside the walls. This other being, this confused and apolitical consciousness in vaguely human form, spreads its ghastly shape among the slain and the executed who lie without burial. It is ghastly because, in its hideous nonsense, we feel the sudden tug of recognition: So am I outside the city. The corpse is a figure of misinterpretation. It is the picture of a self that makes no sense within the walls of meaning. It is, as Socrates says of the body in general, "unintelligible."[31] And yet this meaningless being has some sort of sentience, some emotion, some vague awareness.

The unburied dead are, however, not as powerless as they would seem at first. In a weird, phantasmagorical scene of vengeance, Hegel depicts them as a potent force whose claims will eventually prevail against the injustice done them by the city. Polyneices's demand to be covered in death is as much an expression of the ethical order as Creon's sentence against him, and it cannot, therefore, remain unsatisfied. This is the impulse of history, of absolute spirit working through toward the certainty of itself, and so the last word cannot go to the city, although in his youth, Hegel had imagined it to be the final shape of human destiny.[32] It is, consequently, the slain who, in returning to the place that had exiled them, repair the course of history.

> The dead, whose right is denied, knows therefore how to find instruments of vengeance, which are equally effective and powerful as the power which has injured it. These powers are other communities whose altars the dogs or birds defiled with the corpse, which is not raised into unconscious universality by being given back, as its due, to the elemental individuality [the earth], but remains above ground in the realm of outer reality, and has now acquired as a force of divine law a self-consciousness, real universality. They rise up in hostility and destroy the community which has dishonoured and shattered its own power, the sacred claims of the Family.[33]

This is certainly one of the most vivid passages of the *Phenomenology* and one of the richest in concrete details. Already, it is rare to find an exact quotation or a specific name in the text, and Hegel has already used both in his references to *Antigone*. But here, he also gives himself over to a close reading of specific lines from the play—Tiresias's angry rebuke of Creon—as if the history of absolute spirit were written in them and the work of philosophy had become an act of literary exegesis.[34] And perhaps, at this point in history, that is how he understood the play, for as he would later write, "As ethical spirit . . . Greek spirit is the political work of art."[35] The dead rise up here in arms, though not their own. Their bodies have become pasture for the beasts that feed on carrion and haunt the European imagination of war. The slain have not yet dissolved into unconsciousness; they still, it would seem, retain some glimmer of awareness, and their unsleeping cause becomes that of the outraged cities that circle Thebes, the ones whose houses and altars have been defiled by this alien, thinking filth, similar in kind to what Antigone calls "living neither among mortals nor as a shade among the shades, neither with the living nor with the dead," when she contemplates "the heaped-up mound of [her] strange tomb."[36] As their cause is taken up by other poleis, it thereby attains to the true universality that they alone embody, the impersonal collectivity of those through whom the community loathes and loves. It is now the cities and not just the kinsfolk who do what the dead are imagined to want. The self-consciousness of the corpse is now that of the polluted city. Or to put it the other way around: The self-consciousness of the city is the thinking of the corpse. To be a city is to suffer as the cadaver suffers, but to act on this pain and this injustice. It is to turn filth into the purity of impersonal action through the selfless endeavor of war. Disinterested death cleans the altars of the stains left by a grotesquely material consciousness, a deliquescent self, carried piecemeal in the mouths of dogs and the droppings of birds. But also, in this vision, the city rises up like a saprophyte, finding its substance and sustenance among the dead bodies that defile it. For the city, according to Hegel, "*is, moves,* and *maintains* itself by consuming and absorbing into itself [*in sich aufzehrt*] the separatism of the Penates, or the separation into independent families presided over by womankind, and by keeping them dissolved in the fluid continuity of its own nature [*und sie in der Kontinuität seiner Flüssigkeit erhält*]. . . . The community only gets an existence through its interference with the happiness of the Family, and by dissolving [individual] self-consciousness into the universal."[37] The nature of the city is to contain the violence of the families. The work of the family, in turn, is to handle the dead, to assure that their destructiveness is held in check and that their frightening, liminal powers are forgotten in the very process of memorialization. The city is built on this double containment of the corpse: its burial and then the erasure of that burial.

The corpse is central to *Antigone*, but its meaning, I have argued, is unclear. George Steiner's reading of the play probably documents its effects on the Western imagination more comprehensively than any other, and although he recognizes, in almost hyperbolic terms, the force and significance of the corpse within the play, he has difficulty explaining them. He points, however, to what would seem to be the most promising analysis of the issue, citing a passage from Hegel's *Phenomenology*. Still, Hegel's interpretation of the corpse differs from Steiner's description of it—it differs even from Hegel's own, ostensible intentions, since it incorporates a strange, unacknowledged phantasmatic element: the idea of a persistent sentience in the corpse.[38] The deceased, according to this fantasy, brings to a crisis the indeterminacy between life and death in the individual. In order to determine the larger significance of that fantasy, however, we must see if it resonates in other texts contemporary with the tragedies.

FOUR

States of Exclusion

A strange fantasy, as we have seen, weaves its way through Hegel's interpretation of *Antigone*, and this is not just some stray thread, but a crucial, if hidden, filament that holds his whole argument together. In this fantasy, the corpse retains some dim remnant of sentience, a pathetic neediness that is ready, when confronted by an unbearable injustice, to degenerate into rancor, violence, and pollution. By the logic of Hegel's argument, moreover, this thread must remain secret even to the mourners who project their own imaginings onto the dead, for otherwise the individuation they were supposed to effect would short-circuit, remaining only in their own minds and never reaching the deceased. The role of the dead in the life of ancient Athens would thus function something like a necessary psychotic state, in which subjective projections pass for objective reality and structure the very notion of individuality.[1] Now, although Hegel's reading might express the importance of *Antigone* to the modern experience of subjectivity—via a return to its mythic origins in fifth-century Athens—it is less clear how well that reading describes the experience of ancient Greeks, and so it is worth turning to other documents from the tragic era to see how corpses were understood at the time and to determine, on that basis, whether Hegel's argument can hold up in relation to the ancient past.

It would seem in theory at least that the Greeks of Plato's era perceived a sharp distinction between body and soul, or *sōma* and *psychē*.[2] In the early dialogue *Alcibiades* 1, Socrates identified the individual explicitly and exclusively with the latter while dismissing the former as a mere instrument through which a person's will is expressed.[3] His judgment remained essentially unchanged until the end of his life, for in his last conversation before dying he concluded, after a lengthy analysis of the question, that "the soul is most like that which is divine, immortal, intelligible, uniform, indissoluble, and ever self-consistent and invariable, whereas body is most like that which is human, mortal, multiform, unintelligible, dissoluble, and never self-consistent."[4] Later, in the same dialogue, when Crito asked him how he wished to be buried, the philosopher responded, "Any way you like . . . , that is, if you can catch me and I don't slip through your fingers." A few moments later, he turned toward those around him to playfully upbraid his old friend, who seemed to share Hegel's unspoken fantasy that the corpse retains some form of identity and even sentience:

> He thinks that I am the one whom he will see presently lying dead [*nekron*], and he asks how he is to bury me! . . . You must assure him that when I am dead I shall not stay, but depart and be gone. That will help Crito to bear it more easily, and keep him from being distressed on my account when he sees my body being burned or buried, as if something dreadful were happening to me, or from saying at the funeral that it is Socrates whom he is laying out or carrying to the grave or burying.[5]

This scene from the last hours of Socrates's life would have taken place in 406, thirty-five years after *Antigone* and only a few months before the first production of *Oedipus at Colonus*, yet nothing could be farther from the attitudes of Sophocles's characters than this absolute indifference to the rituals of burial and the handling of the corpse, an indifference that Plato faithfully maintained as time passed. He again dismissed the significance of the body toward the end of his own life, when he wrote about the proper treatment of the dead in book 12 of the *Laws*. There he stated that "what gives each one of us his being is nothing else but his soul, whereas the body is no more than a shadow which keeps us company. So 'tis well said of the deceased that the corpse is but a ghost . . . . We should never waste our substance in the fancy that he who was so much to us is this bulk of flesh that is being committed to the grave."[6] And because he denied the body's significance for personhood, Plato set firm limits on the mourning and ceremonies that may be accorded to a cadaver. It must not be buried in arable land, thus depriving the living of sustenance, nor should it be carried through the streets. A schedule of maximum expenditures for funeral rites was established according to economic class. The "noise of mourning" should not be audible outside the house where the vigil is held, and the body "must be beyond the city wall before daybreak."[7] All in all, the legislator displayed a profound distaste for anything that expressed an emotional attachment to the deceased's physical remains, something like a categorical indignation that nothing should steal from something, that a nonperson should impose on people or be treated like one of them.[8] Although Socrates, at the time of his execution, spoke with more wit and levity than the Athenian of the *Laws*, he betrayed a similar antipathy toward physical existence in general, for when Crito suggested that instead of hurrying to kill himself Socrates should enjoy a last dinner with his friends, the philosopher responded: "I should gain nothing by drinking the poison a little later— I should only make myself ridiculous [*gelōta ophlēsein* = "incur laughter"] in my own eyes if I clung to life [*glixomenos tou zēn*] and hugged it when it has no more to offer [*kai pheidomenos oudenos eti enontos*]."[9] A meal, it would seem, is literally nothing (*ouden*). Given that the real Socrates is the one who "slips through your fingers," there is no need to stay for dinner, since to do so is to choose the false over the real, nothing over being.[10] But something curious is happening here: to enjoy the pleasures of the flesh and of worldly company is to cling, in some humiliating way, to life. There is still space, it would seem, for one affect among the disembodied dead who are the real: shame. Shame for the body and for love of friends, as if the relation between the *psychē* and the *sōma* were one of humiliation. The corpse and the things that fall on its side, like physical and social pleasures, are not quite, therefore, the nothing that they would seem to be, for they carry an embarrassing affective charge.

One finds a similar inconsistency in Plato's *Laws*, for after dismissing the corpse as "a ghost" on which we "should never waste our substance," the statesman then proceeds to sanction punishments against it, as if it did, in fact, have an ongoing significance: "Rites of sepulture, as also the acts which involve loss of the right to sepulture—parricide, sacrilege, and others— have already been made matters of legislation," he observes, "and we may accordingly say that our code is substantially completed."[11] It is true that scholars have understood the treatment of corpses as a way to control the behavior of the living, so that sumptuary laws on funerals, for instance, might have been a means to hold powerful families in check.[12] But in Plato's writings, at least, it seems quite possible that laws concerning corpses were motivated by fantasies about the dead. It is irrational to punish nothing, and yet that is what seems to be occurring here, or rather, the corpse apparently retains some hold on the criminal. To preserve the coherence of the argument, one could interpret this as a gesture not against the dead but toward mastering the sentimental bond that joins the unenlightened to the remains of their deceased. In this way, the violence against the corpse would have no effect on the latter but would hold a minatory value for those unphilosophical criminals who care about the treatment of their own cadaver. Such an approach would permit the emotional power of the corpse to work for, rather than against, the laws.[13] Instead of repressing such impulses, in short, the legislator now harnesses them, thereby incorporating a persistent irrationality into the very structure of the polis. And the crimes that elicit such an unreasonable retribution are those against an older order associated with Antigone and women in general. They are crimes against the gods and the family: parricide and sacrilege. As these archaic familial agencies continue to act at the heart of the city, so too then does the force of the dead body. The unspoken fantasy that permits the conjoining of death with the dead individual in Hegel, the belief that the dead feel, is taken up here to another end by Plato's ideal legislator. The corpse becomes the figure for a persistent irrationality within the rational order of the city.

This fantasy of a feeling corpse is consistent with a larger conception of the interpenetration of life and matter. "All soul," according to Plato's *Phaedrus*, "has the care of all that is inanimate, and traverses the whole universe, though in ever-changing forms."[14] The world, by this reasoning, is a living, sentient thing, down to its least details. Plato stopped sometimes to contemplate the implications of this pan-animism, and at the end of the *Timaeus* he tarried at length with the details of this idea, drawing, in the process, a gloomy picture of the subhuman consciousness that his theory entailed: "On the subject of animals, then, the following remarks may be offered," he wrote. "Of the men who came into the world, those who were cowards or led unrighteous lives may with reason be supposed to have changed into the nature of women in the second generation. . . . Thus were created women and the female sex in general."[15] He went on, following the scale of sentient beings downward with mounting disparagement. So the birds derived, for their part, from "innocent light-minded men" who aspired to heavenly things, but let themselves be fascinated by images and the power of physical sight. The quadrupeds' faces were drawn down toward the earth to reflect the base tendencies of the souls that inhabit them. "God," continued Plato,

> gave the more senseless of them the more support that they might be more attracted to the earth. And the most foolish of them, who trail their bodies

entirely upon the ground and have no longer any need of feet, he made without feet to crawl upon the earth. The fourth class were the inhabitants of the water; these were made out of the most entirely senseless and ignorant of all. . . . And hence arose the race of fishes and oysters [*ostreon*], and other aquatic animals, which have received the most remote habitations as a punishment of their outlandish ignorance.[16]

The oyster, whose ambiguous minerality so revolted Sartre, embodies a lonely and dimwitted consciousness, the frightening image of an undying, but scarcely living mind.[17] It returns in the *Phaedrus* as a figure for the general relation between the crude materiality of the body and the divine soul it shelters: "Pure was the light that shone around us," Plato writes, "and pure were we, without taint of that prisonhouse which now we are encompassed withal, and call a body, fast bound therein as an oyster [*ostreou*] in its shell."[18] The path of degeneration starts with women, keepers of the family and the dead, and then descends from them toward the lowest level of intelligence, that barely perceptible remnant of awareness that haunts the darkest recesses of living matter. In this sense, the oyster plays much the same role in Plato's imagination as does the cadaver in Hegel's reading of *Antigone*. It is the figure of a consciousness that haunts the farthest reaches of the living world, shading off into the absolute stupidity of inanimate matter in the muddy depths of the sea.

In the *Laws*, Plato attempts to master this parlous continuity between inanimate matter, animals, and human beings through a rationalized system of universal laws. This is not a simple case of magical thinking, in the sense that Freud gave to the term—that is, an attempt to work backward along the chain of causality and provoke material events by re-creating their effects.[19] As grotesquely literal as they might seem to modern readers, the results of this legislation reveal instead the desire for a comprehensive justice that could spread equally throughout the physical and psychic worlds, the belief—or at least the hope—that through human intervention the inhuman can be forced to submit to the divine. Plato's sanctions against bestial or even mineral criminality thus express the fantasy that human agency can reconcile material and immaterial existences and that such agency is guided by a transcendental, and therefore generally applicable, ethics. If punishing animals and rocks seems silly to modern sensibilities, that is probably because of the unembarrassed simplicity with which it disguises a more profound anxiety: that the world of rocks and beasts is *unheimlich*—that is, at once intimately familiar and uncontrollably foreign.[20] And even by its own terms this attempt at a universal legislation is only partially successful, since it systematically creates an unmasterable remainder, an elsewhere that, by the very structures of the law, cannot be submitted to jurisdiction.

> If a beast of draft or other animal cause homicide . . . the kinsman shall institute proceedings for homicide against the slayer. The case shall be heard by such and as many of the rural commissioners as the next of kin may appoint; on conviction, the beast shall be put to death and cast out beyond the frontier [*exō tōn horōn tēs chōras*]. If an inanimate thing cause the loss of a human life . . . it shall be sat upon in judgment . . . —on conviction the guilty object [is] to be cast beyond the frontier, as was directed in the case of the beast.[21]

Two points merit particular remark in this passage. First, the author sees a continuity of responsibility linking the human to the animal to the mineral. In the vision of the underworld from the last pages of the *Republic*, accountability for one's deeds may serve to separate individual from individual, but here, in the *Laws*, it cannot even distinguish between the animate and the inanimate. Second, and more complex, the criminal must be excluded from the confines of the state. It is not sufficient that a malefactor be put to death; its remains as well must be cast out from within the circle of the law, and in this way the city creates an exteriority from itself, a place to which its jurisdiction need not—and, in fact, cannot—extend. Even while colonizing the irrationality of lifeless matter, the reason of the state delimits a realm where its power no longer prevails. This is the place for that which cannot be punished enough—like the rock or any other inanimate thing, such as a corpse, that cannot simply be put to death. (And the insistence on homicide in this passage suggests that the crime here is really that of the dead against life itself, against the point of frailty that separates the living from all else.) Beyond the walls, beyond the *horoi* or limit markers of the fields, stretches a zone to which one relegates the last, irreducible remnants of the criminal. If legislation is the mastery of the continuity that joins matter to thought, the sentient to the inanimate, then the place beyond the *horoi* is where that continuity escapes control. The rock or beast is not merely, therefore, a legally accountable entity; it is also, and more profoundly, an image of personal responsibility projected into the natural world. As such, it translates both a phantasmatic indistinction between the

human and inhuman and the will to subjugate that indistinction to the processes of arbitration—and thus distinction—themselves. In being placed
outside the city's precincts, the criminal corpse identifies that nonpolitical
space as essentially, even ontologically hostile to the state, its justice, and its
claim to legitimacy.

After the expulsion of the corpses, probably the most significant form of
exclusion adopted at this historical juncture, and one of the most remarked
on elements in Cleisthenes's political reforms of 507/508 (some ten years
before Sophocles's birth) was ostracism. Although rarely applied, this invention nonetheless played a crucial role in the new state institutions. The
process was relatively simple: Once a year, the citizens could elect to exile
any one of their number for the period of a decade. The name of the punishment derives from the fact that the votes themselves were inscribed on
ostraka, a word that has the dual meanings of seashell and pottery shard.
Although the archaeological record indicates that in practice the chits cast
were bits of ceramic, the original term establishes a lexical continuity
between the oyster (or *ostreon*) and the ostracized—a connection that is
reenforced by the liminal status of both the shellfish and the banished—and
suggests some of the abjection that adhered to the victims.[22] Apparently
the intentions behind the new policy were to prevent any individual from
reestablishing a tyrannical dynasty and to create a means for resolving otherwise intractable struggles among different factions of the body politic.[23]
Although it would seem to be an extremely harsh means to end disputes and
a disturbingly preemptive way to handle what were, after all, only potential
crimes, ostracism has generally been considered a humane reform, since it
replaced older and more radical forms of expulsion, such as *atimia*, which
had been codified under Solon. Permanent and hereditary, that earlier version of banishment institutionalized the concept of miasma, for the entire
genos of the evildoer was cast out of the city and considered polluted until
the end of time.[24] Cleisthenes himself was stained by the guilt of an ancestral transgression under this old law and was, in fact, obliged to flee the city
when his rival, Isagoras, recalled the crime that still hung over his family.[25]
The violence of *atimia* went further, however, for Solon's intention had, in
his own words, been to reduce the culpable lineage to dust. Anyone who
encountered a member of the banished family within the borders of the
state could put him or her to death with impunity, while, at the same time,
the guilty party's property was destroyed and their bodies forfeited all right

of sepulture.[26] The punishment of *atimia* was a codification, in short, of familial miasma. It seems, in turn, to have inherited some of its particularities and violence from a still older and more widespread practice, that of the *pharmakos*. On the sixth day of the Thargelia each year, two men were cast out of Athens, bearing with them the collective guilt of the inhabitants.[27] They were chosen not because of any particular wrongdoing, but for their apparent predestination for such a role—by the fact that through their exceptional ugliness or deformity they manifestly embodied the most extreme abjection.[28]

These victims polluted the state with its own crimes and had, consequently, to be destroyed or expelled from it, but at the same time, insofar as they purged the community, they enjoyed a sacred privilege. As representatives of collective guilt, they personified the city and thus fell within its walls, but at the same time, as precisely all that must be rejected by the city, they had no part in it. "The ceremony of the *pharmakos*," wrote Jacques Derrida, "is thus played out on the boundary line between inside and outside, which it has as its function ceaselessly to trace and retrace. *Intra muros/ extra muros*."[29] The scapegoat thus continually redefined political space and the limits of its meaning, focusing in his person the city's hatred for the alienation that it could never entirely extirpate from itself and materializing an abjection that ritualistically crystallized every year on the same day, thus marking the very time of the political with a recurrent pattern of self-recognition and self-alienation. For Julia Kristeva, moreover, the ceremony reenacted another, more primordial violence that marked the originary moment when the city first took shape, the sacrificial act in which the symbolic order established itself through a rejection of the semiotic as such, or through what she calls "the inaugural split [*coupure inaugurale*]."[30] The community, according to her, thus created itself by more or less the same process of symbolic castration that would permit access to individual subjectivity and the law of the father within the Oedipal structures of a single family. In the case of the city, however, the originary violence was focused against a specific figuration of that semiotic otherness, and this specification of alterity seems to have played an integral role in the self-identification of the state, for over the course of time, as the ceremonies of the *pharmakos* gave way to *atimia* and then to ostracism, the process of exclusion became more and more clearly focused on the individual as such. Indeed, Jean-Pierre Vernant has argued that the ostracized could be considered, in a certain sense, to occupy a position symmetrical to that of the *pharmakos*, since he stood out from the community by virtue of his superiority, whereas the victims of the Thargelia were distinguished by their baseness.[31] In both cases, however, the victims separated themselves from the group. Already, in serving as a solitary example of the whole city, the scapegoat represented a form of individuation, the narrowing of attention onto a single person chosen from the collective. With the practice of ostracism, however, that emphasis on singularity came more clearly to the fore, and as Jérôme Carcopino observed, Cleisthenes "thus effected a profound transformation in the juridical life of his city," for the new form of punishment substituted "the new principle of personal responsibility for the principle of family unity that had always been applied until then."[32] One can, however, go farther and argue that the ostracized is not merely *an* individual, but that he represents, in a deeper sense, the individual *as such*, for as potential tyrant, he is the one who would assume sole power over the city, who would claim to embody its laws in his own person and to speak for its will through his single voice. In the history of civic rejection, the individual itself thus became the object of hatred, the other of the city.

Like the scapegoat, moreover, the ostracized enjoyed a privileged status in relation to the city, for he was both the personification of its subjective coherence and, for that very reason, the figure of its excluded. In contrast, as we have seen in an earlier chapter, the citizen was conceptualized as the subsumption of the individual into the larger body politic. As just such a body, Athens defined itself in opposition to a counterpart, and a rich field of sources—including tragedies such as Aeschylus's *Eumenides*, documents such as the *epitaphios logos* in Plato's *Menexenus*, and the foundational legends that they drew on—located the separation of the city from that other at a specific, mythic moment. The act of ostracism repeated this mythic origin, the theoretical "inaugural split" that the city's very existence seemed to suppose, but it was structurally condemned to repeat it in endless annual cycles, for the instant that such an origin could be figured, the instant that it could be localized in a specific time, place, and gesture, it falsified the symbolic abstraction that this gesture was supposed to inaugurate. The beginning thus revealed itself to be permanently unfinished and therefore in constant need of a supplementary act that could complete the outstanding business of its own paradoxical creation. Insofar, however, as the supplement itself was figurative, and therefore particular, it too remained incomplete and thus led the process of founding the city into an endless regress, or, in practice, a cyclical correction of the interminably faulty origin.[33] This intractable problem of effacing the specificity of the original effacement of the specific was itself mythologized in the accounts that attributed the institution of ostracism to Theseus and then cited him as its first victim.[34] In a similar way, Cleisthenes himself was among the handful of individuals actually ostracized from Athens. Theoretically, at least, the punishment ceaselessly reenacted the separation of the city from its other. And the ostracized, the one on whose person this impossible demarcation was exercised, was also the oyster-man, the ineradicable remainder within the system, the vertiginous point of its own incapacity to close onto itself.

The scapegoat represented a paradox in the definition the state, a necessary but inherently unsatisfying line between inside and outside. Similarly, the corpse, as we have seen, played a phantasmatic intermediary role that was crucial to distinguishing between life and death, between sentience and inert matter—as well as between the "unconscious" of the animal, the family, and woman, on the one hand, and the "consciousness" of the state on the other. These paradoxical indeterminacies reflected, however, a broader theoretical problem that ran through contemporary philosophical texts and that bore, as we shall see, on their attempts to define the city as a rationalized or rationalizable space. This problem was the difficulty of conceptualizing the relation between thought and matter. We find an early expression of this difficulty in Plato's *Parmenides*. The episode in question occurs during a conversation between the young Socrates and the older philosopher of the title. Here, the possibility of subjugating matter to thought (and indistinction to distinction) is expressed through a curious process of denial and subsequent confession. Like the paradoxical structure of inhuman legislation, which simultaneously recognizes and dismisses the possibility of confusing the material and the psychic, Socrates both rejects and acknowledges his intense interest in submitting abject matter to the principles of abstract, formal reason.

> Are you also puzzled, Socrates, about cases that might be thought absurd [*geloia*], such as hair or mud [*pēlos*] or dirt [*rhupos*] or any other trivial [*atimotaton*] and undignified [*paulotaton*] objects? Are you doubtful whether or not to assert that each of these has a separate form distinct from things like those we handle?

Not at all, said Socrates. In these cases, the things are just the things we
see; it would surely be too absurd to suppose that they have a form. All the
same, I have sometimes been troubled by a doubt whether what is true in
one case may not be true in all. Then, when I have reached that point, I am
driven to retreat, for fear of tumbling into a bottomless pit of nonsense.[35]

From the beginning of Socrates's philosophical career to its end, a certain ridiculousness infects the physical world. In the *Crito*, yielding to
the interests of earthly existence provokes ridicule (*gelōta ophlēsein*), while
here the philosopher finds laughable or *geloia* those material things that are
atimotata—stripped, like the victims of *atimia*, of their *timē*. More important, however, they are nothing but themselves: This filth has no higher
vocation, it reflects no reality that transcends it. A vague conception of
uniqueness informs this passage, the notion of a thing without a model or a
type. Beyond the oyster, which ultimately submits to categorization, one
comes to the mud and the slime with which mollusks share the deepest
recesses of their being. These abjections signify nothing, and still they exist.
Even more, they insist. Socrates claims that this strange matter has no value
or importance, and yet there is something shameful about it since it brings
ridicule: *geloia*. And the very idea of formalizing this disorder makes the
head spin, for the border between thought and matter, between the distinctive and the indistinguishable, is guarded not only by embarrassment, but
also by a fearful abyss of infinite meaninglessness. This abyss is the frontier
of formal conceptualization, the place of its *horoi*, where it recognizes the
nauseating intractability of its remainder, the slough of thought. Both
the civil code of the subhuman and the abyss of meaninglessness are examples of *Verneinung*, or denial in the psychoanalytic sense, for in both cases
no means yes. The abject is said to be trivial, but in fact it provokes horror.
Socrates says that he does not wonder about the formalism of the absurd
and yet it turns out that he is terrified by the question. The legal system
claims to master the animal and the rock, but thereby disguises the fact
that the very recognition of communality between thought and matter, that
is the applicability of the law to rocks, raises the unaddressed possibility
that such mastery could fail or, worse, function in the opposite direction.
And this *Verneinung* betrays a more profound refusal of the physical, non-
transcendental world, of the unruly filthiness of material existence. Here
and at the end of his life, Socrates's response will be virtually the same: He
turns away, backing off from the abyss, pushing away the cup of absurdity

in favor of the cup of death. His final statement on the subject—indeed, virtually his final statement altogether—is sooner die than face this nonsense. And so death comes in its purity, its strange immortality, to wash away the horrifying meaninglessness of bodily life, its atypical singularity as filth.

Now, the problem between matter and thought expressed itself also in relation to the theorization of the city, and I am going to argue in what follows that the frightened antipathy that Plato felt in the *Parmenides* toward the particularity of material existence reappeared in the relation between the city and its other, whether that other was the individual, the barbarian, or something less distinct. Plato evoked the world outside the city throughout his writings and with particular force in his one attempt at a funeral oration, the *Menexenus*, where he contrasted the foreign with the autochthonous purity of the Athenians: "So firmly rooted and so sound is the noble and liberal character of our city," the argument goes, "and endowed also with such a hatred of the barbarian, because we are pureblooded Greeks [*eilikrinōs einai Hellēnas*], unadulterated by barbarian stock."[36] Aspasia, the principal speaker in the dialogue, distinguishes Athens from other cities, which she qualifies as only "nominally Greek," because their origins can be traced back not to the soil where they are located, but to the settlements of displaced populations—Thebes, for instance, was founded by Cadmus, who was not himself of Hellenic descent. Seemingly alone among its neighbors, Athens is, however, absolutely Greek, and to say Greek is, therefore, *strictu sensu* to say Athens. In its otherness to the state, the corpse is somehow related to this hateful foreignness and to other operators of indistinction. The terrible ambiguity of that other world can be caught only in glimpses, but it returns to haunt Greek thought, slipping among its interstices and distinctions and troubling not only the laws, the principles of justice, and the subjects that they would create, but also the very possibility of making sense.

Poststructuralist analyses have, in particular, been fascinated by the troubling wealth of these fatal confusions. Nicole Loraux, for instance, deconstructed Plato's use of the term *eilikrinōs* in the above passage from the *Menexenus*. She argued that the supposedly absolute difference between the foreign and the Greek disguised a more fundamental interpenetration of terms, such that the native is always already alien to itself and the alien central to the city. She remarked, as well, that the same word *eilikrinōs* (an adverb meaning "purely," "without mixture," or "absolutely") was also used to describe another putatively absolute difference: that between the body and the soul.[37] The lines of a necessary but impossible separation thus run between various crucial binaries in a Platonic configuration of the intelligible: the borders between the city and its other, between the Greek and the barbarian, between logos and foreign babble, between the soul and the body. For Loraux, this unsatisfiable necessity, this need to distinguish between distinction and indistinction, formed the crux of Plato's work. "I could easily say," she writes, "that, in Plato, everything happens between *khóra* and *khorís*. Between *khóra*—neither sensuous nor intelligible and, consequently, the principle of indetermination—and *khorís*, which separates and isolates."[38] But the *chōra* itself is already a complicated notion. It has the common meaning of "the civic territory, with its well-sealed borders guarded by the distant spaces of the *eskhatía*."[39] It is, in this sense, the physical space of the state—especially the Attic states—outside of which the alien begins. Its semantic field extends, however, much farther than that. In Homer, it also has the more basic sense of a demarcated place, of the area between two limits.[40] It is, in this way, an interval: formed, delineated extension, the rhythmic element of space, the unit of its intelligibility as a distinguishable place. Later it will acquire as well the meaning of post or position in a hierarchical system, further developing the concept of distinctiveness or distinction. In these respects, *chōra* is defined, definitive even.

The word has, however, another specific, but crucial, meaning within Plato's writings, one that would appear to contradict all of its other senses, and it is this other meaning that Loraux seemed to have in mind in the quotation just above. In the *Timaeus*, the term *chōra* is used to designate a third kind of being, or "*triton genos*," between the immutable and intelligible, on the one hand, and the corruptible and sensuous, on the other. Somewhere between the ideal forms of things and their material copies there must lie, according to Plato, a substance from which the copies can be fashioned. Still, if it is to receive the impress of the purely intelligible it cannot simply be gross matter; whence the need, conceptually, for some intermediate kind of existence, a field or place that can articulate between two absolutely distinct forms of being. "If we describe [the *chōra*] as a Kind invisible and unshaped," Plato writes, "all-receptive, and in some most perplexing and most baffling way partaking of the intelligible, we shall describe [it] truly."[41] Ontologically puzzling, the *chōra* occupies a troubling position in relation to knowledge itself as well, for it cannot be apprehended by either of the two principal modes of intellection, that is, reason (*noēsis*) or opinion (*doxa*), which are concerned, respectively, with the "ungenerated and indestructible" forms and perishable objects "perceptible by sense."[42] For its part, the *chōra*,

> which admits not of destruction, and provides room for all things that have
> birth, itself [is] apprehensible by a kind of bastard reasoning [*logismōi . . . nothōi*]
> by the aid of non-sensation, barely an object of belief; for when we regard this
> we dimly dream [*oneiropoloumen*] and affirm that it is somehow necessary that
> all that exists should exist *in* some spot and occupying some *place*, and that
> that which is neither on earth nor anywhere in the Heaven is nothing.
> So because of all these and other kindred notions, we are unable also on
> waking up to distinguish clearly the unsleeping and truly subsisting substance,
> owing to our dreamy condition, or to state the truth—how it belongs to a
> copy—seeing that it has not for its own even the substance for which it
> came into being, but fleets ever as a phantom of something else [*heterou . . .*
> *phantasma*].[43]

To the extent that it can be conceived only through a "bastard" reasoning, the intelligibility of the *chōra* enjoys an ambiguous relation to the familial dynamics of procreation and filiation that, according to this passage, govern intelligibility in general. The *chōra* is part of the family by blood but not by law. The situation is further complicated, however, because this "third kind" of being is also described elsewhere in the same dialogue as a mother (*mētēr*) or nurse (*tithenē*) who receives form from the father.[44] It is at once the mother and the substitute for the mother; similarly, insofar as it is *nothos*, the only kind of thinking that can approach the *chōra* is itself merely the illegitimate offspring of a concubine or slave. It is, in other words, the real daughter of a false mother, progeny of the one who, as nurse or slave, should supplant the wife only in the physical practicalities of child rearing.[45] The *chōra* is, in this sense, trouble in the family, the confusion of different codes of organization within the home itself: on the one hand relations of power, legitimacy, and intelligibility (what one might call the civic or the symbolic order), but also, on the other, affectively charged material relations, the bonds of care and nurturing. For the familial categories of meaning grow inextricably complicated in the attempt to think the very *chōra* that is supposed to bring intelligibility to the material world—in it mother blends with slave and surrogate, while the intellectual legitimacy of the offspring depends on its status as bastard. The mother of distinctions, the mother as such, the one whose nourishing breasts guarantee the identity of filiation—indeed true identity as such in the *Menexenus*—yields here to a phantasmatic chaos, while the family romance of reason degenerates into an endless boudoir farce of undecidable parentages. Member of and yet excluded from the family, the *chōra* threatens to exceed any possible legislation within a symbolic order organized around stable familial relations, let alone by something so precise as the Oedipal complex.[46] But the principle that lends intelligibility to the material world can be perceived only in this way.

Now, a similar genetic imaginary is taken up by Aspasia in the *Menexenus*, where it is again a question of establishing fundamental distinctions. There, the Athenians are said to differ from others, from *the* other in fact, in that they alone spring from a true mother—the earth that they inhabit—while foreigners must satisfy themselves with the nourishment supplied by a stepmother (*mētruia*), who serves as yet another proxy for real maternal agency.[47] This would seem to be a simple enough division between Greek and non-Greek, where legitimacy is patterned on an unproblematic model of biological procreation, but the *Timaeus* shows how unhelpful biological categories can be in establishing rational ones and how the relations between mother and surrogate, in particular, can muddle the pure formality and the legality of the father—indeed of distinction itself. If we read the *Menexenus* together with the *Timaeus*, if we read it, that is, as a particular instance of the larger rules of intelligibility laid out in the *Timaeus*, the notion of the state becomes similarly paradoxical. Although Aspasia traced the origins of the Greeks back to the womb of their own mother earth, the beginnings of the city must necessarily lie elsewhere, as the rituals of exclusion and the tragedies themselves attest. Those origins can be found only in the other that her language of hatred of the foreign strives to reject, in the impurity of a bastard reasoning, for the imposition of legal form (the Athenian state) on a physical, material, and womblike space (the maternal earth) must pass through a phantasmatic breakdown of the family, the biological, and the rational themselves, given that the difference between mother and surrogate cannot be rationally established—and it cannot be rationally established because the distinction between form and matter, between state and land, depends, in the *Timaeus*, precisely on a confusion of mother and surrogate. Only, in other words, if the surrogate mother (that of the other, the barbarians, according to the text) can be identified with the true mother (that of the Athenians) can the state integrate with its "native" land and establish the unique legitimacy of the Athenians as Greeks.

Glimpsed in a hazy dream, the *chōra* flits ghostlike between the worlds of *doxa* and *noēsis*, between, as well, the physical and the intelligible, the body and the soul. This was the abysmal place from which the young Socrates had retreated in horror, the inconceivable transition point between the formless and the formal, between sheer materiality and its potential intelligibility. One has the right to wonder why this juncture should be so frightening, and we had seen hidden in it the threat that filth, that thing of indeterminate borders, might enter into the world of systematic thought, might pollute it too, and this by the very nature of reason, which, in its necessary claim to universality, in its obligation to think that what is true in one case must be true in all, could find itself obliged to drag an uncontrollable, oozing miasma into its very heart. And here it is, that miasma, in the *Timaeus*. The intelligible depends on the unintelligible. The purity of thought depends on the confusion that the material world forces on it. Or rather, it is reason itself that forces this filth on itself. And horror would be, in this respect, the panic of self-recognition, the sudden awareness that by its very constitution rational thought is forced to do that to which it is constitutionally allergic, to do that which is the very denial of itself. As at other frightening moments in Plato's writings, the veil of *Verneinung* falls across this terrifying obscenity that queers the family, the order of the father, the meaning of the mother's nurturing breasts, and the possibility of lucid thought itself: It is a bad dream. But it is a bad dream haunted by a certain uneasy certitude: For all of its absurdity, it bears within it, and even in its strange, woozy form, a legitimate, indeed a crucial insight. It is this reviled thinking, this illegitimate offspring, the object of an axiomatic hatred for the impure, alien and barbarian, that alone can support the very idea of distinction.

This same passage from Plato's *Timaeus* also occupies a significant position in poststructuralist theorizations of the relations between subjectivity, language, and artistic creation. According to Julia Kristeva, the *chōra* can be understood to figure something like a psychic developmental stage, a protosubjective state in which an individual consciousness has as yet no awareness of a separation between what is itself and what is not. Although distinct from the symbolic register, or language considered as a means of signifying, this "semiotic" aspect is nonetheless characterized by other, more primary linguistic properties. As Kristeva describes it, the *chōra* can be conceived of as a condition in which "discrete quantities of energy move through the body of what will later be the subject." *Chōra* thus designates for her "a nonexpressive totality formed by the drives and their stases in a motility that is as full of movement as it is regulated."[48] Her understanding of *chōra* as a designation for a presymbolic and presubjective stage of linguistically articulated consciousness bears a striking resemblance to Hermann Fränkel's description of how Greeks of the Homeric period would have experienced themselves and the world around them.[49] Indeed, Kristeva's analysis can be read as a commentary on the tendency to consider ancient Greek experience as radically different from and, in certain crucial respects, incomprehensible to post-Cartesian subjectivity. As both a non-self-conscious field articulated by intersecting affective forces and as a mode of awareness that cannot clearly distinguish between its own agency and its acts (or even between itself and others), the prepolitical Homeric consciousness described by Fränkel and others would come very close to the infantile realm of the *chōra* as Kristeva construes it.

Now, the semiotic, as Kristeva describes it, is an integral element of language, always active in it but normally subordinated to symbolic functions. At certain moments, however, the semiotic overwhelms this repression and erupts into the foreground as an affectively charged but nonsensical obstruction to meaning. This can be seen in certain poems by Antonin Artaud, for exemple, where intelligible words give way to transcriptions of preverbal voicings.[50] It can be heard in the ululations of mourning, the wordless cries of emotion that accompany the dead to their graves. It can also be detected in more subtle forms, such as the very nature of artistic creation, for when language mimics itself, when it is used to represent its own symbolic functioning, it distances itself from that function. The words of a play do not mean what they say, but only represent the saying of that meaning. The death sentence pronounced on a stage does not carry the weight of law beyond the fictions the words create, nor do wedding vows or promises of love, and in this way speech detaches itself from its own signifying. At this moment, according to Kristeva, language leaves its place within the city, moving beyond the walls and the *horoi*: "By *reproducing signifiers*—vocal, gestural, verbal—the subject crosses the border of the symbolic and reaches the semiotic *chora*, which is on the other side of the social frontier."[51] To a greater or lesser extent, all art thus sacrifices meaning to an emotionally charged field of presubjective consciousness, or, to borrow Nicole Loraux's distinction, subordinates *chōris* to *chōra*.

This is especially true, Kristeva contends, in Attic tragedy. "The reenacting of the signifying path taken from the symbolic unfolds the symbolic itself and . . . opens it," she writes. "The Dionysian festivals in Greece are the most striking example of this deluge of the signifier, which so inundates the symbolic order that it portends the latter's dissolution in a dancing, singing, and poetic animality. Art—this semiotization of the symbolic—thus represents the flow of jouissance into language."[52] For tragedy, as we have seen, is not simply art. The theater of Dionysos is not an entertainment, but a civic duty, a solemnity and a consecration of the polis. As the art of the city, as a ritual self-representation, tragedy is also the city as art, the invention of its meaning and its relation to its phantasmatic others. It is from the very words that are spoken, in the very fact of their fictionality, their absurdity, their meaninglessness and futility, that these dramas draw their power and significance. Not so much from the legal debates and originary myths they enact as from the enactment itself, from the phantom presence that hovers over the crowd and the actors, the nonbeing that intrudes on the assembled citizenry and collects them into the city. That presence that is not one, that veils the stage, is the *chōra* too. And as the tragedy celebrates the mysterious origins of the city, their mysteriousness manifests itself not so much in the myths that are represented as in the irrationality of the aesthetic itself, present in its subversion of the apparent meaning and narratives of the myths, in the meaninglessness that is the tragic performance itself. The tragic is terrifying because it stages, as the staging itself, the other against which both myth and reason define themselves, the other whose minatory presence reminds the citizenry that the enemy of the state is not those against whom it joins battles but rather their own intimations of a passionate meaninglessness. It is not the representation of the myths, but the presence of this alien and yet familiar enthusiasm among the gathered population that lends its horror to tragedy.

Difficult as it might be to define, the divide between the city and its other was marked by powerful affect, and, in a perverse way, this affect became part of the definition of the state as a suprapersonal entity. Like the women of the chorus who can hear the walls groaning in Aeschylus's *Seven against Thebes*, the citizens can feel the boundaries of their polis in their very flesh. Or as Aspasia argues in the *Menexenus*, all that lies beyond is more or less barbarian, and this difference provokes a profound *misobarbaros* antipathy. She is emphatic on this point, reiterating a couple of lines later: "Our people are pure Greeks and not a barbarian blend; whence it comes that our city is imbued with a whole-hearted hatred of alien races [*hothen katharon to misos entetēke tēi polei tēs allotrias phuseōs*]."⁵³ She gives no explanation of why that should be—indeed the *misos* toward the barbarian is treated as axiomatic: Athenians despise others because they are other. The Athenian hates the foreigner. The pure hates the impure. One can actually feel the difference, for autochthony cannot be separated from allergy. And this constitutional loathing is reenacted against the *pharmakos* and the victims of *atimia*. They are not just chased from the city: The scapegoat is loaded down with blows and humiliations; the point of *atimia* was to reduce a whole lineage to dust, to spend the fury of the citizens on a family. Ostracism was a more subtle form of this hatred, and, indeed, one could almost say that with his reforms, Cleisthenes came close to purging exile of its emotional content. In theory, at least. For the punishment, in this case, was not to become other, but rather to dwell among others and thereafter to return. The populace drove a troublemaker from the city and thereby resolved its inner conflicts and contradictions—on the symbolic as well as the pragmatic levels—for ostracism did not only end power struggles between individuals, it also played out the original contradiction of the city itself, the paradox of its origin, the endless need to expel its origin from itself. And by rejecting this originary problem, one also punished its manifestation with an episode of otherness, a long dose of abjection among the barbarians—for all outside the gates of Athens were impure, were tainted with barbarity. The affective charge remained even in ostracism, for that affect was itself the punishment.

In theory and in practice, the city hated its others. And this relationship echoed other fundamental distinctions in Plato's writings. In its delineation of an emotionally charged border between two antithetical states—or, more radically, between the need to establish antithesis (Greek vs. non-Greek) and its impossibility—the *Menexenus* recalls Socrates's discussion of filth in the *Parmenides*. There, the intersection of the formless and the formal was marked by a vertiginous terror. Here, the line between the clean and the adulterated is traced by anger. And in these instances, the very possibility of clear distinction is haunted by a paradox. One separates oneself from the adulterated through hatred and fear, and yet those very feelings introduce impurity. For difference is traced by a failure of difference, by a confusion between thought and affect, by an uncontrollable insistence of feeling within the world of meaning. Athens is constitutionally angry. It cannot be a purely symbolic or rationalized system, for its very identity is indissociable from this anger. And this affective charge returns, in different form, when reason tries to think itself, to establish its own universality. For when thought attempts to achieve its own absoluteness, as Socrates's outburst in the *Parmenides* shows, the head spins, and reason feels. Despite the crucial role of lucid judgment in the eulogists' definitions of the citizen, despite Plato's attempt to create a rationalized state in the *Laws*, the city depends on emotion. More surprising, perhaps, so does reason. What Sophocles's tragedies do, in this respect, is to shift the nature of that emotion. In *Oedipus at Colonus*, the chorus enjoins the protagonist to hate and to love as the city does. In *Antigone* the heroine asserts that she was born not to hate but to love—even the excluded of the city, even the corpse of her brother.

In punishing rocks and corpses by casting them beyond the *horoi* of the city, the Athenian of Plato's *Laws* created a zone outside of the polis for that which can never be punished enough, the place of a potentially infinite regress in which the inanimate is made to suffer beyond death, in which it is made to suffer, in exclusion, the very persistence of its being.[54] It is now the place itself that serves as punishment, and as such it answers to Antigone's question: "Would you now do more than seize and slay me?" This space is not merely alien to the city but hostile to it, for it is the realm of the intractably criminal, of that which persists in its criminality even as it is punished, for the punishment is never sufficient: There is no provision for a reintegration of the criminal dead or inanimate within the city, for a moment when the murderous stone can be brought back through the gates or the guilty man's corpse returned through the streets to repose, finally, among the living. The sentence is never fully served, the time never comes when expiation is done, and for that reason the punishment is not a duration but an extension, a place. Historically, as the city took shape as a political entity, this also became the place to which the dead—all the dead—were allotted, so that the dead became by their very nature criminal. These were not the shades who huddled on the shores of the Styx or those who would later crowd the carceral system of Hades, since the latter's death, the death suffered by the immortal soul, would be colonized by the laws of the living. Those spirits, whom Plato evokes at the end of the *Republic*, inhabited a dusky but faithful image of the state with its own elaborate system of crimes, criminals, judges, and punishments. What remained outside the gates was, instead, what those souls had left behind, the uneasy remnants of the living, still marked by their human traces. All the material dead and *only* the material dead were consigned to this place of ignominy, for what was living and criminal was put to death before being thrown here. Even the outcast, who was driven still breathing from the state, was only apparently alive. As the history of exclusion shows, the *pharmakos*, the scapegoat, and the ostracized were all the objects of a ritual (and not always merely symbolic) putting to death. The subject of *atimia*, who functioned as an intermediary step between the pharmakon and the ostracized, stood in forfeit of his life as long as he remained within the precincts of the city. He was, in other words, legally dead *within* the state and could exist legally only outside of it—*as the dead of the state*. To occupy the zone beyond the *horoi* was, therefore, to be dead either by nature (that is to say biologically) or by definition (as that which was dead to the state). The space outside of the city was, therefore, characterized at least in part by the nature of the corpse. Or rather it is the other way around: The corpse embodies those aspects of the political that are allotted to this extramural space.

But the conceptual richness of the corpse stems, in part, from the special way in which it figures or embodies. It is itself, but in being itself, in being *just* itself, it also exhausts its ability to signify something else and reverts to the materiality and meaninglessness of what is signified by representation in general: the "just itself" itself. By thus representing an entire field of indistinction that must be marked off from political space, the cadaver functions as a figure of the unfigurable, the point where figuration itself is eaten up and collapses into a formless residue. It is the remains of meaning. This ambiguous status as a determination of the indeterminate creates, however, a twofold theoretical danger. To call the corpse a purely arbitrary figure suggests that its "in itself"—that is, the corpse as vehicle of symbolic representation—is utterly undetermined by and therefore perfectly foreign to formal thinking, whereas the horror of the abject derives, according to the *Parmenides*, from its potential involvement in just such thought. In calling the corpse a necessary figure, however, one risks conceiving of it categorically, which is to say, as simply one more element within the abstract symbolic system that produced it. The problem with this approach is that the Platonic texts indicate that the principal interest and power of dead bodies stem from their being located, at least in part, outside of such systems: Insofar as it embodies individuality, the corpse itself is an accident and, therefore, by definition uncontrolled. To thus fetishize the corpse as the sole possible expression for the indistinguishable is to discard the concept of indistinction itself. To the extent that it has meaning, therefore, to the extent that it figures, the dead body turns against itself, deliquescing into a horrifying phantasmatic field where it passes into other images and processes of strangeness. This is why the corpse, in being just itself, is also other than itself: It is not only the corpse as such but also things that happen always just at the borders of the city. So the dead body participates in a wide and semantically fluid range of alienation: the stranger, the barbarian, the foreign tongue, the feminine, the Erinyes, and the mythic fantasy of a prepolitical world.[55]

In answer to our question at the end of the previous chapter, the indeterminacy between life and death that the corpse brought to a crisis did, in fact, resonate through other ancient texts. Plato, in particular, seemed troubled by a potential indistinction between thought and matter—and between distinction and indistinction in thought itself. This indeterminacy, whose articulation passed almost invariably through complicated fantasies of family structure, had to be expelled from civic space, and yet it could never be completely and satisfactorily excluded. In their various ways, the Thargelia, myths, and tragedy all echoed this theme, figuring a preoriginal but ineradicable other of the polis, a remnant from a vague and frightening before. As the instantiation of what cannot be abstractly formalized, the remnant itself played a central but troubling role in the definition of the state, becoming the marker of the individual as such and, thence, of the undying resistance waged by the city's excluded. In its role as the exclusion that is necessarily and paradoxically included in the state, the remnant was similar to Giorgio Agamben's notion of *homo sacer* in the state of exception, but unlike *homo sacer*, the remnant could not be entirely subjugated, even through its paradoxical inclusion.[56] And in its strongest manifestation, as the corpse, the remnant is what death cannot finish, even when the state kills the individual through war or other legitimate means. The corpse, in this sense, is that which can never be punished enough, the individual as such, the filth that will not enter into the typology of the forms or the impersonality of the city. In insistently loving her brother in the person of his corpse, Antigone loves this filth, but because her love is self-sacrificial, because she pays for it with her own individual existence, she elevates that affection to the status of the tragic and, therefore, of the political. Antigone, in other words, grapples with the original paradox of the state, while opening the possibility for a different but still gendered notion of the political— one based on feminine love.

FIVE

Inventing Life

In a sustained analysis of *philia* in Aristotle's works, Martha Nussbaum has argued that the philosopher theorized a love that treats the beloved as an end in himself, valuing him because of his irreplaceable uniqueness. By emphasizing the importance of such friends' "living together," Aristotle seems, moreover, to have premised his notion of friendship on that of life, so that *philia* would establish the value of a specific and *living* individual.[1] But it is a long and difficult passage from the texts that I discussed in the last chapter to that loving and living individual. By examining—and to some extent re-creating—that difficulty, we should be able to appreciate the facticity, fragility, and importance of that new person. *Antigone*, I have argued, plays a privileged role in the invention of a new subjectivity, but that role is largely determined—and revealed—by other texts and practices that resonate through it. In this chapter therefore I will begin the reading of life in *Antigone* by looking back to earlier treatments of the same events. By working through these older texts, and Hegel's reading of the play, I will show how Sophocles brings love and life to bear on each other.

Aeschylus's *Seven against Thebes* offered a purely military vision of its eponymous heroes, describing their acts in battle and their eventual death before the gates of the besieged city. Euripides's *Suppliant Women*, written some fifty years later, returned to the same characters, now some hours after their death, but in an attempt to imagine what they had been like in times of peace. When Euripides's Theseus asks for descriptions of the fallen, he specifically instructs Adrastus, his interlocutor, to omit any reference to their exploits in battle. The reply, accordingly, details how the various soldiers lived, how they treated others, what they loved, how each, in short, "showed his nature" while still among the living.[2] As if in direct contradiction to the earlier play's vision of the world—and, less directly, in contradiction to the *epitaphioi logoi*—Euripides's description explicitly rejects any characterization based on military exploits and thereby asserts the possibility of a new category of person whose "nature" derives from experiences outside of war. The symmetry, as Nicole Loraux remarks, is almost too stark not to be intentional, as if Euripides were consciously rejecting a previous concept of tragic—and civic—individuality.[3] And although the value of those individual existences derives, almost entirely, from a concern for others or for the city itself, one can half glimpse another sort of inward, almost useless virtue here, the seductiveness of a person for who he is. Euripides's Parthenopaeus was "supreme in beauty," but this does not establish him as irreplaceable, since at his disappearance someone else would necessarily become most beautiful. This is a categorical, almost mathematic notion of individuality, a ranking rather than the sign of some-one who establishes his uniqueness on his own terms and who thus demands familiarity and understanding in order to be appreciated.[4] More telling, perhaps, is the observation that although Capaneus was rich he never behaved arrogantly and "kept an attitude/No prouder than a poor man's." It is difficult to image how such conduct could be of any particular service to others, except insofar as it spared their own self-esteem and, in turn, made Capaneus more appealing as an individual. More important than the actual expression of such distinguishing characteristics were, however, the *desire* to express them and the apparent *belief* that they existed. The intuition of such differences in the very movement of desire for them may have exceeded Adrastus's—and the playwright's—ability to identify them in words, but the language in which Theseus frames his request is still precise enough to offer a glimpse of a living individuality.

Hegel took up the question of war in relation to *Antigone*, offering what probably remains the most insightful analysis of its function in the elabora-tion of a tragic individuality.[5] From a careful reading of his interpretation there emerges, somewhat obliquely and almost reluctantly, the afterimage of a living person, caught in his evanescent singularity. Like Euripides, Hegel marks this person more in absence than in presence, more through desire than through recognition, but this fugitive subject is central to his understanding of the play and its role in the history of mind. Indeed, the fascination that *Antigone*—and Antigone—excercised over the philosopher throughout his life probably emanates from this missing figure of desire, this love object inscribed in the character of the heroine.[6] His reading also throws a sharp light on the concept of citizen subjectivity that runs through the *epitaphioi logoi*. By its very status as an impersonal entity, according to Hegel, the polis must resist any tendency to treat a person as an end in himself or herself, and it does so through its eminent domain over lives. In order to maintain itself, the city reduces the individual to an impersonal abstraction and thereby integrates him into the state, simultaneously destroying in its citizens all useless specificity. But the living individual threatens the city, according to Hegel, not because he is political but because he is alive, and so what must be mastered in him—what makes him individual in other words—is life itself. Consequently, everything accidental, contingent, and as yet still potential—which is to say the individual as open-ended existence rather than pure essence—must be abolished from the body politic. By comparison, as an abstract individual, the *anēr agathos*, or "good man," of the eulogists is a product of death, and accordingly the most important instrument with which the state asserts control over the living person is war. For in war, Hegel writes,

> the individuals who, absorbed in their own way of life, break loose from the whole and strive after the inviolable independence and security of the person, are made to feel in the task laid on them their lord and master, death. Spirit, by thus throwing into the melting-pot the stable existence of these systems [i.e., families], checks their tendency to fall away from the ethical order.[7]

Hegel thus differentiates here between the real individuality of the state, which is abstract, and the sensuous individuality of the family, which reduces life to animal biology and meaningless contingency.[8] This passage gives its full human and ontological force to the abstraction that is political individuality: The sovereignty of the state is death, and it is death that calls the wayward back to ethics.

Hegel, moreover, associates the "biological" individuation that the state supersedes with two principles: femininity and desire. Gender difference thus becomes an indicator not only of difference as such, but of life itself insofar as it opposes the integrity of the state. In Hegelian terms, to understand living individuality, one would consequently have to understand female desire. And if woman, in Hegel's pungent phrase, is the "irony of the community," it is because she leads what belongs to the city back toward the family, because she turns the beauty of young men, their strength and virtue, away from the public and toward private ends.[9] "Womankind—the everlasting irony [in the life] of the community—" Hegel wrote in his analysis of *Antigone*,

> changes by intrigue the universal end of the government into a private end, transforms its universal activity into a work of some particular individual, and perverts the universal property of the state into a possession and ornament for the Family [*zu einem Besitz und Putz der Familie*]. Woman in this way turns to ridicule the earnest wisdom of mature age which, dead to singularity—to desire and pleasure as well as to effective activity—[*der Einzelheit—der Lust und dem Genusse sowie der wirklichen Tätigkeit—abgestorben*] only thinks of and cares for the universal. She makes this wisdom an object of derision for raw and irresponsible youth and unworthy of their enthusiasm [*zum Spotte für den Mutwillen der unreifen Jugend und zur Verachtung für ihren Enthusiasmus*].[10]

The universal goal of the government—which is also to say, the goal of the government *as* universal—is premised on the death of singularity, indeed on death itself. In her desire, however, woman delights in Capaneus's modesty or Parthenopaeus's beauty for the sake of that delight itself, transforming the youth's utility into a mere ornament. Woman, in this sense, does not embody the grinding paradoxes of tragic irony; instead, she is irony as a superfluous embellishment, a rhetorical figure that gives no deeper meaning but simply stands to amuse. She perverts meaning, interrupting the great syntagmatic flow of history by drawing down on herself the futile pleasures of meaninglessness itself, or of excessive meaning. For her, war is the cure, and in it, the "brave youth in whom woman finds her pleasure, the suppressed principle of corruption, now has his day and his worth is openly acknowledged."[11] Impurity, corruption, these are the names Hegel gives for woman's pleasure, the longing for an individual as such and not in his abstraction. Her good is no good, for the particularity of her concupiscence taints the clear surface of the ethical itself. She revels in what Nicole Loraux calls the "hypertrophy" of the individual.[12] Taking her own desire as an end in itself, she becomes, in her love, selfishness personified. In having his character Theseus require descriptions of the fallen warriors that omit their deeds of arms, Euripides positioned his dead within what, following Hegel, we could call a new, more feminine order, based on a principle that one can justifiably, if somewhat imprecisely, call life, since it is the alternative to an order of death.

And yet, even among women there are distinctions to be made. The wife, for instance, is not like the sister, for according to Hegel, in the "wife

there is an admixture of particularity, [and] her ethical life is not pure."¹³
An embodiment of womanly irony, she loves the hero for his being rather
than his utility to the state or his service to others, and that love derives
from sexuality and the call of pleasure, so that she pollutes the political
itself. In the *Phenomenology*, however, Hegel describes another, stronger
bond that joins woman to man: that between brother and sister, for through
it she cherishes him in his uniqueness but outside, now, the blinding
force of sexual longing and the contingency that it introduces. "In this
relationship . . . ," Hegel writes, "the indifference of the particularity, and
the ethical contingency of the latter, are not present; but the moment of
the individual self, recognizing and being recognized, can here assert its
right, because it is linked to the equilibrium of the blood and is a relation
devoid of desire. The loss of the brother is therefore irreparable to the sister
and her duty toward him is the highest."¹⁴ Desire falsifies a relationship
precisely because it is desire for an individual in his individuality, his evanescence, his accidentality. But desire is absent between siblings. This
distinction gives the sister's love a certain disinterestedness, and therefore
legitimacy, that offsets its unclean commitment to the particularity of a
single person.¹⁵ Hegel terms that disinterest "blood." Woman's ethical
value thus derives from a biological notion of interpersonal relations in
which sister is bound to brother through a shared animality. By moving
that animality beyond the contingency of the mere individual, by instead
situating that individual within the larger network of the family, the sister
legitimizes female love. Antigone, in Hegel's reading, personifies this legitimacy. She loves another, not her own desire, and her death raises womanly
care for an individual to the role of duty. She secures with her death—and
this is the coin of Hegel's city—the value of the individual, but she does so
only insofar as he represents a larger form of the personal, the network of
biological relations that make up kinship. She represents, in other words,
the ethics of miasma. This is the closest that Hegel gets, at least in his readings of *Antigone*, to approving a love for individual life.¹⁶

Philosophers, especially recent ones, have productively criticized the
notion of blood relationship that subtends Hegel's analyses of *Antigone*,
arguing that it is heteronormative, incoherent, and driven by motivations
external to his own arguments. Indeed, it is difficult to understand how
anyone could use the Labdacids as an example—let alone *the* example—
of kinship when Antigone's relatives wrote the book, so to speak, on the

breakdown of the family.[17] Starting from this observation, Judith Butler has argued that Hegel's reading represents—and indeed *accepts*—nonnormative sexual desire as an entombment or living death.[18] For Jacques Derrida, Hegel's arguments about sibling love were more an expression of the philosopher's own feelings toward his sister than a coherent product of his ethical system.[19] Tina Chanter, in contrast, has argued that Hegel was blinded by his naturalist conception of women as individualistic, natural, and inward, a notion that was itself influenced by his time and the philosophical tradition he was working in.[20] Using an immanent critique of Hegel's texts (including, notably, the *Philosophy of Nature*) and approaching the issue from a different angle, Luce Irigaray has examined the problematic biologism implicit in the idea of blood itself.[21] These are all important objections, but they all ignore another peculiarity of Hegel's notion of kinship: It is not representative of the ancient Athenian practices it is supposed to describe. In my discussion of Aeschylus's *Eumenides*, I have already shown how complicated—and controversial—the idea of consanguinity was, but even aside from that, family relations among the ancient Greeks were much more complex than Hegel seems to have appreciated—and closer, in many ways, to the incestuous confusion represented by the Labdacids.[22] "Because of the frequency of endogamy and adoption within the *anchisteia*," Sarah B. Pomeroy has written, "one person may fill multiple positions within the family tree."[23] Her remarks about brother-sister relations are particularly relevant: "Most societies also find that the relationship between siblings, half-siblings, or step-siblings should not be assimilated to the husband-wife relationship. The Greeks, however, were not strict about considering sibling marriage as taboo."[24] The basis on which Hegel's whole interpretation of sibling love rests—the absence of sexual desire between brothers and sisters—is thus swept away within the Greek world he was ostensibly describing. More important, however, Hegel's understanding of the relationship between kinship and desire led him to extremely misleading conclusions about the role of individual love in Sophocles's play. In a way that has never been appreciated, the original text exceeds the limitations of Hegel's analysis—and, indeed, of the critiques of that analysis—by opening up the possibility of an ethically significant *living* person, and it does this through its handling of the idea of love.

The word *philia* and its cognates covered a range of meanings in ancient Greek that were not always consistent with modern notions of love.[25]

In Homer and the early poets, *philos*, as an adjective, could simply indicate possession.[26] By the classical period, however, it had acquired a more emotional significance that indicated affection for a person or object. As Warren Lane and Ann Lane have observed:

> For the Greeks, *philos* referred to that which is dear, loved, or liked, including kin, friends, allies, or any object cherished. *Philia*, the relationship of affection and commitment among persons, contrasts with hostility (*echthros*) on the one hand and is differentiated from charity (*agape*) on the other. The Greek sense of *philia* in friendship and community carries the idea of genuine regard and loyalty and further implies a mutual knowledge of character, the sharing of words and deeds, and the responsible actions and emulations of virtue that sustain bonds of association.[27]

Although it would be difficult to defend for the Homeric period, this description of *philia* seems, in many respects, plausible for the classical age. Aristotle, for instance, theorized a similar notion of *philia* based on mutual recognition and esteem.[28] But Aristotle was writing in the century following *Antigone*, and his idea of love is both surer and vastly more modern than what we find in Sophocles's tragedies. Indeed, I would argue, it is undoubtedly the fruit of a tremendous intellectual and social labor undertaken through those very dramas. Now, Lane and Lane contend that *Antigone* represents an expansive notion of love that would prefigure Aristotle's. They write that, in contrast to Creon, Oedipus's daughter "exemplifies the cultural understanding that *philia* not only cuts across the distinction between kin and non-kin, but traverses gender and generational distinctions, while moreover setting the standard for what should be considered best in forms of association."[29] In this respect, then, the young heroine would represent that personalized *philia*, based on mutual affection and recognition, that would offer a more supple and enlightened basis for political bonds than Creon's rigidly categorical approach to legislation. Their argument, however, depends on the proposition that Antigone's love cuts "between kin and non-kin," but that seems clearly refuted by Sophocles's play itself. As Mark Griffith has observed: "Antigone's much-quoted claim, 'I was born to share in love, not in hate' . . . is found to have a more specific and limited application than she intends: her 'love' is for her father, and her brother, and extends no farther; indeed it is invariably converted into hatred and rage as soon as it encounters resistance."[30] Lane and Lane seem to recognize this problem, since they are at pains to demonstrate that the *philia* between Antigone and her brother is not a love between siblings but rather the virile friendship that binds soldiers in the field. "In Greek terms," they write, "the language here is appropriate to those who consider themselves close friends and comrades in arms."[31] The only explanation of those "Greek terms," which would sweep away gender difference and family ties along with the literal meaning of the text, is that "Antigone conceives of her burial of Polyneices as a glorious engagement in battle."[32] They offer no textual support, however, for what they take to be Antigone's conception, which consequently appears to exist more in their minds than in hers. In keeping with a long tradition of readership, Lane and Lane thus repress the possibility that Sophocles's play represents incestuous desire, and in so doing they transform its heroine into a man. More significant, for my own argument, they oversimplify and distort the notions of love that are being worked out through it.

At certain moments of *Oedipus at Colonus*, the word *philia*, or some cognate of it, wells up with an almost convulsive insistence, as when the blind old man reunites with his daughters or when he first meets Theseus.[33] This is especially remarkable at the end of the play, when Oedipus asserts that all the suffering of his daughters has been redeemed by his love: "It was hard, I know, my daughters; but a single word dissolves all these hardships. For from none did you have love [*philein*] more than from this man."[34] By my count, variations on *philein* then reappear another eight times in the 107 lines that follow, compared to about seventeen times in the preceding 1616 verses, or with a close to eightfold increase in frequency.[35] Modern sensibilities might well bridle at Oedipus's presumption that his own love is so valuable as to nullify (*luei*) the sufferings of another: To some extent, is the other not delimited for us *as* other by the untransferable isolation of their pain?[36] If so, to assert authority over that hardship is to assume dominion over the very alterity of the other. And what modern would not bristle at being told: "All the pain I've caused you doesn't matter. What's important is that I love you"? There is little that such an argument could not justify, from persistent tardiness to spouse beating, rape, and murder. Some of that disrespect toward the otherness of the beloved, along with some of that latent violence, lingers in Oedipus's use of the verb "to love," and it informs other passages in the play as well. Elsewhere, for instance, *philia* names the collapse of alterity that assures the body politic's solidity, as when the chorus describes love as a means of adhesion to the city itself. They advise Oedipus:

"You are a stranger, poor man, in a strange land [*tolma zeinos epi zenas*]; bring yourself to loathe what the city is accustomed to dislike [*o ti kai polis tetrophen aphilon apostugein*] and to respect what it holds dear [*philon*]."[37] *Philia* toward the values of the city would, in this sense, act as an antidote to strangeness by suppressing the distance that separates the citizen from the *zenos* or foreigner. To become a member of the city, one chooses to love as it does.[38] To love here is to love *as*, and the object of affection is less important than the subject created by it. But if the significance of the object is subordinated to the subject, that subject, in turn, disappears, for I do not personally love the city or what it holds dear. Instead, the city loves through me, dissolving the I into its higher agency. The collective nature of this feeling is emphasized by the fact that these words are spoken through the chorus, in whose role the polis is reduced to a single voice.

This is not, however, the only image of love that emerges in the play, and if Oedipus himself expresses toward his daughters a *philia* that suppresses their alterity, he also, at other points, resists its inherent violence. When, for instance, Creon appears on scene to convince—and failing that, coerce—him to return to Thebes, Oedipus responds with arguments that derive from an understanding of individuality and love very different from that presupposed by his brother-in-law. The latter rebukes Oedipus for his crimes, asserting that the people of Athens "would not receive a parricide and a man impure [*kanagnon*], nor one in whose company were found the children of an unholy marriage [*gamou . . . anosiou tekna*]."[39] In his response, however, Oedipus rejects not only his own guilt, but also the entire principle of genetic miasma, the familial pollution that precedes birth and exceeds the individual agent: "Tell me," he commands, "if a prophecy came to my father from an oracle that he should die at his children's hands, how could you justly make that a reproach to me, whom no father had begotten, no mother conceived but who was still unborn?"[40] Because his act was done "unwittingly [*akon*]." he argues, the guilt is not his. According to this view, the responsible party is the one who knowingly commits an act, and he or she alone must bear its blame. A person is a voluntary agent, the author of a crime, a creator. Similarly, Oedipus rejects his brother-in-law's abusive *philia*. When Creon tries to cajole him into returning to Thebes, Oedipus responds: "When you see this city [i.e., Athens] and all its people kindly [*eunoun*] to me as a resident, you try to tear me away, saying hard things in soft words. Why is it so delightful to be kind to men against their will [*kai tis tosautē terpsis, akontas philein;*]? . . . That is the nature of what you offer me, sounding good, but in essence bad."⁴¹ To be a person, according to Oedipus, is to will, and a love that violates that will in another is bad. It is this different, nonhegemonizing conception of love that allows Oedipus to recognize the alterity of Theseus by addressing him as "dearest of strangers [*philtate zenōn*]," an expression that accepts the possibility of a *philia* for the other in his or her otherness.⁴² Certainly, this idea of an individual, in respect both to itself and to others, as a voluntary actor comes embedded in other world visions that do not comfortably accept it. We have already observed, for instance, that ancient Greece had no real vocabulary for what would subsequently become the category of the will and that the tragic period grappled with the idea of agency itself.⁴³ And for all his strident rejection of the herald's archaic worldview, Oedipus reverts to it easily, as when he speaks of the redemptive qualities of his own love for his daughters. The two versions of *philia* thus coexist uneasily in the play, crossing between and through its characters, dividing and joining them as if they were so many variations on its own lability.

Although less clearly and more tentatively, as if still caught in an earlier stage of development, these divergent understandings of *philia* had already begun to emerge in *Antigone*, written some thirty-five years previously. In a stichomythic passage from early in the play, the heroine tells her uncle Creon that the laws, or *nomoi*, of the underworld justify her insistence on burying Polyneices despite Creon's decree forbidding it. When Creon asserts that even in death an enemy does not become a friend, she responds: "I have no enemies by birth, but I have friends by birth [*outoi sunechthein, alla sumphilein ephun*]."⁴⁴ She is, by her own account, both faithful to the laws of the dead and incapable of joining in hatred. How exactly the two positions go together remains unclear, but we do know that while Creon speaks in the name of an animosity more powerful than death, Antigone counters with a love stronger yet, and it is by this love that she characterizes herself. Creon immediately challenges her to prove the strength of this sacred bond in literal terms: "Then go below and love those friends," he retorts, "if you must love them [*katō nun elthous', ei phileteon, philei/keinous*]."⁴⁵ Later in the play, he will, of course, carry out the threat, ordering Antigone to be buried alive. For the moment, what he has done is to reverse the terms of mortality: Whereas Antigone's lines suggest that her love is lawful because it survives the death of the *other*, Creon demands that

it survive her *own* extinction. She, for her part, must now prove the distint-
erest of her *philia*, and she does this in a violent, proprietary, and original
way. Her sister, Ismene, who had earlier refused to violate Creon's decree
and bury Polyneices, now offers to share Antigone's fate, but the latter,
somewhat surprisingly, rejects her:

ISMENE: I did the deed [*tourgon*], if she agrees, and I take and bear my share of the
blame.

ANTIGONE: Why, justice [*dikē*] will not allow you this, since you refused [to bury our
brother] and I was not your associate!

ISMENE: But in your time of trouble I am not ashamed to make myself a fellow
voyager in your suffering [*pathous*].

ANTIGONE: Hades and those below know to whom the deed [*tourgon*] belongs! And
I do not tolerate a loved one who shows her love only in words [*logois
d'egōphilousan ou stergō philēn*].

ISMENE: Sister, do not so dishonour me as not to let me die with you and grant the
dead man the proper rites!

ANTIGONE: Do not try to share my death [*mē moi thanēis su koina*], and do not claim
as your own something you never put a hand to! My death will be
enough [*arkesō thnēiskous' egō*]!⁴⁶

Not only is Antigone's love stronger than death, it is also uniquely hers,
and it is hers because it derives, in turn, from a deed (*ergon*) that is her own.
At issue here is not *which* person owns the deed so much as *what* an owner
is: Who, in other words, is Antigone? The answer is in part circular: She is
the one who did the deed. But she is also the one whose death will suffice
(*arkesō thnēiskous' egō*), whose death is adequated to the crime and responds
to it. Ownership is that sufficiency, that fit between the deed and the death
that pays for it, and yet the individuality of that death is so unsteady that it
must be jealously protected. The specificity of Antigone's mortality, its
uniqueness as hers alone, is still so fragile that Ismene's love can jeopardize
it. In this sense, Antigone does not only reject her sister, she also rejects a
communal demise, the sharing of a punishment, a finitude, and a guilt that
she wants to stem only from her own agency, that is, from her knowing
violation of Creon's edict.⁴⁷ When Ismene begs to share in her sister's punishment, she acts as the proponent of a more archaic order of justice, in
which honor entails participation in a familial miasma, in a shared pollution
that exceeds the limits of birth, death, and knowing action. Antigone, however, defends her right to an isolated suffering, culpability, and death that

are grounded in her individual agency. The isolation of mortality that will become axiomatic in Heidegger must here be established and then defended.[48] Moreover, it must also be defended against language itself, for, as Antigone says, she does not tolerate a love that is shown in words alone. One might suppose that Ismene was demonstrating her love in the offer of her own death, but since it is the value of that death that is in question here, it cannot serve as a guarantee of itself. Nor can her words, and here, at the risk of doing anachronistic violence to the play, it is worth speculating on why they cannot: Words, I would argue, are not to be tolerated because, unlike acts, they are by their very nature communal. "I did the deed, if she agrees," contends Ismene. But the crime, as Antigone understands it, is not done by committee or consensus.[49] Instead, it does violence against consensus and agreement; it is the voluntary breaking of civic law; it is commitment to one's self and not to the community. Even the laws of the underworld that Antigone adduces refuse the communality of language, for they are unwritten: The *agrapta nomina* that she had earlier assimilated to the divine justice (*dikē*) of the dead.[50]

Antigone's act, as she will have it, is at once loving, uniquely hers, and distinterested. And since it is disinterested, it is also good, in the sense of Aristotle's *Rhetoric* and of the *epitaphioi logoi*. The nature of this goodness is, however, paradoxical, for it is established through Antigone's sacrifice of herself in death, while that death, in turn, serves to define her as an individual. That is to say that she exists as a singular person only in the evanescence of her willing self-immolation, in the period of time between her decision to violate Creon's proclamation and her death. She does the deed that will cost her her life and in that same moment gains the life that she will lose.[51] Were she not to die, there would be no one to die, since the one who perishes is created in the willing choice of death, the knowing violation of the mortal edict against burial of the dead. Her self is, in this sense, selfless. Or she is, in other words, selflessness itself. This is a far cry from the womanly irony of which Hegel had spoken, and yet, this selflessness is directed toward someone. A lonely death is the payment of her crime, but she upholds the justice of her act and its wisdom by referring to the uniqueness of the person for whom it was committed. The passage in which this occurs sets up a somber contrast between *philia* and *eros*, between self-sacrificial love and pleasurable desire. "O tomb, O bridal chamber," Antigone begins and then, somewhat later, continues: "now he leads me thus by the hands, without marriage, without bridal, having no share in wedlock or in the rearing of children, but thus deserted by my friends [*philōn*] I come living, poor creature, to the caverns of the dead."[52] The pleasures of life itself, of lovemaking, motherhood, and friendship prompt her to regret her perishing, but they are counterbalanced by another form of *philia*, which awaits her even in death itself: "But when I come there [i.e., among the dead], I am confident that I shall come dear [*philē*] to my father, dear [*prosphilēs*] to you, my mother, and dear [*philē*] to you, my own brother."[53] In this gloomy affection of the underworld, the I now has its turn to be dear to another, and death emerges, in this sense, as a fantasy of becoming the beloved. The price of this love that falls, at last, on the self, is selfless love for the other. Such is the context in which Antigone describes the uniqueness of Polyneices, the object of her immortal affection:

> And now, Polynices, for burying your body I get this reward! Yet in the eyes of the wise I did well to honour you; for never, had children of whom I was the mother or had my husband perished and been mouldering there, would I have taken on myself this task, in defiance of the citizens. In virtue of what law do I say this? If my husband had died, I could have had another, and a child by another man, if I had lost the first, but with my mother and my father in Hades below, I could never have another brother. Such was the law for whose sake I did you this special honour.[54]

The argument in this passage has aroused controversy, and the authenticity of its lines has been questioned.[55] Goethe, for one, hoped that Sophocles had not written them. The Hegelians tended to believe that he had.[56] Even from the latter perspective, however, the notion of individuality that Antigone represents here is problematic, for although Hegel considered the family to be organized around allegiance to a general principle of individuality, by "general" he did not, as we have seen, mean "categorical." And yet, it is the notion of category that seems to prevail here, since the burden of Antigone's concern falls on Polyneices not as an irreplaceable person, but as an irreplaceable brother. It is not the loss of his unique individuality that makes her feel the dictates of a deeper law, but his position within the structures of kinship. One can imagine the indignation that such a coolly practical conception of love would have elicited in a writer like Goethe, who had developed his own theory of elective affinities between individuals and had committed himself to depicting the absolute need of one specific person for another, as in *Werther*. The pleasures of her brother's company, memories shared from childhood, a communality of outlook, taste, or feeling—none of this is mentioned in the plays. Instead, Antigone speaks of sibling love in terms of duty, law, and obligation. Only at the end of *Oedipus at Colonus*, perhaps, does a notion of pleasure taken in the other make itself felt in her language, but even there it comes in reference to her father, not her brother. After learning of Oedipus's death, she recalls that "what was never dear [*philon*] was dear [*philon*], when I had him in my arms!"[57] The notion of love, even in the mouth of a single, powerful character like Antigone, is unsure, as if it were being worked through. The criteria for determining its definition and meaning are unclear and often in conflict: Is it pleasure or duty, the living person or its ethical evacuation who loves or is loved? Is it the city or the family who should prevail?

Hidden behind the attempt to define Polyneices's irreplaceable uniqueness, another contingent individual traces her ghostly presence. In imagining herself as the beloved (*prosphilēs*), Antigone defines herself through the pleasures and loves that she will not know, the nuptial bed, her own children, the various acts of affection. In thus detailing her destitution, she does in fact offer an image of a living individual, both loved and loving, who is capable of giving and receiving pleasure. If only in the negative, in her lamentation over what she will not know, Antigone represents life, and she represents it as that which cannot be known, which is different from what is said, described, and sung in this strange poem that is caught between an epithalamium and an elegy. Life is different from what she describes; it is what is described *as missing* from the description, the object of lamentation itself: life, or what cannot be told. It is in the sacrifice of that life, that unspeakable existence *in keinem Buchstaben gegeben*, that she becomes *prosphilēs*. Consequently, any subsequent version of Antigone that sees her as a suicide effaces this crucial tension in her person: her desire for the living, among whom she counts herself.[58] She is not a ghoul, a nihilist, or a suicide, and her human tension, the dynamism of her character and person, comes from the fact that for her to embrace life—which is not yet a possibility clearly established in the city—she must embrace her own death. What Hegel saw as the underlying tragedy of the Greeks, the tragedy of tragedies, shapes her person: She attains the plenitude of her being, even to herself, only in the idea of her extinction. Her identity, indeed her life itself, emerges only in reaction to her inevitable but "superfluous death." And yet

Inventing Life 99

the sacrifice does not diminish the fact that in her lament the possibility of an irreplaceable, lovable, and living person does emerge.

Lacan has convincingly demonstrated that Antigone's description of her relation to Polyneices must be authentic, and, indeed, those lines speak to a deep concern that troubles Sophocles's play.[59] In it, the notions that a loved one is irreplaceable, that this uniqueness is valuable, and that it serves to establish a singular identity vie with an opposing conception of individuality, which sees it as an impersonal civic obligation. But both positions are riven by internal paradoxes. On the one hand, as manifested in the beloved, love is the stain of the particular, but it is also the dissolution of that stain in the self-sacrifice of the loving individual. The laws of the city, on the other hand, recognize the need for individuals, but only insofar as they surrender their individuality to that need. These antithetical ideas of personhood move uneasily both throughout the play and across subsequent interpretations. For Vernant, it was the city whose laws toppled the ancient *dikai* of the family. For Hegel, in contrast, neither order prevailed, for both were one-sided expressions of a more general order, the ethical itself. The power of Antigone's selflessness was one of the reasons why Hegel must break, as it were, with Vernant. For Hegel, Antigone's claim was just, and so his notion of history, which saw it as the self-disclosure of Spirit over time, could not accept that Creon triumph over his niece. If he did, the play would collapse into mere entertainment, an insignificant embellishment, rather than the voice of human spirit discovering itself. Because she is right, and because Creon is right as well, history does not merely pass from one to the other, but moves instead toward what lies below them, the field on which both their positions are deployed, the order of thought that maintains them both in their incompatibility. According to Hegel, it is not empty time that supports the opponents, letting one yield to the other in a nonjudgmental variation, but instead a new manner of thinking, which discloses itself, through a deeper insight, as a more truthful way to understand the world.

Antigone contends that she was born for love and sacrifices her life, in the name of that love, for a single person. But one cannot say that either Creon or Antigone simply represents the individual in face of a more impersonal force. If the virgin speaks on behalf of the ancient and prepolitical laws of the family, she nonetheless upholds neither a miasmatic guilt into which the single person disappears nor the heroic figure who attains individuality only at the cost of his own life. She speaks, in hesitant, groping terms, for what Hegel calls the necessary and indelible stain of the particular in the fabric of the ethical, for the duty that is owed to a person for his or her unique being. She may understand her brother categorically, and thereby undermine his vibrancy and uniqueness, but she also struggles against her own kin, in the person of Ismene, to establish her own doubly "ironic" individuality—ironic, in Hegel's sense, because it refuses to sacrifice itself to the dictates of the civil law, doubly ironic because it refuses also to submit to the archaic ethics of a miasmatic and familial guilt. Conversely, Creon figures not only the polis as war maker and hecatomb of youth, the ethical as absolute altruism to the point of death. He speaks also for the laws of the city and the responsible individual agent they recognize— the need, in other words, to find the one who did the deed. In both cases, the two orders create and dissolve individuals. And each is incompatible with the other—indeed, they are traumatically conflictual. This is the crisis of the city that *Antigone* stages. Nor are these the only positions in play. One cannot say that the different versions of personhood can all be parsed according to a simple binary opposition, that they can be lined up in ranks behind the two antagonists. The play, I have argued, bears traces of other kinds of persons: the legal one, the genetic one, the amorous one, the one commemorated in the *epitaphioi logoi*. They all intersect and struggle in a context where the question of the individual is at once insoluble and of the first importance. Tragedies, in this sense, are works of suffering, and their suffering derives from the need for a seemingly impossible answer to the problem of the individual in the city. That problem is to determine how an individual life can have meaning, when meaning is established through communality, through the subordination or sacrifice of that very individuality on behalf of the group. And it *is* a problem, because a strange and powerful erotic desire insists on the value of the individual within the very structures of the city that would eradicate him. This constitutional erotics opens the way, I would argue, for a rethinking of the individual, even in our own times. Or at least that is what I hope to show in the final two chapters.

SIX

Mourning, Longing, Loving

Hegel's powerful and idiosyncratic reading of *Antigone* describes an intimate relation between the treatment of the dead and the meaning of the city. It also establishes the grounds for a sustained analysis of gender's role in that meaning. But his interpretation is also marked by blind spots, curious and identifiable features of his argument that reveal themselves only in absentia, through lapses or contradictions in his reasoning or as necessary but missing elements. It is an indication of the force of Hegel's reading that these blind spots should be so richly productive and should bear sustained scrutiny. The principal one of these has been associated, for us, with his understanding of the function of the corpse in Sophocles's play. George Steiner recognized Hegel's as the most astute analysis of this aspect of the tragedy, but even so, Steiner failed to understand the singularity of Hegel's treatment, confusing his approach to death with Heidegger's, which viewed it as an absolute and untransferable limit to individual consciousness. Hegel, as we saw, was more complicated and truer to Sophocles's own vision, as expressed, in particular, through the mouth of Antigone herself when she fenced, verbally, with her uncle and sister for the right to bear exclusive blame for Polyneices's burial. But if Steiner confused Hegel with Heidegger, this is perhaps, at bottom, an echo of a confusion in Hegel's text, what I am calling one of its blind spots, for even as Hegel treats death as the perfection of the individual, he does not see that perfection as resulting from death's ontological status (i.e., the absolute intervention of nonbeing in being or, as Heidegger will put it, the possibility of the end of all possibilities), but instead treats it as a result of human intervention, a moral construct fashioned by living people who had some familial attachment to the deceased.

That construction of individual death depends, as we have seen, on the necessary but unspoken fantasy of a dim sentience inhabiting the corpse—and here, "inhabits" is used not in a weak sense to mean the behavior of something that can come and go, but in a stronger one, as an indissoluble link between inhabitant and its habitation. For Hegel's interpretation to make any sense, the dead body must be invested with some faculty of awareness and some moral agency, even if that agency is, through a typically Hegelian paradox, purely passive. And this, as we have seen, is foreshadowed in the treatment of inanimate but criminal matter in Plato's writings. The moral and interpersonal aspects of the city that Hegel saw expressed in *Antigone* are indissociable from the unspoken biological fantasy that permits them, such that the moral aspect of the city is grounded in an inability to distinguish between the living and the dead, between sentience and nonsentience, between thought and matter.

This indistinction expressed itself in other forms as well. Notable among these, the poetic aspects of language embodied a persistence of the past in the present, a persistence that depended on the nonsensical elements of language that Kristeva has called the semiotic. These elements, which have no meaning in themselves, speak, nonetheless, of will, thought, and life, the groaning of desire, the trembling of fear, or a multitude of other, inchoate feelings that may have no name. Emotions take form in them, leave their trace, and then that trace remains, with the eerie semblance of life, of a speaking and feeling that persist even after the death of those who had spoken and written. In this sense, language is a place of the dead. It is also a public place, owned by no one in particular but all in common. Here, the dead continue to signal to each other and to the living. But it is also, crucially, a material place, for those signals are embedded in words that must be pronounced or written down. The dead speak in language and in that speaking they seem still to think and to feel, teaching, exciting, and confusing the living, whom they seem almost to inhabit. In the laws they laid down, they still control the living from beyond the grave. In their poems they still move the living to tears. And, as Kristeva observed, in the very fictionality of the theater, language shows its autonomy from meaning, its semiotic force. This autonomy, I would argue, is itself an index of language's ability to survive, to live beyond and after. Theater—and indeed all literature in the sense of linguistic creation—instantiates the ability of language to produce the semblance of thought, affect, character, and, in a word, life. Whether or not Oedipus ever existed outside of language and the images derived from it, we know that he was proud, suffered, and died in a blaze of light.

That apparent, fictitious animation of language that is brought to the fore in literature depends on the semiotic aspect of language and elaborates on it. In its semiotic aspect, language is a dimly feeling thing, a meaningless confusion of thought and matter, and literature takes that sentient matter, separates it from the original moment of its expression, and uses those isolated, seemingly animate traces of thought to create new life. With this new life, it tells the stories of forgotten but necessary origins, the rise of the city, the justification of its laws, and the definition of its citizens. As a civic festival, tragedy does so not as if it were inventing. It carefully hides the facticity of inventions. Instead, it pretends to return to a lost beginning, as if the legitimacy, laws, and citizens of the city had all to have been ordained before and not by the citizens themselves, as if not even democracy could bear itself as a justification. The city finds its legitimation in those who went before and no longer remain, except in the traces they left behind. It insists, in other words, on legitimizing itself through the dead. It legitimates itself, moreover, in the fictitious remnants of the dead, in the words and stories that they supposedly left behind: the material but sentient remains of their invented lives. These remains, I have been trying to argue, are a form of corpse. Or, perhaps it is the other way around: The corpse is an embodiment of this mythical origin of the city, the matter of its literary creation. Poetry is a revisiting of the origin and meaning of the city. The city, for its part, depends on the forgetting of its poetic facticity. It expresses that forgetting through the expulsion of the dead. First, for reasons we do not know, the dead were excluded at the moment that settlements began to reshape themselves as poleis. Then they were excluded again, during the period of Cleisthenes's reforms, just before the tragic period. The city, in short, was established as a place of the living, while the dead were consigned to a place among the criminal and barbarous. Then, a few years later, the dead returned in sublimated form to justify the city. The conceptual link between those two categories of the dead, the criminals and the legislators, is embodied in *Antigone* as Polyneices's corpse. It is Hegel who allows us to see that body as the expression of a concept crucial to the city. It is Vernant who allows us to reintroduce Hegel's insight into the historical specificity of tragic Athens.

Nicole Loraux's work on the funerary discourses honoring soldiers fallen in battle for Athens opened another vista onto the relation between death and citizenship during the tragic period. The citizen, as imagined in these speeches, sacrificed his individuality to the greater good of the state. From the viewpoint of this tradition, he was, as citizen, always already dead. But the sheer need to insist on the nature of citizenship and the repetitive, almost unvarying formulae of the *epitaphioi logoi*, recycled year after year, decade after decade by various orators, betray an ongoing pressure to define the citizen, as if that definition were at threat. In the interest of what follows, I would like at this point to retain three elements from my earlier analysis of the *epitaphioi logoi*, for out of them emerges an image of that insidious enemy of the state who threatened to undermine the creation of citizens—the other of the state that the corpse embodied. First is the simple fact that there was some ongoing threat to the citizens, something that persistently resisted the city's legitimacy and needed to be conjured over the bodies of the dead. Second, this definition of the citizen was related to the treatment of dead bodies, for the orations were spoken at the Cerameicus cemetery as part of official funerary ceremonies. Third, the conception of the citizen as an impersonal embodiment of his own death was related, by Hegel, to gender difference. War, according to him, was the instrument by which the state subjugated individuality to citizenship, subordinating personal interests to what he called their "master, death." What resisted that abstraction of individuality, according to Hegel, was a specifically feminine desire for the individual in his evanescent uniqueness, an "ironic" stain on the history of the city.

In this chapter, I pick up these various threads to argue that an ineradicable desire persisted in the very essence of the city as it was imagined in key texts from the tragic period and immediately after. This was a desire for an origin, both in the sense of a prepolitical condition and as the mysterious, mythical "moment" in which that prepolitical condition yielded to the city and its meanings. As such, it was a desire for the other of the state, for what the state constitutionally reviled, excluded, or dissimulated. It was, moreover, as the gendering of that impulse suggests, an erotic desire, such that the relation between the state and its repressed other was a sexual one, an aspect that will come out more clearly in my analysis of the parable of Leontius in Plato's *Laws* and in my discussion of the legends concerning the enigma of the sphinx. In the last part of the chapter, I argue that the concerns about the past figured by the dead were in fact displacements of other concerns, concerns that focused not on the relation to the dead but on differences among the living. These differences could be categorical, such as gender or family, or they could be individual, such as the characteristics that distinguish one person from another, making him or her irreplaceable and mysterious. The corpse, it will be seen, was an amorous construct.

To begin, let us frame the issues at hand in terms of affect, for the feminine desire that militates against the purity of the citizen in Hegel's reading is an emotion and can perhaps best be understood as such. In this light, let us return once more to Plato's descriptions of the relation between the individual and the state, in order to test the aptness of Hegel's interpretation. Now, one could argue that of the dialogues I have discussed so far, neither the *Menexenus* nor the *Parmenides* is characteristic of Platonic thought. The latter text, after all, represents a very young Socrates, who was only just establishing his credentials as a philosopher and still had not, as his interlocutor observed, achieved the maturity of his own thought. The *Menexenus* presents itself as a parody of funeral orations, and so, while Aspasia's words might be representative of the *epitaphioi logoi* that are being mocked (and even that is questionable), they cannot be considered as unproblematic expressions of Plato's own positions. But a mature and consistent Platonic system is itself only achieved through the rejection of precisely those elements that do not fit into an ideology of coherence, those moments when developmental uncertainty, rhetorical ambiguity, or other inassimilables disturb its integrity.[1] And even if such a coherent and mature system were possible, an affective paradox still returns at what would surely be something like its core, at the point of articulation between the body, the soul, and the individual as described in the *Republic*, a dialogue that can scarcely be dismissed as an aberration within the Platonic canon. There is a passage in its fourth book that describes this point of articulation through the use of a curious and violent anecdote. At issue is the status of *thumos* in relation to reason and desire, which respectively represent aspiration toward the immortal and embeddedness in the transitory. *Thumos* is a kind of emotional energy that can be found in animals and prerational children as well as in adults, and as such it clearly stands in opposition to the *daimōn*, or the transcendental and therefore impersonal aspect of the soul. It is an individualizing element in people, a force that leads them back toward interest in their own evanescent self, in that part of humanity that, as Vernant

observed, the lyric poets "exalted and to which they abandoned themselves."² Throughout the *Republic*, the dialogue in which it is most exten-
sively discussed, *thumos* generally expresses itself as a covetousness of
honor, but this love of distinction is only one example of a more fundamental affective drive, of an animalistic contentiousness that translates a striving
for autonomy and its recognition, a potentially destructive infatuation with
one's own self coupled with the desire to submit others to that same
impulse.³ The difficulty in this matter lies not so much in the relation
between *thumos* and reason, as in that between *thumos* and desire, or *epithu-
mia*. Socrates formulates the problem to Glaucon in the following way:

> These two forms [viz., reason and desire], then, let us assume to have been
> marked off as actually existing in the soul. But now the *thumos*, or principle
> of high spirit, that with which we feel anger, is it a third, or would it be
> identical in nature with one of these?
>
> Perhaps, [Glaucon] said, with one of these, the appetitive [*epithumētikōi*].
>
> But, I said, I once heard a story which I believe, that Leontius the son of
> Aglaion, on his way up from the Piraeus under the outer side of the northern
> wall [*hupo to boreion teichos ektos*], becoming aware of dead bodies that lay at
> the place of public execution [*aisthomenos nekrous para tōi dēmiōi keimenous*],
> at the same time felt a desire to see them and a repugnance and aversion
> [*apotrepoi*], and that for a time he resisted and veiled his head, but overpowered
> in despite of all by his desire, with wide staring eyes he rushed up to the
> corpses and cried, There, ye wretches, take your fill of the fine spectacle
> [*tou kalou theamatos*]!
>
> I too, he said, have heard the story.
>
> Yet, surely, this anecdote, I said, signifies that the principle of anger
> sometimes fights against desires as an alien thing against an alien.
>
> Yes, it does, he said.⁴

Less familiar than the parable of a charioteer and his two unruly steeds
that Plato uses in the *Phaedrus*, the Leontius incident nonetheless tells
a version of the same story about the soul's opposing tendencies toward
the mortal and the immortal. The thrust of the argument here is to
demonstrate that *thumos* and desire are two distinct drives, and Socrates
will quickly proceed to argue that reason must harness the first to help
govern the second.⁵ In other words, a violent emotional energy is the
best—and perhaps only—means for the *daimōn* to master the irrational
forces that would drag it back down into the vacuous world of transitory

appearances and insignificant materiality. But the way Plato portrays these different forces is as important as the lesson he intends to draw from them, for he plays, in the very form of his exposition, on the relations between person and collective. Here, a particular individual, Leontius, is used to represent an impersonal entity, the city, that negates him in his individuality. The anecdote about him is, in this regard, an allegory, since it uses concrete particulars to depict abstract propositions (or relations): the mortal Leontius figures the immortal state that is absolutely different from him. Now the allegory that Socrates uses here is a synecdoche both for the general relation between the city and the individual and for the structure of the dialogue as a whole. As described in book 2, the aim of the work is to "prove that [justice] is better than injustice," and in order to consider the issue closely, Socrates proposes discussing it in relation to the city "and then only examine it also in the individual, looking for the likeness of the greater in the form of the less."[6] Like the tragedies—as was particularly clear in my discussion of *Eumenides*—the goal of this dialogue is to justify justice itself. The entire argument is based on the premise that the state is an enlarged version of the single person, a point that is repeated only a few moments after the Leontius anecdote, when Socrates asks, "Does not the necessity of our former postulate immediately follow, that as whereby the state was wise, so and thereby is the individual wise?"[7] It is this postulate that justifies, in advance, the very use of this allegory, since it treats the possibility of taking one term to figure the other as axiomatic. Or, more precisely, it posits that possibility as a premise. When one reintroduces this postulate into Socrates's discussion of *thumos*, the passage reveals a vertiginous circular structure. The Leontius allegory describes the axiomatic rhetorical mode of knowing the relation between individual and universal that permits— without explaining it—the relation between the body and the soul, between the mortal and the immortal, between the individual and the general. In other words, the relation is possible only because of its allegorical structure—because, that is, allegory is postulated as a legitimate mode of knowing. And since that possibility derives only from that postulate and cannot therefore be grounded in some other, more fundamental sort of knowledge, the relation between the body and the soul is rhetorical in nature. Like the *chōra*, which can be apprehended only through a "kind of bastard reasoning [*logismos . . . nothos*]," the relation between the mortal and immortal is intelligible only through a mysterious (because unjustified and unexplained) allegorical figure. There is therefore no literal version of the Leontius anecdote, no way of translating it into a nonrhetorical statement. Or to put it another way, its literal form is already allegorical.

The city, as conceived in the *Republic*, consequently knows and masters itself by repeatedly submitting the particular to the transcendental, by giving general meaning to the specific, by allegorizing. Similar to the recurrence of the origin enacted in the rituals of the *pharmakos* and its offspring, the city's allegorical mode of self-knowledge demonstrates the submission of the particular to the transcendental. Like the rituals of expulsion, moreover, the process of self-knowledge is interminable, because the key to its intelligibility, the allegorical relation itself, is never justified.[8] Like the *pharmakos*, the figure of allegory itself, Leontius, son of Aglaion, is to be found at once excluded from and central to the polis, simultaneously outside the walls of the city and in the public place. He embodies a violently emotional struggle between an impersonal vocation toward the rational and a focused, idiosyncratic desire. Now the object of that desire is not insignificant, because it is part of a complex figure of the state itself. Given his allegorical status, Leontius's desire is an example of the individual—it means the individual itself or as such—but at the same time he also desires with the quirky, nonexemplary specificity of his own curious tastes. In the *Phaedrus*, the soul's earthly instincts betray themselves through a man's sexual longing, or eros, for a youth's beautiful living body.[9] In the *Republic*, however, that same tendency toward the flesh, toward the irrational materiality of evanescent individuality, is represented as an overwhelming need to look at corpses. And not just any corpses: These are the excluded of the city, the unburied dead cast outside the walls to rot away beneath the sun. The choice of object seems, paradoxically, to be no accident, for, as we have seen, the corpse condenses into itself the body-soul conundrum that Socrates is portraying. Insofar, then, as the city comprises an alien, individualizing drive, that drive is directed toward the remains of its dead.

As an allegory of the republic, the Leontius anecdote indicates that the state longs constitutionally for the cadavers of its deceased, that it cannot tear its eyes away from them, that its unmasterable will is bent toward them. An ineradicable emotional and rhetorical pollution at the heart of the city is thus directed toward a criminal, extramural, unburied cadaver. Structurally therefore this corpse is the exemplary object of (irrational) desire within the polis. The city is built as a longing for that object of exclusion, as the compulsion, in its public space, to see the abject spectacle of what it despises. These bodies are its filthy rejects, the uncovered excrement left behind by what it cannot assimilate into the impersonal abstraction of its rational communality. It is, in short, Polyneices's corpse that the brutal force of mortal individuality wants to see. And so goes the great Platonic revulsion toward the deceased that we had seen earlier in the *Laws*: They are expressions of a longing for the fleshly, the earthly, the material, in all their strange and thoughtless autonomy. Individuality, for the republic, is the violent force of material ignorance, and it is figured by this passion for the dead. The city is not only constitutionally erotic, it is necrophilic.[10] If the corpse is powerful and, by consequence, frightening, that is because powers have been attributed to it by the imagination of the living. Hegel recognizes this when he speaks of the paradoxical passive agency of the dead. The power of the dead and the threat that they represent to the city, among others, is by necessity a phantasmatic construction. What the Leontius parable suggests is that the power of the corpse, that phantasm projected onto the inert, is the desire of the living for the dead.

Leontius's explanatory power derives from the deconstructive force of rhetoric within a philosophical discourse that would try to master it. A similar story is told, however, in a very different kind of discursive tradition, one that is essentially literary and ritualistic rather than analytical. The mythic material about Oedipus's rise to power reaches far back into the pre-tragic period, and in it the encounter between the hero and the sphinx seems to hold a crucial role, only obliquely visible in Sophocles's subsequent treatment of the legend. This encounter bears key features of an originary moment as I have described them so far: a confrontation between two opposing forces that will result in the control of pollution within the city (a plague) and the (re)establishment of civic order (under a new king); an enigma; and a mythic structure. Now, victory over the sphinx also represents the triumph of a certain kind of knowledge. The trial that the monster imposes, the battle for the city, is not a contest of strength but of intelligence, for it consists in a riddle. What is in question in the enigma, moreover, is not some kind of technical knowledge that would be useful to some practical end, but a form of insight, indeed insight into the nature of humanity. The answer to the enigma is a form of self-knowledge.[11] Jean-Joseph Goux has described this kind of knowledge, which overpowers the forces ravaging the city, as philosophical.[12] The state, according to this myth, thus depends on the triumph of philosophical thought over a monstrous scourge. The nature of that scourge and the literary materials that gravitate around it reveal much about the mythical enemy of the city and the sort of power that it was imagined to exercise.

By examining the mythopoetic tradition around the Oedipus legend and graphic images associated with the sphinx, Marie Delcourt concluded that the monster represented the coalescence of two themes. First, the sphinx figured the dead—not death (i.e., the punishment she threatened those challengers who failed to best her), but the souls of the deceased. This can be seen from the folklore and iconography that appear to have given rise to her figure, in which two images of the dead seem to have been fused. "The mythical being that the Greeks ultimately called the Sphinx," Delcourt wrote, "was born in their mind from two superimposed causes. One was a psychological reality, the *oppressive nightmare*, the other was of a religious nature: the belief in the souls of the dead, represented with wings."[13] Insofar as she derived from the former, the monster would thus figure a heavy and physical reality that weighed down on sleepers and filled them with terror. But to the extent that she derived from depictions of souls with wings, the sphinx formed part of a long list of similar monsters that included the Keres, Harpies, Erinyes, and the so-called *noonday demons* that appear in Mediterranean folklore.[14] Oedipus's adversary was, in short, caught between two opposing traditions and, indeed, tendencies: According to one, she was heavy and physical; according to the other, light and immaterial. In this respect, she seems to have conjoined, without necessarily reconciling, two opposite fears: On the one hand, the stifling horror of a crushing, physical death and, on the other, the fascinating terror of transcendence. Taking Delcourt's descriptions a step further, we could say that as the result of an inherent scission derived from two different and not entirely compatible sources, the sphinx figured the separation of body and soul at the moment of death—and, moreover, that she offered an image of each as a condition that could be experienced. The experience of the soul would be like that of a bird, while the condition of the lifeless body would be like the suffocation felt in certain nightmares.

According to Delcourt, this scission, or what she calls "ambiguity," at the very heart of the sphinx

> derives . . . from her name and the manner in which she was represented. Her wings predestined her to incarnate a *soul* in pain, hungry for blood and

love, but seductive and capable of song. Her lioness's body and her name of *the Frightful One* [*Angoissante*] predestined her to embody the oppressive nightmare. As a light vampire, she pursued youths; as a heavy one, she crushed them with all her weight. It was not, moreover, their life that she attacked first or foremost.[15]

The "ambiguity" of the sphinx, I have said, was a representation of the mysterious and incomplete dissolution of the bonds between body and soul at the moment of death. The encounter with this "enigma," I also said, represented the mythical, originary moment of the city, when the powers of self-knowledge, or what Goux has called "philosophy," allowed the hero to triumph over the pollution of death and secure the boundaries of the state. I have described this as a triumph over death, but Delcourt, in the lines I have just quoted, argues that the sphinx did not attack first and foremost the life of its victims. What she wanted, according to Delcourt, was something else. "All of these beings have a trait in common," she wrote in reference to the sphinx and its like; "they are hungry for blood and erotic pleasure."[16] The somewhat ambiguous images of the monster throwing herself on her male victims that Delcourt adduces would seem to support her argument that the sphinx was, essentially, a figure of female sexual desire, as would the folklore and legends surrounding succubae and other, erotically ravenous souls in pain that helped shape the Theban monster.[17] As represented by the sphinx, the relation between the city and its dead would thus conceal another ambiguity: that between horror and longing, such that the relation between the philosopher-hero-statesman and feminine pollution would be one of sexual desire.

By the time of the tragic poets, these brutal anxieties would have found more oblique, if not necessarily less troubling, expression. The suppression of the ravening sexuality—although not the gendering—of the sphinx may have been compensated in Sophocles's version of the tale by the importance given to the role of Jocasta and the attendant horrors of incest.[18] A similar transformation seems to have occurred in the earliest of the tragedies that we have discussed, Aeschylus's *Eumenides*, where the dark goddesses still bore the impress of a repressed eroticism. "The Erinyes, at least in the works that we know," wrote Delcourt, "have completely lost their sexual character to become pure agents of justice. And yet, how is it that no one has ever noticed that *they are never seen pursuing a woman*?"[19] Like Sophocles's version of the sphinx and hideous as they may have been, the Erinyes would thus have represented a more decorous, displaced version of female desire. The verdict of the play is that even in this more palatable form, the goddesses must be subjugated to a specifically male reason and law. This is the justification of Athens as given in the *Oresteia*, and it is roughly equivalent to the story of the sphinx as we have read it through Marie Delcourt's analyses. The city is the mastering of an archaic pollution, and that archaic pollution is female sexuality. But the iconography and mythopoetic traditions related to the sphinx add another, crucial element to this primal phantasm of the city: Female desire was confused with the experience of death. This would be consistent with the Erinyes' role as Furies or avenging goddesses, for in that capacity they recalled blood crimes and murders, embodying the agency of the corpse that Tiresias and Hegel had commented on, its untiring ability to call down retribution on the guilty. They are, in this respect, memories of death, figures for its lingering in the consciousness and conscience of the living.

One last point about the sphinx warrants comment in the present context. She sang. For Delcourt, this is part of her seductiveness and danger. "But the Sphinx, like the Sirens," she wrote, "is a *soul*, and *souls* sing in order to cast their spell."²⁰ Because of this quality, according to Delcourt, the monster would later reappear in desexualized form as the "*lioness*-rhapsode of the tragedians."²¹ A beastly, bestial singing was thus associated with the sphinx, and this aspect was picked up by the tragedians themselves. Now, singing is not speaking. It is a very different kind of language use than the philosophizing embedded in the enigma. It is a characteristic that would, instead, relate her to the affective, irrational elements in language that Kristeva named the semiotic and that she saw as the condition of possibility for all literary discourse, especially tragedy. In the song of the sphinx would thus linger the memory of tragedy's archaic origins and the recollection that they reach back to the birth of the city. Locked in caverns beneath Athens, renamed the benevolent ones, the Erinyes, in this way, still called out through the voices of the poets. And just as often, even in those calls themselves, they must be resubjugated by myth and civic theater.

The sphinx and her like thus essentially represented two things: woman's erotic desire and the dead. The origin of the city, according to the Oedipus legend, would consequently have been marked by an encounter with the desire of the dead. That desire was seen as frightening, destructive, and profoundly disruptive of the order of the city. In Plato's parable, it was the

living Leontius who desired the dead, whereas according to the mythopoetic tradition behind Oedipus's encounter with the sphinx, it was the other
way around: The monster represented the erotic longing of the dead for the
living. But once again, we must remember that the desires of the dead are
merely fantasies projected onto them by the living: It is the latter who
understand the deceased in terms of a fearful erotic hunger. The two visions
of the city that I have teased out of Plato and the sphinx would thus share
a common vision of its relation to the dead. In both cases, they are a remnant of the originary moment of the state and, as such, an object of desire.
I do not want to level any of the richness that would derive from the infinite
differences between these two versions, their histories, contexts, or tendencies, but I do want to bring out from them the signs of a repressed emotion
in the relation between the polis and the deceased, an emotion that must
have imbued the culture as a whole if it can be found in two such different
but iconic sources. It would, undoubtedly, have made itself felt more
strongly at certain, crucial moments. The story of the Labdacids, I would
argue, is one of these. The figure of the sphinx, as Marie Delcourt observes,
is unique to that story. The sphinx belongs to Oedipus just as much as his
accession to the throne belongs to her overcoming. It is part of his legend,
his identity, and his meaning. And insofar as he is part of Antigone's story,
the sphinx is part of her meaning too. Part of her force comes from this
persistent monster of female desire, displaced and purified into a tragic act
of piety.

Cognate to a series of operators—the *pharmakos*, the criminal, the
female, the foreigner, the language of the barbarian, presubjective gesturing, art (and especially tragedy) itself—the corpse plays along the line of
distinction and indistinction, between *chōra* and *chōris*, blending with these
deliquescent figures that the city never stops rejecting from itself and to
which, at the same moment, it clings as the source of its own possibility. But
the corpse is not simply an indistinguishable mess that can be interchanged
with these other functions, for—like them, moreover—it also participates
in the codes of definition and intelligibility. It figures within the city, delim-
iting the permeability of the social, focusing it into certain, distinctive
points. The places of entry for the city's other, like the seven gates of
Thebes, have their own characteristics, their own effects, their own functioning within the walled enclosure. The corpse does not fall entirely outside the systems of laws, of political structures, of individuality, and of

meaning that define the interiority of the polis, but instead it positions trouble within them. And as a trouble spot, the corpse operates differently from the terms that Derrida, for instance, analyzes—the *pharmakon*, the *chōra*, writing, and so on. For one thing, the cadaver is affectively charged in ways that those others are not. It is more directly related to questions of the individual body and to individuality as such, since it always bears some remnant of the particular person whose disappearance it betrays, some attachment to their history and irreplaceability, even if the abstractness of death simultaneously negates that uniqueness. Most significant, it traces along the crucial but unintelligible line of body and soul, between matter and thought, in a peculiar way. Indeed, Hermann Fränkel has observed that in Homeric Greek, there was no word to designate either the soul or the body of a living person: *psychē* always referred to the departed spirit of the deceased, *sōma* to their mortal remains. "Not in his lifetime," Fränkel writes, "but only in death (and in a lifeless swoon), was Homeric man divided into body and soul. He felt himself not as a cloven duality but as a unitary being."[22] R. Drew Griffith has similarly argued that the corpse was the indicator, par excellence, of the body as such, and that the ancient Greeks otherwise had trouble imagining the body as a whole.[23] So it would seem that the distinction between *psychē* and *sōma* originated in death, that the body first took shape in the corpse. The latter would then be the original figure, the catachresis for the division between the self as mortal and the self as immortal. And from that figured separation, the personified *Urspaltung* of the personal, derive the material and immaterial halves of the individual. The remainder forces the distinction, makes manifest an absence, compels the notion not merely of the corpse but also of the disappearance that makes it other than the living being that it once was. The soul is born, in short, from the cadaver. The individual subject, or rather its very possibility, originates in this visible remnant, the manifest sign of someone lost. The mortal remains are, therefore, the figure not only of the body, but of the self in its intangibility, the material sign of its immateriality, the specific possibility of thinking that particular abstraction and everything that derives from it, such as individual responsibility, legally accountable agency, and the sublime and vanishing point of the single citizen. Stranger to the city, barbarian, passionately desired, as the sign of all that is lost in death, the corpse, weirdly, is the original figure for life itself.

A dead body, from this perspective, becomes such only through the loss of something not previously recognized as a determinable entity, that is, the soul. The individual is the point of contact or interpenetration between the material and the transcendental. That point of contact is situated in the *chōra* and is expressed in the vertigo of the young Socrates. The possibility of meaningful individuation, of the person in his or her specificity, is consequently caught up in a zone of abjection and phantasmata, of bastard thinking and inextricable familial lineages. The complexity of this interpenetration means, moreover, that death does not simply divide two elements, body and soul, but rather that it reorganizes a series of inscrutable but necessary connections between the two. For it is not certain that the individual is possible without a body or that a body, even dead, can ever be detached from the living person it was. If the conjunction of matter and idea in a person is mysterious and irrational, so too is their separation. The tragedy of *Antigone* makes this manifest, for it shows that one cannot be sure what an individual is and, consequently, that one cannot be sure either at what point he or she ceases to be. The materiality of the body, we have seen, determines an evanescent singularity, but it is not enough. The other element or elements for defining a living person have nonetheless remained elusive, seeming to escape the attempts, sometimes pathetic (as in Euripides's *Suppliant Women*), sometimes contemptuous (as in Plato's *Laws*), to identify them. My discussions of Leontius and the sphinx suggest, however, that the individualizing supplement to materiality may lie in the affect that is attached to it, an affect that seems to play such a significant role in distinguishing the abject of the city from the impersonal citizen. For if the individual is born of the cadaver, that is not to say that he or she is born from death. Heidegger and George Steiner would have one believe as much, but we have already seen how their approach fails in face of Sophocles's drama, since death, in *Antigone*, is an abstraction that must be appropriated by an individual whose uniqueness consequently derives from elsewhere. That elsewhere, I have argued, is the love that the protagonist feels for others and that others feel for her. Even Hegel, when commenting on the play, saw in death a purely natural event, an accident whose externality to the deceased must be reconciled through the intervention of survivors. And those survivors, for Hegel, gain their ability to connect individual to death through an interest in the ironically meaningless particularity of the deceased. This particularity takes the form of an irreplaceable uniqueness. The state, in contrast, emphasizes the impersonality and, therefore, the interchangeability of its fallen heroes. Without completely achieving a notion of living individuality through affection, *Antigone* nonetheless opens the possibility for such an entity and such a process of recognition.

My work on *Antigone* is now essentially finished, for I have done what I set out to do. I have described how the role of Polyneices's dead body related to the state as it was imagined in the tragedy. I have shown how that role resonated with other, contemporary attitudes, which are attested in sources ranging from funerary rites to philosophy and legend. I have found in Attic fantasies about the corpse a site for working through anxieties about human individuality, about the legitimacy of the state, and about the possibility of meaning. And I have shown how those functions, which the very nature of the corpse—i.e., its status as remnant or leftover—embedded in the past, yield to the possibility of another kind of conceptualization, one that was based instead on affections toward the living and their open-ended, futural possibilities. But if, at the end of these discussions, I have described *Antigone* as a turning point in the history of love, that claim now places me under some obligation to indicate, at least in broad terms, how conditions changed afterward. Nicole Loraux spoke of the "hypertrophy" of the individual in the century that followed the tragedians.[24] I will not enter into the fine grain of that new enthusiasm, since we have already seen how tortuous and hesitant its expression could be, as in the *epitaphioi logoi* of Demosthenes and Lysias. Instead, I would like to turn to two very different but eloquent artifacts to show how much had changed in the aftermath of *Antigone*. The first is a funerary stele that postdates the tragedy by several decades. The other is even more distantly removed, separated from Sophocles by centuries and a language. This last move may be unbearably speculative for some, but I hope that even they will recognize the value of working in larger, quicker strokes to evoke the picture of a world radically different from the one I have been discussing so far—a world radically different and yet, I would argue, profoundly related.

Let us look first at a representation of death in the century following the tragedians. The *epitaphioi logoi* were still being pronounced in the Cerameicus, but in contrast to fifth-century practices, private citizens had begun erecting funerary stelae in memory of their own dead. Youths and women now figured alongside grown men among the remembered, and all,

as a rule, were depicted in quiet scenes of bas relief. In general, these monuments were more intimate than those of the preceding century and more
oriented toward the family.[25] This would seem then to be the place to find
a depiction of personal loss, of an affectively based value for human life that
had meaning outside—and even *against*—the values of the state. These
images are at once familiar and hard to decipher. In them, the dead and the
living are almost indistinguishable, and it is difficult to understand who is
being memorialized.[26] Survivors and deceased take leave of one another,
but who is who? A father shakes hands with his departed son, as if death had
no hold on the latter, his body still full, beautiful, and erect. Only the
somber tone of the embrace suggests that this is a separation, the restrained
movements, the soberness of the treatment, the absence of smiles, the very
decorousness of the representation. Insofar as it is present, death is indicated in the solemnity of gazes and in the stoic sadness of the faces, so that
it hangs over these scenes in their mood and style. It is indicated, so to
speak, through a rhetorical effect rather than a specific sign. As a result,
each of these encounters is like Orpheus's fatal glance toward Eurydice. It
is the instant of disappearance, the figuration of an absence, in which the
missing one wells up momentarily only to manifest that he or she is lost
forever. The dead are portrayed, then, as Euripides's Theseus had requested
in the *Suppliant Women*. They are shown as they were in life—but just as
categorically as in Euripides, for most of these images are not portraits but
presculpted stock figures.[27]

In some of these stelae, however, the rhetorical tone gives way to a more
defined symbolic representation. Here the grip of the living on the deceased
has loosened, so that a literal space separates the departed from their kinsfolk. In one, from 370–360 B.C.E., a maidservant holds up an infant, who
reaches out toward its mother, while she in turn gazes down into the eyes of
the child (frontispiece).[28] A small interval separates their two hands. That
space is the death in this monument. It is condensed into the distance
between two persons, depicted through the bodies of the living and their
emotions. On one side, the child reaches for a mother it can never again
touch, while on the other a mother holds her own hand curled under her
chin, in meditative reflection on her offspring. Abrasions to the stone
obscure some of its passages, and in particular the child's hand, but it is
clear, nonetheless, that that hand is in very low relief, as if it were disappearing into the materiality of the stele, into the background void that had taken

on the significance of death. This sketchiness is surprising, given that it comes at the focal point of the composition, both in terms of space and meaning. I would suggest that this sketchiness is not a negligence on the part of the sculptor, but instead an integral part of how he understood the subject he was representing, whether in conscious or unconscious terms. In the very execution of its images, in the differences in relief, the stele thus makes an argument about life, indicating that the merest trace distinguishes the living, who are constantly being called back into a primordial indistinction. The materiality of death, its strange, liminal—and crucial—position at the juncture between matter and thought, distinction and indistinction, *chōra* and *chōris*, is indicated, in this stele, through the depth of the modeling. But—and this is key—that primordial indistinction only becomes apparent as such, only takes figure, through the people it separates, for rather than a mere blank in the composition, the void acquires meaning from its status as a gap between two other elements. That gap, I have said, is the figurability of death and as such the basis of its potential intelligibility. Its meaning, in turn, derives from the relation between people and, indeed, from the relation between *living* people, for even the dead, as I have observed, are represented as they were in life. Death, in other words, is an effect of their longing for each other, since what charges the space between them as a separation rather than a mere distance is their manifest desire to touch.

Although Fränkel's linguistic observations indicated that at a certain historical moment the ancient Greeks could grasp that a person was alive only through his or her demise, the mother and child stele would argue otherwise, seeing the conceptualization of death instead as a by-product of relations between living individuals. For the funerary artist, in short, death would be revealed in and by life. And the stele makes more sense, in my opinion, than Fränkel. One cannot use his arguments to absolutize death as the ground and limit of individuality, even at the historical moment he is studying, because for a person's death itself to be noticeable, the deceased must have previously been alive and must have been sufficiently memorable for his or her absence to be remarked. We should try to imagine how it could have worked otherwise. An anonymous cadaver washed ashore is an impersonal and categorical entity, a dead stranger whose particularities can, perhaps, be reconstructed in part through the clues of their person and effects, but that can occur only through analogy to other experiences of the living. The body of a loved one, however, reflects an irreplaceable uniqueness that derives from previous knowledge of him or her. The beloved is both recognizable and absent: recognizable in absence and therefore recognizably absent. For that loss to have specific, individual meaning, for it to be the loss of an individual, the individual must already be known. Now, the corpse plays a special role in this relation between individuality and death because in it the beloved is both identifiable and manifestly absent. It forces the awareness of death through a precise and familiar figure. The deceased does not simply vanish into oblivion. Instead, a corpse in his or her likeness remains to indicate the specificity of the one who has been lost. And this body must manifest itself, for otherwise death is uncertain and a terrible, unanswerable longing persists—not a longing for the lost, which haunts the living long past the rites of mourning, but a longing for the loss.[29] For without that loss, the survivor hesitates between life and death, not knowing whether to wait for the beloved to return or to mourn them. Absence takes on a fragile fictionality in the possibility of death. The gestures that one still continues to make in view of the absent one's return— the preparations for his or her homecoming, the prayers to the gods for protection and safe passage, and all the infinite fabric of expectation and familiarity—go futile without one's knowing it. And because the beloved has not renounced the lover, it is the corpse that must do so. Only the beloved has authority to take final leave, and if he or she can no longer speak the words of absence or perform the rituals of rejection, then it is the corpse that must speak instead. It says two things: I am the one you know, and I will not return.

Perhaps the clearest expression of this comes only centuries after Euripides's death and in another language. When king Ceyx drowns far from home in Ovid's *Metamorphoses*, it is only the ghostly vision of his dead body that can prove to his wife Alcyone that he has died and that she must stop her prayers on his behalf.[30] Evidently, it is not enough that a god come bearing the evil tidings or even that the deceased appear in the form that he had known in life. Instead, the likeness of his drowned body bends over her in sleep and whispers, "Oh wretched wife,/Do you not recognize your husband? Have I changed/Too much in death? Look at me! You will know me,/Your husband's ghost, no more your living husband./I am dead, Alcyone."[31] Ceyx's death is recognizable only through a fantasy that supplements the loss of his loss and fills the sheer, abstract absence into which he has disappeared. Only when the dead body surfaces—even in semblance—can he die. It is the corpse that gives death. It is the corpse alone that can utter on a literal level, but with the force of its whole person, "I am dead."[32] And yet the corpse only gives death through the love of the one who will recognize it, through the care of the spouse to whom it can appeal. Only because Alcyone can perceive her living husband in the wreckage of his life can he die for her. And, as Hegel contends, it is only because he can die *for her* that the gratuitous and alien event of his death can be attached to his individual person. The stranger, in contrast, takes identity only through a story of love that is not his, that is projected onto him in the place of the one who genuinely knows him, for when, the next day, Alcyone sees a body washing toward the shore, she invests it with her own experience and only thereby gives it meaning and particularity. It is the vision of her husband that allows her to feel for this unknown person: "It was a body, whose, she could not tell, / But someone shipwrecked, and the omen moved her / To weep for the unknown dead: 'Alas poor fellow, / Whoever you are, poor wife, if you are married!'"[33] The sight of a corpse itself is not enough to spark the moment of recognition that would join it to a lost life. That recognition comes, instead, from the omen, which symbolizes the bonds of love forged in familiarity that had tied her, and still tie her, to Ceyx.

In retrospect, death may formulate a singularity that had not previously been finalized, but that singularity already existed, even if not yet articulated in a determinate and closed shape. It was experienced, felt (as love), and still open-ended. It was, in short, alive. Death figures that singularity, but only as dead, that is, as a closed and finite end of possibilities. One lives as infinite. One is bound by inscrutable connections to the endless world of material existence, to the absolute distances of other people, with their own opaquenesses and their own infinite variety. The dead body, because it too is material, because it partakes of the accidentality that gives to the beloved his or her irreplaceable particularity, marks not simply that there is death, but that a certain person has died. The concept of individual death depends on the individual corpse, and the individual corpse, in turn, is a product of affective engagements made in life. The corpse alone can speak the event of death from beyond death. It alone can say, "I am dead." It alone can speak in the voice of the one authority that counts: the beloved. And the lover can answer it, can continue the conversation of loss and death beyond loss and death. To it alone, the lover can respond, "Yes, you are dead."

Only an emotional investment—I have spoken of love, but it could be hatred or friendship, or a multitude of other attachments—can create this conversation over and through death. As its funerary orations attest, the city can only produce the proposition "there is death"—an anonymous dying for an impersonal collectivity. In contrast, only affection can produce "she is dead." The corpse is a figure for life itself—for a meaningless, non-symbolic but affectively charged plenitude. And from that affect derives the individual person—not from death, for death itself derives from that emotional, material construct.

Although it was written centuries later and although it does so in stylized form, the story of Ceyx and Alcyone takes up key aspects of the tragic world. The questions of statehood are condensed into the heroes' status as king and queen and, therefore, heads of state, but are not otherwise developed. Meanwhile, the issues of individuality and death have turned inward, relocated in the workings of the married couple. But instead of viewing this stylization as a decadence or enervation of the tragic undertaking, one should consider how it allows the focus to sharpen on the structure of the single person and his or her relation to a social context. Ceyx's question: "Have I changed too much in death?" summarizes the antinomy of individual death in Hegel: Death changes the I too much for it to be an I anymore, for it to be recognizable as the one who died. The I, in this sense, cannot die—or rather, it cannot die unaided. The connection between the dead and the living that the family had previously performed through the "supplement" of funerary rites has now been supplanted by feelings of sadness and pity. In other words, ritual mourning has given way to psychological mourning, relocating individuation from codified procedures and institutions to spontaneous emotions. This has several significant implications. First, the body is identified and death reconciled with the person who is lost in the bereavement that the survivor feels and that, in turn, results from the person the beloved had been in life. Instead of depending on the intervention of people bound to it only by relations of categorical—that is to say, familial—individuality, the dead person now relies on the feelings that his death provokes and that result from the person he was in life. Second, in place of the fantasy that the corpse can feel comes the genuine and native language of the corpse, its ability to speak in the first person the death of the beloved. The dead body becomes language—the idiolect that only he can speak and that only the mourner can understand. Third, the emphasis in Ovid's story is on the married couple: Ceyx's ghost addresses Alcyone as "wife" and asks her to look at him so that she can recognize in him her husband. The elective family, so discredited in the arguments of the Furies in *Eumenides*, here takes precedence over the biological one. And it is, finally, the woman who assures the continuity of the self into death, who allows the subject to die. It is the "ironic" element of the state, as Hegel described her in his reading of *Antigone*, that creates and finishes the individual.

Affect, in Ovid's account of Ceyx and Alcyone, lends individuality and content to human life. And the corpse plays a special role in that process of individuation. Ovid rereads, so to speak, Hegel's description of funerary rites in *Antigone*, which the philosopher had argued were necessary to attach the individual posthumously to his death and identity. Ovid suggests that it is only through the corpse—through its unique linguistic status—that death can be attached to the individual, and that it is only through affect—in life—that the corpse can, in turn, be recognized as that of a particular person. His version of the Ceyx story is, in this sense, a thinking-through of the process of affective, familial individuality that was adumbrated in Sophocles's tragedy. But it tells us more. Fränkel argued on linguistic grounds that the notion of life emerged historically from death. His argument was convincing but seemed to be contradicted by the funerary stele of the mother and child. We should reconsider, for a moment, those two opposing "arguments" a little more carefully. Fränkel was describing the appearance of life as a notion but not, obviously, as an experience. My brief overview of the years following *Antigone* indicates, however, that it would take time for the importance of that experience to be integrated into the conceptualization of life. That integration stems from a discernible if not explicit recognition, attested to by the mother-and-child stele and Ovid, that death must be represented through the living, who thus take on a primordial value. Consequently, even if life's emergence as an idea depends on death, the latter depends on a perhaps as yet unconceptualized *experience* of life. The living are, in this respect, recognized to be more valuable epistemologically than the dead for determining the nature and limits of individuality. Simultaneously, experience and affect are given legitimacy in relation to abstract, formal thought, since the latter is shown, in this case at least, to derive from them. Now, all of this would seem unsurprising, if strong proponents of an alternative view, including Plato, Hegel, and the authors of the *epitaphioi logoi*, had not argued that individuality depends on death. To this, *Antigone*, the stele, and Ovid offer a counterargument: No, death depends on individuals and the affectively charged differences among them.

Perhaps if the corpse served as the emblem of the erotically ethical individual—the individual, that is to say, whose ethical legitimacy is established through the erotic love felt toward him or her—that was because the legitimacy of such individuality was not easily accepted at the time that *Antigone* was written, and especially not in the sacred rituals of the city itself. It could make itself felt only through negation, that is, as a revulsion toward the individual, the woman, the corpse. That persistence in negation—what Hegel would, from a different perspective, call *Aufhebung*, and Freud the return of the repressed—made itself felt in the remnant that could not be eradicated from crucial theorizations of reason and the state. Leontius thus became against his will a spokesman for the individual and, as such, an object of revulsion to himself, Antigone a pariah. But this may be the nature of true revolutionaries before they are recognized as such: to appear as the proponents of causes that are deemed not so much frightening as ignoble, laughable, or revolting. As that rejection loosens its grip on the imagination, yielding to the force of desire and changing circumstances, the cause in question should, theoretically at least, be able to assert itself in more positive, or at least cleaner, terms. One could say that Antigone's defiance and her shamelessness about it represent two steps forward in such a revolutionary direction. That she would have to legitimate that shamelessness with her life is one step backwards, toward an older ethos. Nonetheless, her play marks a turning point in the history of love, an uneasy, sloppy turning point, perhaps, but a crucial one all the same. It represents, I have argued, a defiant love of the living. That love is expressed, paradoxically, toward a corpse, but the love felt toward it was weighted with the abandonment of life that it demanded, the lament and epithalamium that the condemned Antigone sang for the marriage and life that she had sacrificed. The corpse, as viewed from this subterranean history, was not the individual, but the point of access for rethinking individuality in new terms. By its very nature, it was, I have tried to argue, a point of defiance, the grounds for rethinking personhood in terms of a noncivic, abject, and specifically feminine affectivity. According to this other history, the private subject was born out of the corpse but then revealed itself as a product of emotional life.

Maybe, as Derrida has argued, the Greeks as such never existed.[34] They are only, perhaps, a fantasy, but if so, they are a long-standing one and, as Aspasia demonstrates in Plato's *Menexenus*, a fantasy of the Greeks themselves, a fantasy that has shaped others, that has created an illusion of coherence and direction over centuries and continents. A fantasy of philosophy and history. And insofar as there were Greeks, they indicate to us in their tragedies, their philosophical disputes, and even in their archaeological remains that statehood is an ontological and epistemological question, that it is inextricably bound up with such issues as the difference between thought and matter and the constitution of an individual human being. And in this dream, a specter returns, a ghostly figure of incomprehensibility, pointing with its ghastly face toward the fantasy itself, gesturing from beyond death and beyond the walls to a meaningless and arbitrary origin, when there was, as yet, no fiction of the city. To this repulsive and fascinating figure the city endlessly returns when it needs to think itself. It may not always be the corpse, but at a crucial turning point in the history of the city, I have tried to argue, it did take the specific form of the material dead.

SEVEN

Exit Tragedy

Everything that I have written so far, and indeed a huge body of work spanning centuries and disciplines, argues that *Antigone* is important. That Sophocles's tragedy continues to generate scholarly debate in philosophy, psychoanalysis, literary studies, and feminist theory indicates that it is still timely. And if *Antigone* is so important, even now, that must be because it raises some crucial and unresolved questions. By arguing, as I do, that the interest of the play extends beyond mere literary appreciation or historical interest, that it reaches beyond fact to concerns about meaning and meaningfulness, I place myself under the obligation to attempt an answer to those problems and questions. In this regard I am following a precedent set by some of the most imposing figures of the last two centuries, and my own interpretations will build on what they have done. In Hegelian (and Lacanian) terms, the tragedy of *Antigone* is the inability of human beings to escape the inevitable loss of material individuality that ensues when that individuality and materiality become objects of consciousness. Tragedy is, according to them, the impossibility that the self recognize itself as anything other than dead. This is the life-in-death that echoes throughout the play and finds embodiment in the corpse around which all its actions turn.

Some readers, taking both Sophocles and Hegel in earnest, have tried to escape that fatal aporia by seeking indications or presentiments of a living individuality in the play. In the move from the readings of *Antigone* in the *Phenomenology of Spirit* to those in the *Philosophy of Right*, Hegel imagined that the resolution of tragic Greece lay in the advent of Christianity and, more specifically, in the shift from familial obligations and inherited guilt to another sort of kinship based on the free choice of the wedding contract, but this approach still negated the contingent accidentality of the individual—his or her individuality, his or her life—because Hegel placed more importance on the contract than on the individuals it unites.[1] Luce Irigaray attempted to exit this Hegelian determinism by revealing the repression of sexual difference in Hegel's reading and the latter's unwitting compliance with unexamined cultural stereotypes. Whereas Hegel saw woman as one form of unconsciousness that history must supersede, Irigaray argued that it was, instead, Hegel's masculinist presuppositions about the feminine that formed the unconscious of his system. In her rereading of *Antigone*, she inverted his historical model by understanding the biological unconscious as a good in its own right and a countervalue to the masculine instead of as a primitive state that needed to be overcome. In so doing, she opened the way to feminist critiques of how Hegel handled Sophocles's play by arguing that materialized and irrational affections, associated with the maternal, have value in themselves and can constitute the basis for creating a human individual. My own approach to the play is deeply indebted to Irigaray and her readers, especially in their concern with the contingent and the emotional, and, indeed, in their focus on Hegel. I would like, however, to move away from Irigaray's emphasis on materiality and biology toward what I see as a different conception of life hinted at in *Antigone*, one that puts less emphasis on emotions themselves than on the way those emotions reveal our relatedness to others. To do so, however, it will be necessary to trace through the history of affection in the Hegelian and post-Hegelian readings of the play. I will then return to Sophocles's version to examine the way in which an often neglected character, Antigone's fiancé, Haemon, throws the heroine's tragic status into relief and points the way to other, post-tragic conceptions of individuality.

In the *Phenomenology*, which dates from 1807, Hegel placed the familial and feminine within the material realm, as when he wrote that in death, "this particular individual who belongs to the Family . . . is taken as a *universal* being freed from his sensuous, i.e. individual, reality."[2] Within the family and the feminine, to be individual is to be sensuous and consequently contingent, an unthinking, unconscious stage that spirit must overcome in order to achieve its full identity. For the Hegel of the 1827 *Lectures on the Philosophy of Religion*, however, the situation is somewhat different, for in this reading of *Antigone*, blood relations are no longer governed by biology alone but obey as well the dictates of "sentiment."[3] In this later work, moreover, he explicitly raises the question of life, affirming that the love felt by one spouse for the other is directed toward the latter's living individuality. This, he wrote in *The Philosophy of Right*'s analysis of *Antigone* (1821), is the "ethical moment" in marriage, the emotion felt for a person rather than his or her abstraction.[4] Hegel hesitates, in this respect, between two different registers for understanding familial bonds and the individuals they create: on the one hand sheer, animal drives and on the other affection and love, which have other, nonbiological implications. And Hegel recognizes these other implications, for while *The Philosophy of Right*'s discussion of *Antigone* subsumes the sentiment of erotic love into the marriage contract, that love still retains a positivity that was absent from the *Phenomenology*, where feminine desire was described as an ironic perversion of male civic value and a mere ornament.[5] Whereas the *Phenomenology* had counted on war to correct woman's fascination with the sensuous individual, the *Philosophy of Right* looks to marriage as a means to justify heterosexual love and the individuality implicit in it. Patricia Mills has pointed out the incoherencies in Hegel's theory of marriage, but it nonetheless indicates an important evolution in his understanding of *Antigone*, the shift from a death-based or lethal idea of individuality to one derived from the codification and sublimation of love through marriage.[6] Despite the recognition it gives, somewhat indirectly, to the values of affect and life, this later reading still promotes the supersession of the sensuous individual and advances a heteronormative notion of individuality. In arguing for the unique role of brother-sister relations in individuation, the *Phenomenology* had limited individuality to those fortunate enough to have an opposite sex sibling. In shifting that role to husbands and wives, *The Philosophy of Right* admitted erotic desire into the process of individuation, but limited the latter to married couples.

When Luce Irigaray returned to Hegel's reading of *Antigone* in the *Phenomenology*, she sought to restore the value of the repressed aspects within it and to open up not only Sophocles's play to new interpretations, but also to argue, more generally, for the legitimacy of the feminine. Aside from two paragraphs and their *Zusätze* in the *Philosophy of Nature*, the passages on Sophocles's tragedy are the only place in Hegel's writings where he offered a sustained analysis of sex difference, and Irigaray's focus on his interpretation of a single play was thus a means to open the whole Hegelian system to feminist critique.[7] While her emphasis on sex difference (rather than gender) has led critics to accuse her of biologism, Tina Chanter has persuasively argued that Irigaray's conception of sex is dynamic rather than essentialist.[8] This emphasis inflects Irigaray's reading of *Antigone*, especially in its attempt to recuperate the biological aspects of human experience. For Hegel, the family, as Mills puts it, "is the sphere of 'merely natural existence,' 'mere particularity'; as such its supreme value is essentially inactive biological existence or animal life."[9] That biological existence is negated, over the course of the *Phenomenology*, in the increasing self-consciousness of human spirit. This would seem to represent, and has long been taken to represent, the triumph of thought over animality, but I would like to argue that it codifies, as well, a preference for death over life, since the instrument that subordinates animality to consciousness in the *Phenomenology* is the power of the negative. This is how Hegel describes that humanizing faculty in the preface to the *Phenomenology*:

> That an accident as such, detached from what circumscribes it, what is bound and is actual only in its context with others, should attain an existence of its own and a separate freedom—this is the tremendous power of the negative; it is the energy of thought, of the pure "I." Death, if that is what we want to call this non-actuality, is of all things the most dreadful, and to hold fast what is dead requires the greatest strength. Lacking strength, Beauty hates the Understanding for asking of her what it cannot do. But the life of Spirit is not the life that shrinks from death and keeps itself untouched by devastation, but rather the life that endures it and maintains itself in it.[10]

Here, Hegel describes the transformation of the accidental or contingent individual into something higher. The individual attains that higher status by separating itself from others and by bringing the force of negativity to bear on its connection to the circumstances surrounding it. Humanizing thought, in this respect, is not merely the power of the negative; it is, more specifically, a form of death. According to the broader scheme of the *Phenomenology* as a whole, the supersession of animality by humanity is thus, in fact, the supersession of life by death. This general scheme reasserts itself in the reading of *Antigone*, where the feminine and familial, as manifestations of mere biology, are superseded by the state through the action of war. Even within the family, as we have seen, true individuality is attained only postmortem. But the figures of Antigone and Polyneices indicate another meaning for the life-in-death that Hegel refers to here. Both of them embody the unhappy and unresolved persistence of animality within the male city, indeed the persistence of accidental life under its oppressive laws. In arguing for the value of the biological within Hegel's reading of *Antigone*, Irigaray is thus arguing for the value of a living individuality connected to others and the rejection of a political scheme based on the repression—through death—of that individual. Chanter is quite right to view this as a dynamic rather than essentialist notion of biology.

In a cagey and unexpected way, Irigaray orients her reading of *Antigone*'s function in the *Phenomenology* by connecting Hegel's idea of kinship as consanguinity to his physiological writings on blood. This allows her to relate the categories of the female and the biological in a richer and more problematic way than would be possible by simply reading the Antigone sections alone. "Woman," she writes, "is the guardian of the blood. But as both she and it had had to use their substance to nourish the universal self-consciousness, it is in the form of *bloodless shadows*—unconscious fantasms—that her subterranean subsistence perpetuates itself."[11] Woman, she observes, thus exists within the Hegelian system as the repressed and unconscious, a sensuous materiality that must be transformed into universal will.[12] In that transformation, however, matter—and the biological—lose their ability to constitute a living and autonomous subjectivity, leaving behind only a ghostly remnant.[13] But although that remnant is exsanguine, according to the blood-logic that Irigaray traces, it seems strange to call it a ghost, which hardly evokes the abandoned sensuousness that woman otherwise represents throughout her reading. Indeed, calling woman a ghost identifies her instead with the masculine negation of that materiality, since spirit—the *Geist* (alternatively spirit, mind, or ghost) whose progress Hegel traces in the *Phenomenology*—is the death of the bodily individual. I would propose, therefore, that a better choice for that repressed remnant, especially within the context of *Antigone*, is the corpse, that bloodless leftover that embodies, as we have seen, all that the state can neither successfully repress nor entirely exclude. Like the corpse in its phantasmatic sentience, woman is, moreover, "the still undifferentiated opacity of sensible matter, a reserve (from) substance for the sublation of the self."[14]

The crucial move in this critique of Hegel is Irigaray's contention that consciousness relates to woman not through an *Aufhebung*—the "determinate negation" that preserves what it annihilates and that is the instrument of spirit's progress, according to Hegel—but by "refoulement," or repression. This moves the overall narrative away from a progressive, idealist history of mind to a psychoanalytic structure of uneasy recurrence and uncontrolled repetition. It also allows a new critique of the positivity of consciousness by viewing it as a violence against something otherwise meaningful and valuable. Irigaray herself does not pursue that possibility in her reading of *Antigone*, but Lisa Walsh has shown how some of Irigaray's later writings might be brought to bear on that question. In *Sexes et parentés*, Irigaray describes gender as "the moment of passage of the infinite into the finite, insofar as each gendered individual is finite and potentially infinite in his/her relation to gender."[15] This would seem to offer a new, nonlethal way to resolve the apparent antinomy between contingent individual and universal community. Walsh focuses on the way in which this view of gendering might allow individuals to recognize themselves and each other "through permeable, desiring bodies."[16] As she puts it, quoting from another section of the same volume that contains Irigaray's discussion of *Antigone*:

> These living, breathing bodies and their fluid exchange and interchange depose the culture of death, "*la culte du mort et la culture de la mort*," as foundational moment of the ethical order: " . . . the pleasure of an endless exchange with the other in a touching that no privileged identification might hinder in its resorbtion [*sic*]. Neither one nor the other being taken as terms, any more than is this excess of their passage into each other—which is nothing: what is lacking in the circularity of a movement turning back on itself, the gap which always already refers back to another."[17]

Erotic, gendered desire would thus be redeemed as a means of creating human individuality while guaranteeing to it an ethical value as something universal and interpersonal. As Walsh observes, in *Sexes et parentés*, this revaluation of desire allows one to conceptualize a nonlethal subjectivity. Irigaray pursues this approach by differentiating her notion of gender from another central feature of the Hegelian system, describing it as "a temporalization which passes neither through destruction nor the *Aufhebung*, but rather through an attention, a knowledge, a culture of the sensible as such and through an access to levels of intensity and a contemplation of nature in the self, of the self, of the self and the other."[18]

Despite the tremendous promise that it holds for a gendered, non-Hegelian notion of human subjectivity, Walsh points to what she describes as the principal shortcoming of Irigaray's approach: Since "Irigaray often argues that a symbolic engendered of sexual difference is impossible to

conceptualize, above all because the only available tools of conceptualization are determined in and by a masculine symbolic," she ultimately defers
to a Lacanian model of language, in which a paternal "Symbolic order . . .
inescapably bounds our conscious and unconscious experience."[19] The
escape from Lacan's symbolic order would come, according to Walsh,
through a recognition of maternal desire and the way that it reintegrates
materiality and affection into the determination of individuality. This is
a provocative idea: A maternal order of the otherwise repressed would
counterbalance the domination of the paternal, leading to a truly gendered
subjectivity, in which the feminine was no longer relegated to unconsciousness and silence. To examine the value of Walsh's approach, however, one
needs to look at Lacan's own reading of *Antigone* and the role of the symbolic in it. Ultimately, I would argue, Walsh's solution to the Hegelian
impasse of life and subjectivity remains so bound to the Oedipal familial
structures of psychoanalysis that it limits the notion of gender and individuality to the recurrence of the repressed. I would propose, instead, that
the exit from Hegel's lethal model of subjectivity would derive less from a
recognition of maternal desire than a more general acceptance of the role of
others in desire, the ways that desire both determines an individual and
involves him or her in the interest of others. This is a paradigm of individuality that would recognize the value of a contingent and irreplaceable single
person as a dynamic process among various, interconnected people. Instead
of a Hegelian binary relation of repression between the self and the natural,
the male and the female, based on family structures and kinship, this model
would allow for both the inexplicable spontaneity of desire and the elaboration of that desire into (self-)recognition. As the other loves me, I become
increasingly clear and meaningful to myself, "symbolic" insofar as I have a
significance to others. And as I love the other, I reciprocate that process,
which, because it is a process and because it is reciprocal, is theoretically,
at least, unending. It is this work of and with desire, rather than kinship,
Oedipal relations, or gender, that would produce a unique but meaningful
individual. This is the promise that Sophocles buries, tragically, in sepul-
chral nuptials between Antigone and her fiancé, Haemon.

To understand how this would work, let us first look at Lacan's analysis
of *Antigone*. Lacan's reading of the play is found in his seminar on ethics
in psychoanalysis, which he delivered during the academic year of 1959–60.
His understanding of the drama as a whole centers on the person of

Antigone herself and the tragic pain that she personifies. That pain, according to Lacan, derives not from issues of sex difference or gender—he dismisses Hegel's reading quickly and unceremoniously—but from her relation to the symbolic order, which he sometimes assimilates to the paternal law.[20] In this respect, and despite his ostensible rejection of Hegel, Lacan nonetheless reproduces the basic structure that underlies his and so many other readings of the play: It is organized around the incompatibility between two laws. The symbolic order is, very roughly speaking, language, insofar as it negates the material world it signifies and insofar as it generates individuals as abstracted, dynamic entities defined by their relations to each other and to the materiality they both negate and desire. Here too, Lacan is surprisingly Hegelian, building on the idea, laid out in the "Sense Certainty" chapter of the *Phenomenology*, that language negates sensuous experience and even, at points, adopting Hegel's concept of *Aufhebung* to describe the functioning of the symbolic.[21] To live in the symbolic is, consequently, to live in the negation of sensuous, contingent experience.

Now, for Lacan, Antigone is defined, above all, by her desire. That desire, however, fixes not on the objects that she claims she wants—for example, her sisterly duties or the matrimonial pleasures whose loss she so bitterly laments—but on what she ostensibly fears, namely the death that she will eventually achieve.[22] Through her embodiment of that desire, she lives, affectively and effectively, in death. "In fact," Lacan writes, "Antigone herself declares, and always has declared, 'I am dead and I want death.'"[23] He consequently construes the drama of the play—and of individuation in it—as structured around an *agōn logōn* that pits life against death in an endless impasse. Tragedy *is* that impasse. But it is, according to Lacan, also the human condition, since what Antigone represents is not a specific historical situation but rather the human relation to language. Butler sees Antigone's "life in death" as the existence of those whose sexual desire is repressed as deviant by societal norms. For Lacan, it is instead the fact that the only way to achieve human subjectivity is through language and the negation of sensuous existence that it entails. According to him, Antigone lives in death because she embodies the "signifying split [*coupure signifiante*]," the scission that the symbolic order effects between itself and what it signifies.[24] But it is only through that scission, according to Lacan, that the individual can establish "the unique value of his being."[25] In choosing to phrase the problem in just those terms, Lacan, I would argue, sidesteps a potential paradox in the theory of the subject. What has a unique value has, perhaps, no value at all, since it cannot be compared or exchanged. Money, the common term that explains so much for Creon and underwrites, as we have seen, so much of his worldview, is precisely a means for abstracting from what is unique so that, in that abstraction, it can have a value in relation to others. To speak, as Lacan does, of a "unique value" is thus to assert the value of the unique, the contingent, the material as such. But as he explains how that is, he quickly undermines the promise of such an alternative subjectivity.

> This value comes essentially from language. Outside of language, it could not even be conceived, and the being of him who had lived could not therefore be detached from everything—good and evil, destiny, consequences for others, feelings for himself—for which he had been a vessel. This purity, this separation of a being from all the characteristics of the historical drama that it has traversed, is itself the limit, the *ex nihilo*, around which Antigone holds herself. It is nothing other than the split that the very presence of language institutes in a man's life.[26]

Antigone lives "autour de" or "around" the split between history and meaning that is language. This is "the image of the horizon, of the limit . . . on which she sets herself up," and that establishes, according to Lacan, her legal authority in the play.[27] Her life is thus divided between linguistic purity, on the one hand, and the morally ambiguous historical drama that is an actual existence, on the other. Understood in this way as purity, language is freed from the characteristics that would make for a character, but it is still capable of individuating. And to explain how it can still individuate, Lacan plays on the relation between individuality and spontaneity, on the unforeseeableness that separates a unique person from the predictability of laws or abstract theories. He uses the term *ex nihilo* to describe that spontaneity of the unique individual, but in so doing he draws on the idea of nothingness contained in the word *nihilo*.[28] To be spontaneous is to come from nothing. And Lacan identifies that nothingness as the negativity of language. This nothing is what transforms character into value. But because the worth of Antigone's individual existence is language, that worth is, in fact, the negation of her existence, and in this respect, Lacan reproduces Creon's abstracting approach to value. Consequently, Antigone, as character, represents for Lacan the desire for death that is, more profoundly, the desire for an autonomous subjectivity possible only through the death that is language. Her passion is, in other words, for herself, albeit for a self that does not yet exist. Her pain, though, derives from her embeddedness in a sensuous contingency that prevents her from attaining that subjectivity.

This is the ahistorical value not only of Antigone as an individual character, but of the "drama" itself that is Sophocles's play. *Antigone* and its heroine continue to be timely and important, according to Lacan, precisely because they negate history and character.[29] There are, however, certain limits to Lacan's reading. The most important of these is probably his use of the *ex nibilo* to articulate between individuality and value, for to be unforeseeable and unique is not necessarily to come from nothing. To assert as much is, instead, simply to view the question from an absolute viewpoint (i.e., as unforeseeable to anything, anyone, anywhere), and frames subjectivity from a metaphysical and essentially theological perspective. One could imagine unforeseeable in other terms, as "unforeseeable *to*"—as that which surprises not absolutely but that, instead, surprises another person.

To imagine the unforeseeable in this latter way is to move individuality out of its Hegelian grounding in death toward an ethics of the other. And Lacan, in fact, gestures toward just such an evolution. He ended his series of seminars on *Antigone* with the following words: "Antigone perpetuates, eternalizes immortalizes that *Atè*."[30] *Atē* was, he had earlier explained, not simply misfortune or unhappiness, but the death that Antigone longed for, "the limit that human life can only briefly cross."[31] And yet, he had also positioned that limit elsewhere, not as the division between life and death but instead as the separation between individual people: "*Atè*," he had written, "which derives from the Other, from the field of the Other, does not belong to Creon. It is, instead, the place where Antigone is situated."[32] At the end of his analysis of *Antigone*, he again alluded to this displacement of the "signifying split" from mortality to intersubjectivity, writing: "Antigone takes right to the limit the fulfillment of what one could call pure desire, the pure and simple desire for death as such. She embodies this desire. Think about it. What's going on with her desire? Shouldn't it be the desire of the Other and plug into the desire of the mother?"[33] The desire for death would thus translate another, more fundamental desire "of the Other." The genitive here should undoubtedly be taken in a double sense as objective and subjective—the desire for and from the Other. Now, one can hardly accuse Lacan of undertheorizing how the desire of the Other affects subjectivity, but he does not address the question in his readings of *Antigone*. One would have to turn, instead, to other of his writings, such as the seminar of 1957–58 or his article on the phantasm in the 1970 issue of *Scilicet*.[34] The latter is the more pertinent to us, since it indicates in some detail the connection between the desire of the Other and the negative properties of language. Here again, however, the self and Other live in the scission between being and signifying.[35] Within the terms of Lacan's reading of *Antigone*, this means that they exist toward each other as the impossible relation between life and death. And so Lacan brings us back around to the primacy of death within subjectivity, even as he hints that death itself derives from another, more fundamental register.

But death itself, I would argue, is a product of the relation between people. We have already seen it figured as such in the funerary stele from the Cerameicus cemetery in which a mother and child almost touch hands, separated only by a minute gap of empty background whose blank negativity takes on meaning only through the delicate features it divides and the pathos of their gestures. Death, in that sculpture, was intelligible—and therefore derived imagistically and conceptually—from the distance between two people. In *Antigone* as well, another conception of individuality, based not on mortality but choice, derives from the difference between two characters. Those characters are not Antigone and Creon, who seem so manifestly to be the focus of the drama, but rather Antigone and her fiancé, Haemon. Except for Martha Nussbaum, readers of the play generally devote little attention to Haemon, although they usually describe him as an admirable and sympathetic figure. Because he argues, in face of his father's intransigence, that the state depends on a plurality of opinions, Nussbaum sees in him the voice of democracy in the play and a representation of the "fragility of goodness."[36] The attention of her analysis focuses on the politics of difference that she sees sketched out in the drama. My interest goes to a somewhat different issue: a subjectivity of difference, and more particularly, a subjectivity of living, erotic desire. Like Lacan, Nussbaum sees Antigone as in love with death and the dead rather than the living, and in this respect she draws a contrast between the heroine and her fiancé.[37] "Haemon's advice," she writes, "is that the true way of being humanly civilized requires the preservation of the mystery and specialness of the external, the preservation, in oneself, of the passions that take one to these mysteries. Such a life has room for love; and it also has room, as Tiresias's life shows, for genuine community and cooperation."[38]

Haemon is, in this sense, the good citizen. But he is also, through his acts, deeds, and emotions, the proponent for a kind of individuality that differs radically from those embraced by both his father and his lover. The most important indicator of this difference comes in the way that he chooses Antigone and remains faithful to that choice. The contrast between Haemon's notion of erotic affection and his father's is brought into focus in a stichomythic passage between Creon and Ismene. When the latter asks, "But will you kill her who is to be your son's bride?" Creon answers, "Yes, for the furrows of others can be plowed!"[39] His choice of metaphors is typical for the period—it was part of the Athenian marriage contract—but it also affiliates his notion of marriage and the erotic with the models of political identity propounded in the *epitaphioi logoi*, since the latter understood legitimate statehood as autochthony, which itself was construed as derivation from a female-gendered, maternal earth.[40] The relation between plow and native soil thus symbolized the connection between the citizen and his legitimacy. By playing on this other, civic register, Creon's metaphor makes Haemon's erotic desire a matter of state.

Whereas Creon's rhetoric of statehood asserts that women are interchangeable, Haemon, through his behavior, treats Antigone as irreplaceable, thus consciously and directly contradicting his father. By choosing a wife and remaining faithful to that choice, he rejects Creon's subordination of individual inclination to the larger identity politics of the city. He also differs, in this respect, from Antigone herself. Like Haemon, she proved willing to die for the object of her love, but she chose that object, as we have seen, because of his categorical identity: Polyneices was irreplaceable not because of his individual character or "history," but because of his role as orphan brother (ll. 905–12). Antigone's reasoning is consistent with Creon's in this respect: If it is, as she argues, the categorical relation that must be cherished, there is nothing that makes her, in her categorical role as betrothed, irreplaceable in Haemon's affections, for unlike the orphaned brother, a fiancée can be replaced. But Haemon does remain true to his choice, even to the point of death. No rationale is given to explain his behavior, although reasons are given against it, which makes it, within the play, an untheorized act. As such, it remains unsubordinated to law or concept—spontaneous in the sense of Lacan's *ex nihilo*, although free from the burden of absolute negativity that the Latin term carries. Within the economy of the play, then, Haemon chooses Antigone because of who she is, and in that sense he individuates her. At the same time, he chooses her because of who he is, and thus his choice also individuates him. He is consequently the character who indicates most powerfully the possibility of creating a living individual through interpersonal choice, an erotics and philia of reciprocal self-identification.[41]

It is more through her contrast with Haemon than with Creon that Antigone emerges as a tragic figure. In her vocation for death, she remains caught in the aporia of a living subjectivity, while the figure of Haemon—unnoticed by critics such as Lacan and Hegel—indicates that her impasse results not from fate but from her own categorical blindness. She sacrifices herself for a dead brother, but never even mentions her intended husband, while her epithalamium points to some abstract family that she will have lost. Haemon, however, resolutely chooses her and her alone, a specific wife, whom he holds in his arms at the end of the play. He embodies, in this way, the move away from marriage as a contract or civic institution toward marriage as a free decision based on character. The move, as well, away from kinship to choice. And in that choice, even if it is unexplained—indeed *because* it is unexplained—emerges the specificity of the individual, determined in the unspoken, unwritten, *in keinem Buchstaben gegebene* laws of erotic desire. Antigone *is* tragedy. Haemon represents an exit from that tragedy.

That exit is legible, but literally unwritten. For the interpersonal subjectivity Haemon points to remains absent from the text of the play. His choice, I have argued, is a matter of character, but character could be understood to be an immutable force that bends events to its will or breaks, tragically, against a still greater resistance. This is not spontaneity—it is a form of predetermination. But spontaneity, if it is to ground subjectivity, cannot be aleatoric, for otherwise character would be happenstance. It would seem to bring individuality to an impasse, caught between predetermination and chance, but the figure of Haemon suggests a resolution. If we take spontaneity to mean "unforeeable *to*" and see character as something open to change, contingent individuality might have meaning and value in its very contingency. To see this, we would have to imagine the unwritten of the text, a scenario in which Antigone reciprocated Haemon's love on its own terms, in which she chose him uncategorically and faithfully. In this unscripted drama, he loves her for who he perceives her to be, and through this choice he discovers what he desires. In this sense, he discovers both himself and her. Antigone, meanwhile, reciprocates this love, thereby discovering both herself and him. But this is only half of the story, since both partners are still limited to their own perceptions. Imagining further, we see that in his love, Haemon presents to Antigone an image of the person he perceives her to be, and insofar as she accepts this image (consciously or unconsciously, willingly or not), she is shaped not only by her own character but also by Haemon's view of it. And this is not a static image, for as Haemon is shaped by Antigone's view of him, his perception of her changes. In their reciprocal love, in their exchange of images, the two characters evolve, in a process of mutual determination whose open-endedness derives from the infinite distance that separates two people. Because of this difference, or what Nussbaum, in another context, calls "mystery," each member of the couple must live in a constant and constitutional state of surprise.[42] We can call this mutual, open-ended determination of the contingent a living individual.

To base that mutual determination on the specific affect of love could, however, seem arbitrary. In my discussion of the Ceyx and Alcyone story in the last chapter, I did acknowledge that an enemy might have enough intimacy with a person to link a corpse to the person it had once been. The relation between two living individuals is different, however, since it is mutual. The lover *affirms* the character of the beloved and thereby gives to his or her uniqueness a positive value. Enemies may also affirm each other's value, but only as a negative. The lover's positivity is the inducement that leads the beloved to accept the self-image supporting that positivity, the inducement to enter into the mutual determination that creates the living individual. Through the positivity of love, the lover affirms the contingent in its uniqueness, while the interpersonal aspect of mutual determination gives to that same unique individual (what Hegel called "an accident" in the preface to the *Phenomenology*) a nonabstract, noncategorical, and nonsymbolic meaning.[43] This means, moreover, that the play points, through the figure of Haemon, toward a subversion of heteronormativity, since affection need not depend on written laws, social conventions, or kinship relations. Indeed, the crucial intervention of Tiresias in the play's denouement serves to reinforce this subversive tendency, since the seer's interpretive abilities derive from the ambiguity of his own gender. But because it does not determine individuality, gender would now have to be considered a derivative of mutual determination, a consequence of living individuation rather than a cause of it.

I have argued for the continuing importance of *Antigone*—an importance that is indissociable from a specific history reaching from the "cultural" context in which it was written, through Hegel, to contemporary concerns about ethics, subjectivity, and gender. My principal goal has been to understand how this play works through the relation between individuality and life. Sophocles's drama stages various, conflicting notions of individuation, most of which derive from death, but in the figure of Haemon it indicates another possibility, an exit, as it were, from the tragic condition. This is the promise that an individual could be valued not through her abstract negation but in the specificity of her character and being, as evidenced in the love and desire another person bears for her. That love links those it binds to an infinite transcendence, for the absolute difference between them opens their evolution to an endless futurity.

Appendixes

APPENDIX A

Summary of Sophocles's Labdacid Cycle

Antigone is the last of three plays about the ruling family of Thebes. The cycle begins with *Oedipus Rex*, in which Antigone's father discovers that he has ascended to the throne by unwittingly murdering his father and marrying his mother. After his wife and mother kills herself, he gouges out his eyes and sets off into exile, led by his daughter Antigone. In the central play of the series, *Oedipus at Colonus*, the two wanderers arrive in a grove outside of Athens. The old king is on the point of death. Aware that the parricide's body will bestow divine protections on the state within whose precincts it is buried, Oedipus's brother-in-law, Creon arrives to bring him back, either by threats or enticements, to Thebes. Theseus, the ruler of Athens, promises, however, to protect the famous criminal. Polyneices, one of Oedipus's sons, arrives to beg his father's blessing. The young man is traveling with an army from Argos to lay siege to Thebes, from which the new king, his twin brother, Eteocles, has driven him. Instead, Oedipus curses Polyneices, who sets off to face his destiny, asking first that Antigone promise to secure the burial of his own, now doomed, body. At the end of the play, Oedipus walks alone into a sacred wood, where he vanishes into a burst of light. The action of *Antigone* begins after the end of Polyneices's failed attack on Thebes. Both he and his brother Eteocles have perished in the battle. Creon, having just been made king, orders that Eteocles, whom he has succeeded to the throne, be buried but that Polyneices's corpse be left to rot outside the city. Invoking an authority higher than human laws, Antigone secretly covers Polyneices's body with dirt. The crime is discovered and then the criminal. Faced with her refusal to repent, Creon orders that she be buried alive. After his rash words, he consults with the seer Tiresias, who upbraids him for his impiety. Creon hurries to undo the wrong he has set in motion, stopping first to bury Polyneices and then to release Antigone from the cave where she had been entombed. He arrives only to discover that she is already dead, and his son, Haemon, who was betrothed to her, kills himself after threatening his father. On hearing the news of her son's death, Creon's wife, Eurydice, commits suicide. At the cycle's close, Creon is left alone to contemplate the disaster that he has brought down on himself.

The three plays were not, however, written in narrative sequence. Sophocles completed *Antigone* first, then *Oedipus Rex* and finally *Oedipus at Colonus*, which were produced in 441, 428/427 and 405 B.C.E., respectively. The long duration and confused order of their composition led to several inconsistencies of plot, especially concerning the succession to the throne after Oedipus's departure from Thebes and the responsibility for sending him into exile. Elements from the story were also taken up by Aeschylus, in his *Seven against Thebes*, and Euripides, in *The Suppliant Women* and *The Phoenician Women*. For the sheer number of extant tragedies devoted to them, the Labdacids, as Oedipus's family was called, rank second only to the household of Agamemnon, also stained with guilt.

Timeline of Relevant Events in Ancient Greece

Unless otherwise noted, all dates are B.C.E.

Eighth century: Panhellenic rise of the polis

c. 750: Initial expansion of the burial group[1]

c. 640–c. 558: Solon. "The social advance of the individual" in funerary testaments[2]

End of seventh century: Addition of likenesses and writing to funerary stelae[3]

527/8: Death of tyrant Peisistratus

c. 525/4: Birth of Aeschylus

510: End of Peisistratid dynasty

510–480: Sumptuary laws limit size and ostentation of funerary monuments in Athens[4]

507: Democratic constitution of Cleisthenes

End of sixth century: In Attica, tombs generally individual[5]

Fifth century: Second widening of the burial group: a large increase in the ratio of burials to size of Athenian population in comparison to sixth and seventh centuries[6]

c. 500: "Latest burial in the Athenian agora. Probable date of ban on intramural burial at Athens."[7]

c. 500–c. 425: Period of restraint in Athenian funerals and burials[8]

97/6: Birth of Sophocles

490: Persian invasion of Greek mainland under Darius I; battle of Marathon

c. 490: Aeschylus's *Suppliant Maidens*

487–c. 380: Gorgias

480–79: Persian invasion of Greek mainland under Xerxes

480: Battles of Thermopylae (August) and Salamis (September); Athens invaded and torched by Xerxes's armies

c. 480: Birth of Euripides

c. 480–30: Suppression of funerary monuments in Athens[9]

469/70: Birth of Socrates

467: Production of Aeschylus's *Seven against Thebes*

460–45: First Peloponnesian War

458: Production of Aeschylus's *Oresteia*, comprising *Agamemnon*, *The Libation Bearers*, and *Eumenides*

c. 456/5: Death of Aeschylus

Second half of fifth century: The funerary stele is now addressed to the urban public.[10] Acme of the abstraction of Athens in the *epitaphioi logoi*[11]

Second half of fifth century to early fourth century: "Notable extension . . . of the right to 'written death'"[12]

441: *Antigone*

440–c. 380: Lysias

431–404: Second Peloponnesian War

431: Pericles's funeral oration for Peloponnesian War dead in Cerameicus cemetery, Athens

427/8: Sophocles's *Oedipus Rex*

Last quarter of fifth century: Rise of private funerary practices and memorials. Aside from public funerals, "in which the individuality of each deceased person is as it were drowned in the common glory of the city, the custom of familial tombs begins to take hold," with an emphasis on "personal feelings of affection and regret . . . between husband and wife, parents and children."[13]

420–415: Euripides's *Suppliant Women*

406: Deaths of Sophocles and Euripides

405: Sophocles's *Oedipus at Colonus* (first production)

End of fifth or beginning of fourth century: Gorgias's *epitaphios logos*

Fourth century: Consolidation of *bios politikos* and the emergence of death as a reality "incommensurable with all civic value."[14] Emphasis in funerary monuments shifts from polis to family.[15]

399: Death of Socrates

394–386: Lysias's *epitaphios logos*

384–322: Aristotle

c. 375: Plato, *Republic*. Move from ancestral *miasma* to penal individuation[16]

366–347: Plato, *Laws*

348: Death of Plato

Third century: Change in testamentary practices to emphasize the individual over the *oikos*[17]

c. 60–after 7: Dionysius of Halicarnassus

43 B.C.E.–17 or 18 C.E.: Ovid

8 C.E.: Ovid's *Metamorphoses*

46 C.E.–120 C.E.: Plutarch

NOTES

INTRODUCTION: TRAGEDY, THE CITY, AND ITS DEAD

1. "By its very nature, tragedy entails an *opposition of two discourses*, an *agōn logōn*" (Nicole Loraux, *L'invention d'Athènes: Histoire de l'oraison funèbre dans la "cité classique"* [Paris: Payot, 1981], p. 217). Unless otherwise indicated, all translations are mine. Although an English translation of *L'invention d'Athènes* exists, it is based on a second, abridged edition, which does not contain many of the passages I cite, and so I have not used it (see *The Invention of Athens: The Funeral Oration in the Classical City*, trans. Alan Sheridan [New York: Zone Books, 2006]). See also Simon Goldhill, *Aeschylus: The Oresteia* (Cambridge, U.K.: Cambridge University Press, 1992), pp. 16–17.

2. Loraux, *Invention*, p. 290.

3. See Jonathan Strauss, *Subjects of Terror: Nerval, Hegel, and the Modern Self* (Stanford: Stanford University Press, 1998), pp. 63–73.

4. Sarah C. Humphreys, *The Family, Women, and Death: Comparative Studies* (Ann Arbor: University of Michigan Press, 1993), pp. 101, 82. For a good overall history of burial practices from the protogeometric (eleventh–tenth centuries) through the Hellenistic periods, see Donna C. Kurtz and John Boardman, *Greek Burial Customs* (Ithaca, N.Y.: Cornell University Press, 1971). For a descriptive inventory of Greek bronze-age burial sites see Carla M. Antonaccio, *An Archaeology of Ancestors: Tomb Cult and Hero Cult in Early Greece* (Lanham, Md.: Rowman and Littlefield, 1995).

5. Ian Morris, *Burial and Ancient Society: The Rise of the Greek City-State* (Cambridge, U.K.: Cambridge University Press, 1987), p. 109. In a sustained analysis (pp. 130–34), Humphreys contests many of Morris's arguments, but her criticism focuses on the composition of the burial groups under study. Humphreys is attempting to refute the nineteenth-century Hellenist Fustel de Coulanges's thesis that a prepolitical society organized around familial veneration (including the graves of the dead) gave way to the political state, so this aspect of Morris's analysis is important to her. She does not, however, contest

the two points important to us—the exclusion of the dead from inhabited spaces and the democratization of burial practices (p. 130). And although she does complain that Morris's sample groups are small, she also acknowledges that this problem affects all archaeologically based studies on death in ancient Attica and Greece.

6. Morris, *Burial and Ancient Society*, p. 11. This dating for the origin of the polis is widely accepted. See, for example, Siegfried Froriep, *Frühzeit der Städte: Entstehung und Entwicklung im Abendland bis zum Ende der Antike* (Frankfurt: R. G. Fischer, 1989), p. 92. Jean-Pierre Vernant speaks of "the most archaic forms of the city, at the end of the 8th century" (*L'individu, la mort, l'amour: Soi-même et l'autre en Grèce ancienne* [Paris: Gallimard, 1989], p. 218).

7. Morris, *Burial and Ancient Society*, pp. 205, 210.

8. See Aristotle, *The Constitution of Athens* 22.1–2, trans. F. G. Kenyon, in *The Complete Works of Aristotle: The Revised Oxford Translation*, ed. Jonathan Barnes, vol. 2 (Princeton: Princeton University Press, 1984), pp. 2354–55, and Jérôme Carcopino, *L'ostracisme athénien* (Paris: Presses Universitaires de France, 1954), pp. 15–30.

9. Humphreys, *Family, Women, and Death*, p. 157.

10. On this period of restraint and democratization, see Kurtz and Boardman, *Greek Burial Customs*, pp. 89, 106, 124–25; Humphreys, *Family, Women, and Death*, pp. 102, 104, 105; and John H. Oakley, *Picturing Death in Classical Athens: The Evidence of the White Lekythoi* (Cambridge, U.K.: Cambridge University Press, 2004), pp. 215, 226. On sumptuary laws concerning funerals and tombs, see Josh Beer, *Sophocles and the Tragedy of Athenian Democracy* (Westport, Conn.: Praeger, 2004), p. 68; Humphreys, *Family, Women, and Death*, pp. 85, 86, 118, 121; Sarah B. Pomeroy, *Families in Classical and Hellenistic Greece: Representations and Realities* (Oxford: Clarendon Press, 1997), pp. 100–105; and Robert Garland, *The Greek Way of Death* (Ithaca, N.Y.: Cornell University Press, 1985), chaps. 3, 7.

11. Aeschylus's birth date is traditionally given as 524/5, but Richmond Lattimore has convincingly argued for 513 or 512 (Introduction to *Aeschylus I: Oresteia*, trans. Richmond Lattimore, ed. David Grene and Richmond Lattimore [Chicago: University of Chicago Press, 1953], pp. 1–2). It should be noted that 535 B.C.E. is the probable date for the beginning of the tragic competitions or "Dionysia" (see Luciano Canfora, *Histoire de la littérature grecque d'Homère à Aristote*, trans. Denise Fourgous [Paris: Editions Desjonquères, 1994], p. 163).

12. Morris, *Burial and Ancient Society*, pp. 63–65.

13. Ibid., p. 63.

14. Ibid. See also pages 65–68. Garland (*Greek Way of Death*, pp. 42–43) places the date for the exclusion of the dead from Athens at c. 500 B.C.E., but he is using a much earlier and less reliable source (R. S. Young, "Sepulturae intra

urbem," *Hesperia* 20 [1951]: 67–134) than Morris. Kurtz and Boardman also use the date of c. 500, but it is little more than a speculation based on vague literary evidence from centuries later (*Greek Burial Customs*, p. 70). They note, however, that in classical Athens, almost all grave sites were located just outside the walls and gates of the city (p. 92). Garland similarly observes that except for some infants, there were no intra-muros burials in Athens in the fourth and third centuries B.C.E. (*Greek Way of Death*, p. 82).

15. There is other evidence of a more general shift in beliefs about death during this period. Jan N. Bremmer describes a "complete change of attitude" between the Homeric and classical periods, "even though the old ideas did not die" ("The Soul, Death and the Afterlife in Early and Classical Greece," in *Hidden Futures: Death and Immortality in Ancient Egypt, Anatolia, the Classical, Biblical and Arabic-Islamic World*, ed. J. M. Bremer, Th. P. J. van den Hout, and R. Peters [Amsterdam: Amsterdam University Press, 1994], pp. 95–96). Bartel Poortman argues that during the fifth century a "shift in the focus of philosophical attention . . . has cosmological thought replaced by anthropocentric thought" ("Death and Immortality in Greek Philosophy: From the Presocratics to the Hellenistic Era," in *Hidden Futures*, ed. Bremer, van den Hout, and Peters, p. 198). This anthropocentric shift, according to Poortman, made death for the first time a subject of philosophical concern (pp. 198–99).

16. Jacques Brunschwig, "Aristote et l'effet Perrichon," in *La Passion de la Raison: Hommage à Fernand Alquié*, ed. Jean-Luc Marion and Jean Deprun (Paris: Presses Universitaires de France, 1983), p. 376.

17. Alain Badiou, *Ethics: An Essay on the Understanding of Evil*, trans. Peter Hallward (New York: Verso, 2001), p. 54. Fränkel: "If man is, as it were, a field of energy, whose lines extend into space and time without limit or restraint, then external forces, for their part, operate in him without hindrance, and it is meaningless to ask where his own force begins and that from outside ends. In what they receive and suffer also, there men are wholly open to the outside world, so wide that our own basic antithesis between self and not-self does not yet exist in Homeric consciousness" (Hermann Fränkel, *Early Greek Poetry and Philosophy: A History of Greek Epic, Lyric, and Prose to the Middle of the Fifth Century*, trans. Moses Hadas and James Willis [New York: Harcourt Brace Jovanovich, 1973], p. 80). Jan N. Bremmer makes a similar argument ("Soul, Death and the Afterlife," pp. 92–94), and cf. Bruno Snell, *The Discovery of Mind: The Greek Origins of European Thought*, trans. T. G. Rosenmeyer (Oxford: Blackwell, 1953), pp. 1–22. For an account of recent scholarship on ancient Greek individuality, see Vernant, *Individu*, p. 224. Fränkel summarizes the difference between modern and ancient experiences of individuality: "The premise must be that Homeric man in fact has a structure different from what we know today" (*Early Greek Poetry and Philosophy*, p. 76). Like most of the

writers mentioned here, he is echoing the essential points from the first chapter of Georg Lukács's *The Theory of the Novel: A Historico-Philosophical Essay on the Forms of Great Epic Literature*, trans. Anna Bostock (Cambridge, Mass.: MIT Press, 1971), pp. 29–39, originally published in 1920. In a similar vein, Jacques Derrida has commented at length on the mutual incomprehensibility that binds us to the Greeks: "In the texts we are speaking about, I have tried above all to read 'Greek' words (which are already difficult enough, indeed impossible, to read and translate, and that impossibility is without respite), which is to say words working in sentences, in scenes of discourse and writing, in works that, for that very reason, could not close back up on themselves (nor on the Greeks, nor on philosophy, nor on books, nor on a system, nor, above all, on language) and had therefore already been marked by the effraction of the other (the non-discursive real, the non-Greek, etc.)" ("Nous autres Grecs," in *Nos Grecs et leurs modernes: Les stratégies contemporaines d'appropriation de l'antiquité*, ed. Barbara Cassin [Paris: Seuil, 1992], p. 269). On the relations between individual and law in ancient Greece, see also Vincent Farenga, *Citizen and Self in Ancient Greece: Individuals Performing Justice and the Law* (Cambridge, U.K.: Cambridge University Press, 2006), which includes an important discussion of the role played by the dead in constructing individual legal identity.

18. Vernant, *Individu*, p. 225.

19. James Redfield, "Le sentiment homérique du Moi," *Le Genre humain* 12 (1985): 104 ("Les usages de la nature"), (qtd. in Vernant, *Individu*, 224). Brunschwig, "Aristote et l'effet Perrichon," 375 (qtd. in Vernant, *Individu*, p. 225n.14).

20. Gilbert Romeyer Dherbey, "L'âme est en quelque façon tous les êtres (Aristote, *De anima*, T 8, 431 *b* 21)," *Elenchos: Revista di studi sul pensiero antico* 8, no. 2 (1987): 380.

21. Martin Heidegger, *Introduction to Metaphysics*, trans. Gregory Fried and Richard Polt (New Haven: Yale University Press, 2000), p. 157.

22. Simon Goldhill has emphasized the instability and importance of the notion of individuality in Greek tragedy in general and *Antigone* in particular. He writes that "it is precisely the defining of such notions as 'man' that is put at risk in tragedy, which often focuses on the grey areas and boundaries of such a process of categorization or defining" (*Reading Greek Tragedy* [Cambridge, U.K.: Cambridge University Press, 1997], p. 60). On this aspect of *Antigone*, see ibid., pp. 91 and 105–6.

23. George Steiner, *Antigones* (Oxford: Oxford University Press, 1984). Martha Nussbaum, for instance, treats individual and character as identifiable and nonproblematic concepts (*The Fragility of Goodness: Luck and Ethics in Greek Tragedy and Philosophy* [1986; Cambridge, U.K.: Cambridge University Press, 2001], p. 66). She also, somewhat oddly, treats Hegel's notion of synthesis as a

denial of opposition (p. 73). Mark Griffith also treats "individual personality" as a relatively straightforward issue ("The Subject of Desire in Sophocles's *Antigone*," in *The Soul of Tragedy: Essays on Athenian Drama*, ed. Victoria Pedrick and Steven M. Oberhelman [Chicago: University of Chicago Press, 2005], p. 110). Tina Chanter's otherwise brilliant reading simplifies Hegel's very complex concept of the individual in his reading of *Antigone* (see *Ethics of Eros: Irigaray's Rewriting of the Philosophers* [New York: Routledge, 1995], pp. 95–96). Even Patricia Jagentowicz Mills ("Hegel's *Antigone*," in *The* Phenomenology of Spirit *Reader: Critical and Interpretive Essays*, ed. Jon Stewart [Albany: State University of New York Press, 1998]), who finds Hegel's notion of the individual inadequate, sometimes oversimplifies it. See, for example, pages 244 and 246, where she seems to take Hegel's opposition between the individualism of the family and the universalism of the state as the opposition between a unique individual person and the collective. I will discuss Bonnie Honig's arguments about individuation in some detail in the following chapter.

24. Judith Butler, *Antigone's Claim: Kinship between Life and Death* (New York: Columbia University Press, 2000); Tina Chanter, "Looking at Hegel's Antigone through Irigaray's Speculum," in *Between Ethics and Aesthetics: Crossing the Boundaries*, ed. Dorota Glowacka and Stephen Boos (Albany: State University of New York Press, 2002), pp. 29–48; Kelly Oliver, "Antigone's Ghost: Undoing Hegel's Phenomenology of Spirit," in "The Family and Feminist Theory," special issue, *Hypatia* 11, no. 1 (1996): 67–90; and Jacques Derrida, *Glas*, trans. John P. Leavey Jr. and Richard Rand (Lincoln: University of Nebraska Press, 1986), pp. 141–94. As Simon Goldhill has observed, "Since Hegel's reading of the play, it has been difficult not to consider the text of the *Antigone* in terms of dialectic and opposition. Even critics who have added important qualifications to Hegel's interpretation have felt, like Reinhardt, that conflict in this play 'emerges finally as a kind of "dialectic" in spite of everything'" (Goldhill, *Reading Greek Tragedy*, p. 88).

25. See the discussion of Lacan in Chapter 7, below.

26. See, for example, Mills: "When we adhere to what actually happens in the play and put it within Hegel's interpretative framework . . ." ("Hegel's *Antigone*," p. 253); and Oliver, "Antigone's Ghost," pp. 76–77. I do not mean to nitpick, but rather to illustrate a general tendency in readings of the play. Both of these articles are important pieces of scholarship. Mills offers an "internal or immanent critique" of Hegel's interpretations of *Antigone* in the *Phenomenology of Spirit* and the *Philosophy of Right* by using "Seyla Benhabib's understanding of the 'doubled vision' of feminist theory, a method that takes traditional issues into account but does so by simultaneously focusing on gender issues that have been 'traditionally' marginalized" (p. 243). She finds internal incoherences in Hegel's dialectical treatment of gender difference in the play

and ultimately argues that Adorno's negative dialectics offers a better way to recognize both that difference and the (self-)conscious particularity of woman (pp. 251, 265–66). Oliver will be discussed later.

27. "We cannot know whether concepts such as 'maternal instinct' or 'conjugal love' or visual depictions of family groups have an emotional content and range similar to that which such words and images provoke in the author and readers of this book" (Pomeroy, *Families in Classical and Hellenistic Greece*, p. 11).

28. For an overview of the major critical stances adopted by post-Nietzschean readers of Greek literature, see Simon Goldhill, "Modern Critical Approaches to Greek Tragedy," in *The Cambridge Companion to Greek Tragedy*, ed. P. E. Easterling (Cambridge, U.K.: Cambridge University Press, 1997), pp. 324–47. Like Pomeroy (p. 11; see preceding footnote), Goldhill recognizes the dangers of anachronism in modern interpretations of the Greeks, but he offers a more complicated and open-ended response, recommending an ongoing vigilance to inevitable (and justified) charges of "appropriation and distortion" (p. 342). When Goldhill adopts this stance in some of his own readings, they can become vertiginously self-aware. For an example, see his deconstructive analysis of Aeschylus's *Oresteia* and Euripides' *Electra* in "The Failure of Exemplarity," in *Modern Critical Theory and Classical Literature*, ed. Irene J. F. De Jong and J. P. Sullivan (Leiden: E. J. Brill, 1994), pp. 51–73.

29. Rush Rehm, *Marriage to Death: The Conflation of Wedding and Funeral Rituals in Greek Tragedy* (Princeton: Princeton University Press, 1994), and Piero Pucci, "Reading the Riddles of *Oedipus Rex*," in *Language and the Tragic Hero: Essays on Greek Tragedy in Honor of Gordon M. Kirkwood*, ed. Pietro Pucci (Atlanta, Ga.: Scholars Press, 1988), pp. 131–34.

30. On Vernant's importance and his significance in relation to issues of subjectivity in the Greek world, see Goldhill, "Modern Critical Approaches," pp. 334–35.

31. Similarly, Simon Goldhill has written, "Re-telling—reanalysing—the *Antigone* is part of political theory's commitment to changing thinking" ("Greek Drama and Political Theory," in *The Cambridge History of Greek and Roman Political Thought*, ed. Christopher Rowe and Malcolm Schofield [Cambridge, U.K.: Cambridge University Press, 2000], p. 67).

32. Heidegger, *Introduction to Metaphysics*, p. 162.

33. See Walter Kaufmann, *Goethe, Kant, and Hegel*, vol. 1 of *Discovering the Mind* (New Brunswick, N.J.: Transaction, 1991), pp. 173–85, 215–16.

34. Letter to Niethammer, October 13, 1806, in *Hegel: The Letters*, trans. Clare Butler and Christiane Seiler (Bloomington: Indiana University Press, 1984), p. 114. For an account of the events surrounding Hegel's finishing of the *Phenomenology*, see the commentary by Clark Butler in the same volume, pp. 109–10, 113.

35. G. W. F. Hegel, *Phenomenology of Spirit*, trans. A. V. Miller (Oxford: Oxford University Press, 1981), p. 6. Cf. the allocution from his last lecture of the academic year 1805–6, as quoted by Alexandre Kojève in the epigraph to *Introduction à la lecture de Hegel: Leçons sur la* Phénoménologie de l'esprit *professées de 1933 à 1939 à l'Ecole des Hautes Etudes*, ed. Raymond Queneau (Paris: Gallimard, 1947), n.p.: "Gentlemen! we find ourselves in an important epoch, in a fermentation, when Spirit has leapt forward, moving beyond its previous concrete form and acquiring a new one. The whole body of ideas and concepts that were valid up until now, the very bonds uniting the world, have dissolved, collapsing under their own weight like a vision in a dream."

36. "We know from Hegel's philosophy of history that individuality is the principle that elevates the modern world to a higher plane than that reached by antiquity" (Georg Lukács, *The Young Hegel: Studies in the Relations between Dialectics and Economics*, trans. Rodney Livingstone [Cambridge, Mass.: MIT Press, 1976], p. 327).

37. To address only one of the most significant and influential counterarguments to this proposition: Even Althusser's attempt to demonstrate that the putatively autonomous agency of the individual subject simply expresses larger ideological state apparatuses could not take account of itself except as a self-representation of those apparatuses. This reflexivity pervades his description of the social order. It is not, for instance, my friend who calls my name and it is not I who respond, but rather the state that calls to itself. Althusser has not, in short, evacuated the structure of self-perceptive subjectivity; he has merely moved it from the individual to the state. One could argue, in fact, that his own work is the final step in that *prise de conscience* of a collective, state subjectivity. See *Positions (1964–1975)* (Paris: Editions Sociales, 1976), pp. 67–125.

38. More than by its continuators—its Kojèves and Lacans—the strength and pervasiveness of a philosophical approach is probably best reflected through the brilliance and repetitiveness of the attempts to overcome it. So, in their very different ways, Marx and Engels's system of dialectical materialism, Heidegger's concept of *Dasein*, and Levinas's ethics of the other themselves express the significance of Hegel's theories on the world-historical subject. But so, in a different way, are attempts to think away from an ethics of the other, which itself stems from the problems of reflexive subjectivity, since the ontological primacy of caring for the other can become apparent only in an intellectual environment that has identified an other as such. In questioning the legitimacy or desirability of such an ethics, Badiou and Gillian Rose reaffirm the ongoing significance of the reflexive subject's exiled other for contemporary modes of thinking and experience. Rose is explicit about this: "Far from absorbing otherness back into self-consciousness or subjectivity (Fichte's position which Hegel designed the *Phenomenology* to oppose), the presentation of otherness [in the *Phenomenology*] has a motility which the post-modern gesture towards otherness

is unable to conceive" (*Mourning Becomes the Law: Philosophy and Representation* [Cambridge, U.K.: Cambridge University Press, 1996], p. 74). See also Badiou, *Ethics*, pp. 18–29.

1. TWO ORDERS OF INDIVIDUALITY

1. Christian Meier, *The Political Art of Greek Tragedy*, trans. Andrew Webber (Baltimore: The Johns Hopkins University Press, 1993), pp. 219, 48. Or as Simon Goldhill has written: "The institution of tragedy . . . represents the remarkable process of the developing city putting its developing structures of thought at risk and under scrutiny in the public arena of a civic festival. It is in this that we can locate the role of tragedy in the 'politicization of the citizen'" ("Greek Drama and Political Theory," p. 74). For an overview of the civic and political aspects of Attic tragedy, see Canfora, *Histoire de la littérature grecque*, pp. 159–61, 172–78. On the political engagement represented by spectatorship at the tragic festivals, see Goldhill, "The Audience of Athenian Tragedy" in *The Cambridge Companion to Greek Tragedy*, ed. E. Easterling (Cambridge, U.K.: Cambridge University Press, 1997), pp. 54–68. Claude Calame has similarly written that fifth-century Athens was "a culture which seems to achieve its political and democratic aims in and through performance" ("Performative Aspects of the Choral Voice in Greek Tragedy: Civic Identity in Performance," trans. Robin Osborne, in *Performance Culture and Athenian Democracy*, ed. Simon Goldhill and Robin Osborne [Cambridge, U.K.: Cambridge University Press, 1999], p. 126).

2. Meier, *Political Art of Greek Tragedy*, pp. 51–61, esp. pp. 56–57 and Goldhill, "Audience," pp. 55–57.

3. See Meier, *Political Art of Greek Tragedy*, p. 166 and Demosthenes, "On the False Embassy," §247 (cited by Beer, *Sophocles*, pp. 70–71). For a skeptical evaluation of such interpretations, see Goldhill, "Greek Drama and Political Theory," pp. 67–69. Despite his reservations, Goldhill recognizes that specific contemporary political issues are addressed in the *Oresteia*.

4. Beer, *Sophocles*, p. 67.

5. Meier, *Political Art of Greek Tragedy*, pp. 3–5.

6. Ibid., pp. 23, 32, 41–42. On the relation between the rational and the irrational, see pp. 133, 135.

7. Heidegger, *Introduction to Metaphysics*, p. 166.

8. According to Meier (*Political Art of Greek Tragedy*, pp. 97, 110–15), the *Oresteia*, and in particular its final play, *Eumenides*, concerns a contemporary change to the institution of the Areopagus. In 462–461 B.C.E., or some three years before the first staging of the trilogy, the Areopagus's jurisdiction was limited to questions concerning bloodlines. The focus on kinship in *Eumenides*

would thus derive from this reassignment. The Furies, moreover, would represent an irrational and unconscious fear about the foundations of the polis (pp. 119–21, 128).

9. Aeschylus, *Agamemnon, Libation-Bearers, Eumenides, Fragments*, trans. Herbert Weir Smith, Loeb Classical Library 146 (Cambridge, Mass.: Harvard University Press, 1926), p. 319.

10. Aeschylus, *Eumenides*, pp. 337–39.

11. Ibid., p. 317.

12. Ibid., p. 319.

13. Ibid., p. 293.

14. Ibid., p. 327.

15. Ibid., p. 311.

16. Jean-Pierre Vernant, "Tensions and Ambiguities in Greek Tragedy," in *Myth and Tragedy in Ancient Greece*, by Jean-Pierre Vernant and Pierre Vidal-Naquet, trans. Janet Lloyd (New York: Zone Books, 1990), p. 46.

17. Aeschylus, *Eumenides*, p. 323.

18. Redfield, "Sentiment homérique," p. 95.

19. Marie Delcourt, *Oedipe ou la légende du conquérant* (Paris: Droz, 1944), p. 66.

20. Aeschylus, *Eumenides*, p. 335. Simon Goldhill places this discussion of motherhood in relation to earlier scenes from the *Oresteia* and sketches out its political implications (*Language, Sexuality, Narrative: The* Oresteia [Cambridge, U.K.: Cambridge University Press, 1984], pp. 169–71).

21. See Pomeroy, *Families in Classical and Hellenistic Greece*, pp. 95: "In Athenian tragedy some characters maintain that the father is the true parent of the child, and that the mother supplies merely a fertile field in which the father's seed is nourished (see Aes. *Eum.* 658–61; Eur. *Or.* 551–52; Soph. *Ant.* 569; cf. Plato, *Timeaus* 91D1–2). Much attention has been paid to this remarkable view. Not only does it appear in the context of tragedy, but it is stated from time to time by Aristotle, who rejects preformation theory, and instead asserts that the father's semen provides the active principle that shapes the embryo, while the mother merely provides passive matter (*Gen. An.* 738b20–6, 729a10, etc.)." Pomeroy also observes that the "Greek scientific, medical, and philosophical corpus dealing with human reproduction is enormous" (p. 95).

22. Aeschylus, *Eumenides*, pp. 343–45.

23. In this respect, my reading of the treatment of women in *Eumenides* falls in line with what Simon Goldhill characterizes as the "Marxist and feminist" responses to the play (see Goldhill, "Greek Drama and Political Theory," p. 79, and *Reading Greek Tragedy*). On the role of gender—and Athena's peculiar gender identity—in the final scenes of the *Oresteia*, see Goldhill, *Aeschylus*, pp. 42–44 and *Reading Greek Tragedy*, pp. 29–32.

24. "The true material of tragedy is the social thought peculiar to the city-state, in particular the legal thought that was then in the process of evolving [*en plein travail d'élaboration*]" (Jean-Pierre Vernant, "The Historical Moment of Tragedy in Greece: Some of the Social and Psychological Conditions," in Vernant and Vidal-Naquet, *Myth and Tragedy*, p. 25).

25. This narrative, which dates back in its general outline to Fustel de Coulanges, has been nuanced by other Hellenists such as Sarah B. Pomeroy, who has written: "The old notion that the family disintegrated progressively from the huge *genos* ('clan') is no longer acceptable. Instead, the *genos* appears to be an artificial construct. . . . The effective kinship network rarely extended more than three degrees either horizontally or vertically" (*Families in Classical and Hellenistic Greece*, p. 140). What is important for Vernant, however, is less the "disintegration" of the family than its replacement by the state, and about this there is more general agreement by scholars. See, for instance, Nicole Loraux, *La cité divisée: L'oubli dans la mémoire d'Athènes* (Paris: Payot [Petite Bibliothèque], 1997), p. 216; Helene Foley, *Female Acts in Greek Tragedy* (Princeton: Princeton University Press, 2001), p. 195; Beer, *Sophocles*, p. 71; Eva Canterella, *Les peines de mort en Grèce et à Rome: Origines et fonctions des supplices capitaux dans l'antiquité classique*, trans. Nadine Gallet (Paris: Albin Michel, 2000), p. 8; Trevor J. Saunders, *Plato's Penal Code: Tradition, Controversy, and Reform in Greek Penology* (Oxford: Clarendon Press, 1991), pp. 9–32; and Chapter 2, below.

26. Vernant and Vidal-Naquet, *Myth and Tragedy*, p. 27.

27. For example, Vernant speaks of "the divine justice that often makes sons pay for the crimes of their father" (Vernant and Vidal-Naquet, *Myth and Tragedy*, p. 39, trans. modified). Others have written on more specific aspects of the connection between family and miasma. Garland describes pollution rites and miasma as a familial "privilege" associated in particular with women (*Greek Way of Death*, pp. 41–42), whereas Pomeroy (*Families in Classical and Hellenistic Greece*, pp. 106–7) notes that miasmatic contamination by corpses spread not only through physical contact with the dead but through familial relations, so that even relatives who came nowhere near the body could be considered polluted, while nonrelatives present at the funeral remained unaffected.

28. G. W. F. Hegel, *Frühe Schriften*, in *Gesammelte Werke*, vol. 1, ed. Friedhelm Nicolin and Gisela Schüler (Hamburg: Felix Meiner, 1989), p. 368; *Phenomenology of Spirit*, pp. 278–89; *Philosophy of Right*, trans. T. M. Knox (Oxford: Oxford University Press, 1952), §§166–81 (pp. 114–22); *Hegel's Lectures on The Philosophy of Religion. Vol. II: Determinate Religion*, ed. Peter C. Hodgson, trans. R. F. Brown et al. (Berkeley: University of California Press, 1987), pp. 664–66. Steiner (*Antigones*, pp. 19–42) traces the development of Hegel's thought on the play. For a close analysis of differences between the

versions in the *Phenomenology* and the *Philosophy of Right*, see Mills, "Hegel's *Antigone*," pp. 259–65.

29. Hegel, *Phenomenology*, pp. 287–88. Cf. Hegel's description of Polyneices: "The youth comes away from the unconscious Spirit of the Family, and becomes the individuality of the community" (p. 285).

30. Ibid., pp. 287–88.

31. Critics have observed that Hegel's overall argument belies his assertion that both Creon's and Antigone's positions hold equal weight, since it is ultimately the state that prevails over women in the history of *Geist*. See Mills, "Hegel's *Antigone*," and Oliver, "Antigone's Ghost."

32. Hegel, *Philosophy of Religion*, 2:665–66.

33. On the role of death in Kojève's reading of Hegel and the importance of that reading for the later twentieth century, see Strauss, *Subjects of Terror*, pp. 54–63.

34. On the difference between the two kinds of death in Hegel, see Jonathan Strauss, "After Death," in "Post-Mortem: The State of Death as a Modern Construct," special issue, *Diacritics* 30, no. 3 (2000): 91–92.

35. Sophocles, *Antigone*, l. 926. One of only three lines from the play quoted in the *Phenomenology* (pp. 284, 261), it is, as Mills observes, mistranslated to create an Antigone conscious of her guilt (see Mills, "Hegel's *Antigone*," p. 253). Mills also points out that the *Phenomenology*'s reading of Sophocles's play as the tragedy of the pagan world will yield, incongruously, to the *Philosophy of Right*'s argument that it represents a transhistorical, but essentially Christian, notion of ethics (Mills, "Hegel's *Antigone*," pp. 159–65).

36. Vernant and Vidal Naquet, *Myth and Tragedy in Ancient Greece*, p. 34.

37. Ibid., pp. 36, 35.

38. Ibid., p. 42.

39. Ibid., p. 41.

40. Ibid., p. 42.

41. Ibid., p. 41.

42. Ibid., p. 35.

43. Carcopino, *Ostracisme athénien*. p. 31.

44. "Guilt is not an indifferent, ambiguous affair, as if the deed as actually seen in the light of day could, or perhaps could not, be the action of the self, as if with the doing of it there could be linked something external and accidental that did not belong to it . . . . On the contrary, the action is itself this splitting into two, this explicit self-affirmation and the establishing over against itself of an alien external reality" (Hegel, *Phenomenology*, p. 282). See also p. 283: "A power which shuns the light of day ensnares the ethical self-consciousness, a power which breaks forth only after the deed is done, and seizes the doer in the act. For the accomplished deed is the removal of the antithesis between the

knowing self and the actuality confronting it. The doer cannot deny the crime or his guilt."

45. As Kierkegaard puts it, in a discussion of Sophocles's Theban plays: "Inherited guilt contains the self-contradiction of being guilt, and yet not being guilt" (*Either/Or: A Fragment of Life*, trans. David F. Swenson, Lillian Marvin Swenson, and Walter Lowrie, vol. 1 [Princeton: Princeton University Press, 1944], p. 122).

46. Sophocles, *Oedipus at Colonus*, ll. 960–77.

47. Vernant and Vidal Naquet, *Myth and Tragedy*, p. 35.

48. Ibid., p. 36 (trans. modified).

49. Bonnie Honig, "Antigone's Laments, Creon's Grief: Mourning, Membership, and the Politics of Exception," *Political Theory* 37, no. 1 (2009): 5.

50. Ibid., p. 7.

51. Ibid., p. 9.

52. See ibid., esp. pp. 10–12.

53. Gail Holst-Warhaft, *Dangerous Voices: Women's Laments and Greek Tragedy* (London: Routledge, 1992), p. 3.

54. Ibid., pp. 5, 110, 111, 112.

55. Ibid., p. 112. The single possible exception to this impersonality that Holst-Warhaft cites is Helen's lament over Hector (p. 112). Another of Honig's sources is Sarah Brown Ferrario, but here again, the article in question undermines Honig's arguments. Honig refers to the publication as "an article that provides archaeological evidence for this claim [about individuation] and supports my reading of the play" ("Antigone's Laments," p. 13, n. 34). But the page that Honig cites argues that the prepolitical individual of the archaeological record gains significance "as the member of an *oikos*" (Ferrario, "Replaying *Antigone*: Changing Patterns of Public and Private Commemoration at Athens c. 440–350," *Helios*, 33, supp. [2006]: 104), not as an autonomous individual. According to Ferrario, prepolitical burials would appear to memorialize an individual, but that individual, in turn, served less to signify himself or herself than an *oikos* or "shared elite values" (p. 85; see also pp. 95, 104, 105). Indeed, Ferrario refers to "the archaic dead, whose relevance was drawn from their membership in a kinship group and their perpetuation of its unchanging values" (p. 86). The conflict that Ferrario describes pits *oikos* against *deme* rather than individual against the group. Honig also cites Olga Taxidou (*Tragedy, Modernity and Mourning* [Edinburgh: Edinburgh University Press, 2004]), but the relevant passages are themselves based on Holst-Warhaft (*Dangerous Voices*, e.g., pp. 8, 31).

56. In this respect, Honig's argument that "the thirst for vengeance is whetted, not slaked, by the belief that dead relatives are . . . irreplaceable" ("Antigone's Laments," p. 11) is somewhat circular: The dead must be avenged because they

are irreplaceable, and we know they are irreplaceable because they must be avenged. Indeed, Honig's argument seems in general unable to reconcile two conflicting propositions about Antigone's attitude toward the role of death in individuality. On the one hand, Honig asserts that Polyneices's death individualizes him for Antigone: "When Antigone underlines Polynices's irreplaceability (the parents who bore him are dead) and grounds upon it her loyalty to him, she puts the lie to the idea that his death (but maybe also any death) can be responded to by way of an economy of substitution" (p. 17). On the other hand, she asserts that death, for Antigone, abolishes that same uniqueness: "'A death is a death. Trojan or Achaean.' This is Antigone's view. On it is premised her refusal to differentiate as the democratic Creon wants her to between Eteocles and Polynices" (p. 15).

57. Honig, "Antigone's Laments," p. 12. Highly calculating and almost monetary, the notion of revenge on which the laments insist is, for its part, essentially depersonalizing. See Holst-Warhaft, *Dangerous Voices*, pp. 77, 81, 84, 140, 145. Honor is another motivation for revenge, but it is more the survivor's honor than the dead person's (see, e.g., p. 88).

58. See Margaret Alexiou, *The Ritual Lament in Greek Tradition*, revised by Dimitrios Yatromanolakis and Panagiotis Roilos (1974; Cambridge, U.K.: Cambridge University Press, 2002), p. 103: "Early instances point to the *thrênos* as more ordered and polished, often associated with divine performers and a dominant musical element. This is reflected in the extant choral *thrênoi* of Pindar and Simonides, which are characterised by a calm restraint, gnomic and consolatory in tone rather than passionate and ecstatic; the *góos*, on the other hand, while less restrained, was from Homer onwards more highly individual-ised, and since it was spoken rather than sung, it tended to develop a narrative rather than a musical form."

59. Foley, *Female Acts*, pp. 174–75, 183, 184–85.

60. Ibid., p. 185.

61. See Sophocles, *Antigone*, ll. 295–303 and 1033–47.

62. Nussbaum (*Fragility of Goodness*, pp. 58, 60, 62) also remarks on the congruence between Creon's generalizing nature and his tendency to see money as the primary motivation for criminal or otherwise aberrant behaviors.

63. Luce Irigaray, *Speculum of the Other Woman*, trans. Gillian C. Gill (Ithaca, N.Y.: Cornell University Press, 1985), p. 220.

64. Hegel, *Phenomenology*, p. 286.

65. Approaching Hegel's analysis of *Antigone* in the *Phenomenology* from a feminist perspective, Patricia Jagentowicz Mills describes some of this com-plexity in ways somewhat different from the present discussion. She sees the family, as Hegel describes it in these passages, as a place of particularity and individualism ("Hegel's *Antigone*," pp. 244, 246, 251). In her account, the family

represents animal or mere biological life in opposition to the polis, which, for its part, depends on the sacrifice—or at least risking—of that life (pp. 244–45). She argues that although in the Hegelian family woman represents "the spirit of individualism" subversive to the polis (p. 251), she is not consciously particularized (pp. 246, 251), and, indeed, not particularized at all (p. 255). Mills thus points to another way in which the notion of particularization in the family is more complicated than a simple opposition between the individualism of the family and the universalism of the state (although she seems to take this opposition at face value on pages 25 and 246).

66. This would be section A. a. of "Spirit" in the *Phenomenology*, comprising §§444–63, or "The Ethical World: Human and Divine Law: Man and Woman." Later in the *Phenomenology*, Hegel will again use the word "individual" in this sense to describe the different political factions that vied with each other during the French Revolution (see §585, p. 357).

67. This would be section A. b. of "Spirit" in the *Phenomenology*, comprising §§464–76, or "Ethical Action: Human and Divine knowledge. Guilt and Destiny."

68. Hegel, *Phenomenology*, p. 279.

69. At the end of the first part of his argument, Hegel writes: "The ethical realm is in this way in its enduring existence an immaculate world, a world unsullied by any internal dissension. Similarly, its process is a tranquil transition of one of its powers into the other" (ibid., p. 278).

70. Ibid., pp. 267, 284.

71. Ibid., p. 286. See also the following footnote, below.

72. Hegel seems to understand the universal particular in part as an abstract relational category: "In the ethical household, it is not a question of *this* particular husband, *this* particular child, but simply of husband and children generally; the relationships of the woman are based, not on feeling, but on the universal" (ibid., p. 274). But this is not the main thrust of his development of universality, which is based on the death of the individual and in some ways contradicts the categorical approach. For instance, if Polyneices as brother is already universal, why does he further need to die to attain status as an ethical entity? Hegel seems to be arguing that the only real brother is a dead one and that the universality of familial relationships is derived from the universality of death.

73. Ibid., p. 270. Commenting on Hegel's analysis of *Antigone*, Jacques Derrida notes that the essence of individuality is found in death: "Death," he writes, "is its essential object" (*Glas*, p. 142).

74. Hegel, *Phenomenology*, p. 270.

75. Ibid.

76. Vernant, *Individu*, p. 83.

77. As we shall see in Chapter 7, below, this equivalence between death and language is key to Lacan's reading of *Antigone*.

78. Vernant, "L'individu dans la cité," in *Individu*, pp. 211–32.

79. Hegel, *Phenomenology*, p. 270.

2. THE CITIZEN

1. In Homeric times "executions . . . did not take place 'in the public square,' but inside the house. The head of the family (called not incidentally the *anax oikoio*, the sovereign of the house) possessed an absolute and unlimited personal power over all the members of his group, all of whom were indiscriminately subject to a disciplinary power that included the right to put to death those who did not respect his authority" (Canterella, *Peines de mort*, p. 8). See also Saunders, *Plato's Penal Code*, pp. 9–32. Saunders defines the Homeric household as follows: "The basic unit is the 'home' or 'estate' (*oikos*); it consists of a 'hero' at its head, his wife, children, first workmen and slaves, and their families" (p. 10).

2. "At first, adoptions between living persons do not concern the individual as such. . . . The practice of testamentary adoption follows the same principle: it is always a question of the house, whose upkeep must be assured. What is at issue is the *oîkos*, not the individual. On the other hand, when, starting in the 3rd century, the testament properly speaking begins to be instituted in matters concerning the extension of bequests at death, it has become something strictly personal . . . Between an individual and his wealth, whatever form it might take—inheritance and acquest, furniture and real estate—the bond is henceforward direct and exclusive: to each his own belongings" (Vernant, *Individu*, p. 222). For other examples of this precedence of the *oikos* over the individual, see pp. 221–22.

3. Saunders, *Plato's Penal Code*, p. 11.

4. For a detailed discussion of the term *dikē* in fifth-century Greek tragedy, see Goldhill, *Reading Greek Tragedy*, pp. 33–56. On the role of writing in ancient Greek law, see Michael Gagarin, *Writing Greek Law* (Cambridge, U.K.: Cambridge University Press, 2008). For ancient Greek law in general, see Douglas MacDowell, *The Law in Classical Athens* (Ithaca, N.Y.: Cornell University Press, 1986) and Michael Gagarin and David Cohen, eds., *The Cambridge Companion to Ancient Greek Law* (Cambridge, U.K.: Cambridge University Press, 2005).

5. Henry George Liddell and Robert Scott, *An Intermediate Greek-English Lexicon* (1889; Oxford: Clarendon Press, 1978), p. 169; see also p. 202.

6. Sophocles, *Antigone*, in *Antigone, The Women of Trachis, Philoctetes, Oedipus at Colonus*, ed. and trans. Hugh Lloyd-Jones (Cambridge, Mass.: Harvard University Press, 1994), ll. 450–55.

7. As part of a larger discussion of the difference between *nomos* and *physis*, W. K. C. Guthrie details the tension between written and unwritten laws for the Greeks of Sophocles's era (*The Fifth-Century Enlightenment*, vol. 3 of *A History of Greek Philosophy* [Cambridge, U.K.: Cambridge University Press, 1969], pp. 117–31). In opposition to written laws, which varied from state to state and were the work of men, the unwritten laws were considered to be not only more archaic, according to Guthrie, but also universal, natural, and divine. In contrast to Adolfo Levi, Guthrie sees Antigone's notion of unwritten *dikē* as an example of the broader concept of natural law (pp. 119–20). As evidence of the influence of Sophocles's drama on the legal thought of his time, cf. Aristotle's quotation of *Antigone* in a discussion of written and unwritten laws from the *Rhetoric* (see Guthrie, *Fifth-Century Enlightenment*, pp. 124–25).

8. Hegel, *Frühe Schriften*, p. 368 (from the fragment "Jedes Volk . . .").

9. Vernant and Vidal-Naquet, *Myth and Tragedy*, p. 36 (trans. modified).

10. Goldhill has remarked that one of the principal concerns of tragedy is the problematic relation between the individual and the community: "The hero is a central figure in Sophoclean drama not just because of connections with a significant literary tradition or with religious institutions of the polis, but most importantly because this is the figure through which the basic political issue of the relation between an individual and a community can be most strikingly broached. Commitment to self, commitment to family, commitment to polis, are seen as *conflicting* obligations, as tragedy again and again depicts the tensions within the normative constructions of the citizen's political role in society" ("Greek Drama and Political Theory," p. 72). Elsewhere, Goldhill describes the tensions arising from the conflicting imperatives of the state and the individual as the "central dynamic of Athenian social life" ("Audience," p. 60).

11. Gustave Glotz, *La solidarité de la famille et le droit criminel en Grèce* (Paris: A Fontemoing, 1904), p. 455.

12. As Carcopino notes, this was not the case throughout the Greek world: "While in Eresos during the last third of the 4th century and in Ilion circa 281, the entire *genos* of a tyrant or oligarch was prosecuted, [the Athenians] had voted in 410/409 to adopt the decree of Demophantos, by which the oligarch was sentenced to death but his family spared" (*Ostracisme athénien*, p. 251).

13. Plato, *The Republic*, 614a, trans. Paul Shorey, in *The Collected Dialogues of Plato*, ed. Edith Hamilton and Huntington Cairns (Princeton: Princeton University Press, 1961), p. 838.

14. Ibid., 615a, in *Collected Dialogues*, p. 839. Cf. the account of the afterlife in *Phaedo*, 112e–114e, trans. Hugh Tredennick, in *Collected Dialogues*, pp. 93–95, where Socrates similarly describes the various rewards and punishments meted out to souls.

15. Catherine Joubaud, *Le corps humain dans la philosophie platonicienne: Etude à partir du "Timée"* (Paris: J. Vrin, 1991), pp. 262–63.

16. Cf. Vernant, *Individu*: "In crimes of blood, the passage from prelaw to law, from the vendetta, with its procedures for compensation and arbitration, to the establishment of tribunals, frees up the idea of a criminal individual. It is the individual who henceforth appears as the subject of the crime and the object of judgment" (p. 221); "there is a rupture between the prejuridical conception of crime, which views it as a *miasma* or pollution, both contagious and collective, and the notion of crime that the law elaborates—i.e., as the transgression of a singular individual entailing various degrees that correspond, in turn, to different tribunals, depending on whether the crime was 'justified,' committed 'against one's will,' or 'willingly' and 'with premeditation'" (p. 221); "it is the individual who is at stake in the judicial institution through the more or less direct relation he has to his criminal act. This juridical history has a moral counterpart, since it entails the notions of responsibility, personal culpability, and merit. It equally has a psychological counterpart, since it raises the question of the conditions and constraints, the spontaneity or deliberate planning, that presided over the decision made by a subject" (pp. 221–22); and "these problems will be echoed in the Attic tragedies of the 5th century, for one of the traits that characterize this literary genre is its constant questioning about individual agency, about the human subject confronted by his action, about the relations between the hero of the drama, in his singularity, and his deeds and decisions—deeds and decisions whose weight he bears but that nonetheless exceed him" (p. 222).

17. Ibid., p. 88. See also pp. 85–89.

18. Ibid., pp. 85, 89, 86. Other scholars have seconded Vernant's account of death in "mythic" or "pre-tragic" Greece. James Garland describes the "loss of personality at death" among the Homeric heroes (*Greek Way of Death*, pp. 1–2). On the "gibbering shadows" of the Homeric dead, see Redfield, "Sentiment homérique," pp. 96–97. According to Jan N. Bremmer, an essentially Homeric notion of the deceased held sway for centuries. From this archaic perspective, "the souls of the dead are depicted as being unable to move or to speak properly; when the soul of Patroclus leaves Achilles, he disappears squeaking (*Il.* 23.100–101)" ("Soul, Death and the Afterlife," p. 100). "When the early Greeks spoke of the souls of the dead," Bremmer continues, "they referred to them as 'the wasted ones', 'the outworn ones', or 'the feeble heads of the dead'. Important here, it seems to me, is the plural. The dead are clearly considered to be an enormous, undifferentiated group. In Sophocles they are compared to a swarm of bees: 'Up (from the underworld) comes the swarm of the souls, loudly humming' (fr. 879)" (p. 101). In *Odyssey* 24.5–14, the dead are likened to a swarm of gibbering bats (*nukterides . . . trizousai*), while the same verb, *trizō*,

is used to describe the sound made by Patroclus's ghost when it leaves Achilles in *Iliad* 23.100–101 (*psuchē . . . tetriguia*). In book 11 of the *Odyssey*, the impersonality of the dead is evoked both through collective nouns and references to their powerlessness or stupidity, their dreamlike quality, and their numerousness. See ll. 11.29 (*polla . . . nekuōn amenēna karēna*); 11.222 (*psuchē d'ēut'oneiros apoptamenē pepotētai*); 11.475–76 (*entha te nekroi/aphradees naiousi, brotōn eidōla kamontōn*); 11.491 (*nekuessi kataphthimenoisin anassein*); and 11.632–33 (*ethne'ageireto muria nekrōn/ēchēi thespesiēi*).

19. Starting with Homer and continuing up through Plato, Alan E. Bernstein examines the history of the "survival of personality beyond death" (*The Formation of Hell: Death and Retribution in the Ancient and Early Christian Worlds* [Ithaca, N.Y.: Cornell University Press, 1993], p. 21). By describing the emergence of the beliefs that the soul survives death and that in the afterlife it reaps the rewards for its behavior in life, he recounts as well the creation of a soul whose individual responsibility—and therefore individuality—survives death (pp. 21–98). On retributive justice in the afterlife, see Garland, *Greek Way of Death*, chap. 5. Like Bernstein, Jan N. Bremmer also charts the historical rise of the idea that souls of the dead retain some individuality. As an example of this change, he contrasts the undifferentiated mass of the dead in Homer with a passage from Pindar (fr. 131b): "Here then the soul is described as a typical free-soul (although it is called *eidolon*), but—and this is totally un-Homeric—it is considered 'divine': 'this alone comes from the gods'. In other words, an enormous revaluation of the soul. Apparently, in addition to a growing unification, the soul was also considered as being more valuable, more important, and the converging of these two developments can hardly be a coincidence: if the soul is gaining in importance, its fate in the hereafter will also become more important" ("Soul, Death and the Afterlife," p. 101). Other significant currents of thought, however, contested the idea that the soul is immortal. Jan Maarten Bremer describes the history of this other belief ("Death and Immortality in Some Greek Poems," in *Hidden Futures: Death and Immortality in Ancient Egypt, Anatolia, the Classical, Biblical and Arabic-Islamic World*, ed. J. M. Bremer, Th. P. J. van den Hout, and R. Peters [Amsterdam: Amsterdam University Press, 1994], pp. 109–14), while Poortman observes that for Aristotle, the personal soul does not seem to survive death ("Death and Immortality in Greek Philosophy," pp. 200–201) and that among the Epicureans, death was thought of as anesthesia or total loss of sentience (p. 202).

20. Plato, *Menexenus*, trans. R. G. Bury (1929; Cambridge, Mass.: Harvard University Press, 1989), pp. 279–81 (249b–c). The oldest of the genre is Pericles's funeral oration, delivered in 430 B.C.E. and freely transcribed in Thucydides's *The Peloponnesian War*, 2.35–46. Lysias's funeral oration for the fallen of the Corinthian war was delivered some time between 393 and 386 and

has been transmitted largely intact. Demosthenes's eulogy for the dead of Chaeronea dates to 338, and Hypereides's eulogy for the soldiers of the war of Lamia would have been written in 323–322. Plato's *Menexenus* contains a lengthy *epitaphios logos* attributed to Aspasia, and although its status is unclear (pastiche? satire?), Cicero writes that it was so appreciated by the ancients that it was read publicly in Athens every year (*Orator*, 151, trans. G. L. Hendrickson in *Brutus, Orator*, Loeb Classical Library 342 [Cambridge, Mass.: Harvard University Press, 1939], pp. 424–25). Dionysius of Halicarnassus asserts that it was the most powerful (*kratistos*) of Plato's political speeches (*On the Style of Demosthenes* 23, in *The Critical Essays*, vol. 1, trans. Stephen Usher, Loeb Classical Library 465 [Cambridge, Mass.: Harvard University Press, 1974], pp. 328–29). For a detailed study of Greek funeral orations, see Loraux, *Invention*. Useful overviews can be found in Kurtz and Boardman, *Greek Burial Customs*, pp. 108, 112; and Humphreys, *Family, Women, and Death*, p. 89.

21. Demosthenes, "Funeral Speech," in *Funeral Speech, Erotic Essay LX, LXI, Exordia and Letters*, trans. Norman W. DeWitt and Norman J. DeWitt, Loeb Classical Library 374 (Cambridge, Mass.: Harvard University Press, 1949), p. 13.

22. Lysias, "Funeral Oration," §§8–9, in *Lysias*, trans. W. R. M. Lamb, Loeb Classical Library 244 (1930; Cambridge, Mass.: Harvard University Press, 1967), p. 35.

23. *Menexenus* 249b–c (pp. 279–81).

24. Ibid.

25. Lysias, "Funeral Oration," §17, p. 39.

26. Demosthenes, "Funeral Speech," pp. 9–11. The same idea also figures in *Menexenus* 237b, 238, 425a–c, 425d, which will be discussed below.

27. Plato, *Menexenus* 238a, trans. Benjamin Jowett, in *Collected Dialogues*, 190. Nicole Loraux has examined this topos in *Né de la terre: Mythe et politique à Athènes* (Paris: Seuil, 1996), arguing that the idea of women imitating the earth is a "metaphor without metaphor" (146) and that it is, consequently, women who provide the imaginary field connected with the earth in classical times. What matters for us, however, is the *will* to discredit the female and, more importantly, the maternal in the foundational fantasies of the Athenian state, a will that is made only more visible through Loraux's analysis.

28. Aeschylus, *Eumenides*, ll. 657–59 (pp. 334–35, trans. modified).

29. Demosthenes, "Funeral Speech," p. 33; Lysias, "Funeral Oration," §23, p. 43.

30. Demosthenes, "Funeral Speech," §§4–5, p. 19.

31. Ibid. This is not an isolated or aberrant idea. Elsewhere in the same oration, Demosthenes will again insist on the importance of the dead men's decision in the value of their actions: "Of the glory and honor [of the dead] the

source is found in the choice of those who willed to die nobly" (p. 37). J. M. Bremer has found an analogous relation between choice and glory in a two-line epitaph to war dead at Megara: "The verb *déchomai* is of decisive importance here: it highlights the heroic choice of the fighters and gives them the glory about which Sarpedon speaks in the *Iliad*" (p. 111).

32. Lysias, "Funeral Oration," §25, p. 43.

33. Demosthenes, "Funeral Speech," p. 9.

34. Ibid., p. 35.

35. Lysias, "Funeral Oration," §73, p. 65.

36. Michel de Montaigne, *Essais*, bk. 1, chap. 28, "De l'amitié," in *Oeuvres complètes*, ed. Albert Thibaudet and Maurice Rat (Paris: Gallimard [Pléiade], 1962), 187.

37. Lysias, "Funeral Oration," §§73–76, pp. 65–67.

38. Aristotle would seem to belie this exclusion of affection from the state when he writes, in the *Nicomachean Ethics*: "Friendship also seems to keep cities together, and lawgivers seem to pay more attention to it than to justice" (1155a23–25; trans. Christopher Rowe [Oxford: Oxford University Press, 2002]). Aristotle, moreover, also seems to define a form of friendship, the highest in fact, in which one appreciates the other purely for himself: "It is the friendship between good people, those resembling each other in excellence, that is complete; for each alike of these wishes good things for the other in so far as he is good, and he is good in himself. And those who wish good things for their friends, for their friends' sake, are friends most of all; for they do so because of the friends themselves, and not incidentally" (1156b7–12). But the "in himself" of the friend is not the same as the "because it was he [*par ce que c'estoit luy*]" of Montaigne or the irreplaceable uniqueness we have been discussing. Instead one likes "the other in so far as he is good," which is to say, insofar as he conforms to an abstract notion that infinitely exceeds his particularity as this individual person.

39. Aristotle, *Rhetoric*, trans. W. Rhys Roberts in Barnes, ed., in *Complete Works*, ed. J. Barnes, vol. 2, p. 2175 (1.9.1366b36–1367a1). It is Nicole Loraux who makes the connection between the *epitaphioi logoi* and this passage from the *Rhetoric* (*Invention*, p. 103), although to different ends. In the *Nicomachean Ethics*, Aristotle similarly subordinates personal interest to the interest of the state, establishing the latter as the object of all human striving and the true goal of ethics: "The end of this [i.e., political] expertise will contain those of the rest; so that this end will be the human good. For even if the good is the same for a single person and for a city, the good of the city is a greater and more complete thing both to achieve and to preserve; for while to do so for one person on his own is satisfactory enough, to do it for a nation or for cities is finer and more godlike. So our inquiry seeks these things, being a political inquiry in a way"

(1094b5–12; p. 96). One does not find in the latter text, however, the same insistence on selflessness and death that appear in the *Rhetoric*, even if the notion of excellence detailed in the *Ethics* generally negates the individuality of those it characterizes.

40. Loraux, *Invention*, p. 105. In a similar vein, Plato remarks that philosophers are "dead to existence [*tōi onti hoi philosophountes thanatōsi*]" (*Phaedo* 64b4–5).

41. Loraux, *Invention*, p. 106.

42. This "pathetic" individuation of the dead during the tragic period is indicated in several ways. As Armando Petrucci has reported, the number and type of people commemorated by incribed stelae broadened considerably: "During the whole of the fifth century and down to the early years of the fourth century B.C., Athens produced a very high number of inscriptions, certainly a very much greater number than was produced during the previous century. It is also clear that the passage from tyranny to the democratic regime must have led to a notable extension (in no way quantifiable) of the right to 'written death' to strata of the population until then excluded from a practice largely reserved for aristocratic families" (*Writing the Dead: Death and Writing Strategies in the Western Tradition*, trans. Michael Sullivan [Stanford: Stanford University Press, 1998], p. 12). At the same time that "written death" became more democratic, the incriptions themselves moved away from the heroic to the more personal. See Vernant, *Individu*, pp. 219–20: "Beginning in the last quarter of the 5th century, beside and beyond the public funerals celebrated in honor of those who died in combat for the fatherland and in which the individuality of each of the deceased was, as it were, drowned in the communal glory of the city, the custom of familial tombs arose. Funerary stelai henceforth associated the living and the dead of a household, while their epitaphs celebrated personal feelings of affection, regret, and esteem between husband and wife, parents and children." On the inclusion of such personal sentiments in the *epitaphioi logoi* themselves, see Loraux, *Invention*, p. 114.

43. Loraux, *Invention*, p. 105.

3. LOSS EMBODIED

1. For a catalogue of tragedies mentioning burials or corpses, see R. Drew Griffith, "Corporality in the Ancient Greek Theater," *Phoenix* 52, no. 3–4 (1998): 241.

2. Maurice Merleau-Ponty, *Phenomenology of Perception*, trans. Colin Smith (London: Routledge and Kegan Paul, 1962), p. 185; Redfield, "Sentiment homérique"; and Snell, *Discovery of Mind*, pp. 1–22.

3. Steiner, *Antigones*. p. 140. Although Steiner provides scant argument for his interpretation, Meister Eckhart drew the same etymological connection between the two words some three hundred years before Garnier: "One who is

not humble ('from the ground') is not a man, for the word 'man' (*homo*) is taken from the 'ground' (*humus*)" ("Commentary on John," in *Meister Eckhart: The Essential Sermons, Commentaries, Treatises, and Defense*, trans. Edmund Colledge and Bernard McGinn (New York: Paulist Press, 1981), p. 158.

4. Steiner, *Antigones*, p. 141.

5. Ibid., p. 100.

6. Ibid., p. 287.

7. "In short, our pollution behaviour is the reaction which condemns any object or idea likely to confuse or contadict cherished classifications" (Mary Douglas, *Purity and Danger: An Analysis of the Concepts of Pollution and Taboo* [New York: Routledge, 1996], p. 37).

8. Steiner, *Antigones*, p. 32.

9. Ibid.

10. On the problems with Heidegger's argument about the nonrelationality of death, see Jean-Paul Sartre, *Being and Nothingness: An Essay on Phenomenological Ontology*, trans. Hazel E. Barnes (New York: Philosophical Library, 1956), p. 534, and Paul Edwards, "Existentialism and Death: A Survey of Some Confusions and Absurdities," in *Language, Metaphysics, and Death*, ed. John Donnelly (New York: Fordham University Press, 1978), pp. 53–56.

11. Hegel, *Phenomenology*, p. 270.

12. Ibid., p. 271.

13. The passage in question is as follows: "Death is the fulfilment and the supreme 'work' which the individual as such undertakes on its [i.e., the ethical community's] behalf. But in so far as he is essentially a *particular* individual, it is an accident that his death was directly connected with his 'work' for the universal and was the result of it; partly because, if his death was such a result, it is the *natural* negativity and movement of the individual as a [mere] existent, in which consciousness does not return into itself and become self-consciousness; or partly because, since the movement of what [merely] exists consists in its being superseded and becoming a being-for-self, death is the side of diremption in which the attained being-for-self is something other than the mere existent which began the movement" (ibid., pp. 270–71). The first "partly" addresses the natural, or unconscious aspect of the body, whereas the second addresses the abstraction of consciousness.

14. For a sustained and provocative analysis of the "unconscious" aspect of women in Hegel's reading of *Antigone*, and the implications of that aspect for the overall argument of the *Phenomenology*, see Oliver, "Antigone's Ghost."

15. Why the family? Hegel's reasoning seems unclear—or perhaps simply circular—on this point. Irigaray's commentary on Hegel's notion of woman tries to explain: "Powerless on earth, she remains the ground in which manifest spirit has its dark roots and draws its forces. And self-certainty—of virility, of

the community, of government—possesses the truth of its speech and of the oath that binds men among themselves in that substance that is common to all, repressed, unconscious and mute, in the waters of forgetting. It is thus understandable that femininity should consist essentially in placing the dead back into the bosom of the earth, in giving him life again for eternity" (*Speculum*, p. 225, trans. modified). Still, it is unclear why the mortal remains must be remanded to the earth (and therefore woman) and not subtilized—e.g., through burning—which would submit them finally and permanently to the male order. Why, in short, must there be a cadaver—and the female unconscious it represents—if that cadaver can no longer provide the living material needed by the state? Derrida, in contrast, sees in the funerary rites discussed here the displacement of a deeper and more frightening anthropophagic desire (*Glas*, pp. 143–45). By thus interpreting Hegel's "unconscious" in psychoanalytic terms, Derrida would relocate it into the familial structures of the Oedipus complex. But from the latter point of view *everything* is familial in origin, and so his approach does not explain why the dead should be the special duty of blood relatives. It is true that in Sophocles's time responsibility for burial fell on the family of the deceased (see Kurtz and Boardman, *Greek Burial Customs*, pp. 142–44 and Humphreys, *Family, Women, and Death*, p. 83), but Hegel does not explain in nonhistorical terms why that should be so. He seems simply to argue that the family buries the dead because it is the nature of the family to take responsibility for the dead.

16. The distinction Hegel makes between natural death and the willing individual is consistent with the language of the *epitaphioi logoi*. Demosthenes argued that the defeated dead shared in the same glory as the victorious ones, because, "if, as a moral being, he meets his doom what he has suffered is an incident caused by chance, but in spirit he remains unconquered by his opponents" ("Funeral Speech," p. 21). For the orator, the actual event of death remains inherently alien to the ethical individual it affects. Similarly, Lysias asked, "So why . . . be so extremely distressed by the calamities of nature [*epi tais tēs phuseos sumphorais*]? . . . It is fitting to consider those most happy who have closed their lives in risking them for the greatest and noblest ends; not committing their career to chance, nor awaiting the death that comes of itself [*ton automaton thanaton*], but selecting the fairest one of all [*ton kalliston*]" ("Funeral Oration," §§77–79, pp. 67–69). Charles Taylor convincingly argues that the attempt to reconcile this "diremption" between an "expressive" nature (that is, one that embodies meaning) and human autonomy or individual freedom (that is, human being as something more than a simple repetition of that natural meaning) was the fundamental intellectual challenge of the late eighteenth and early nineteenth centuries (see *Hegel* [Cambridge, U.K.: Cambridge University Press, 1975], pp. 3–50). Although Hegel's reading of funeral practices in ancient

Athens may have been motivated by concerns typical to his own period, he nonetheless captured a conception of death that emerged in the original texts themselves. And so, although he may seem a product of his own times, more philosophical than philological and prone to subordinate classical authors to his own world vision, Hegel was, as this example shows, a surprisingly astute reader of the Greeks.

17. Steiner's misreading of Hegel seems to stem both from his understanding death, generally, in Heideggerian terms (see *Being and Time*, trans. John Macquarrie and Edward Robinson [New York: Harper and Row, 1962], pp. 279–311) and from the influence of Kojève's powerful but highly idiosyncratic interpretations of the *Phenomenology*, which Steiner quotes here. (For a critique of Kojève's reading of death in the *Phenomenology*, see Strauss, *Subjects of Terror*, pp. 54–63.)

18. Steiner, *Antigones*, p. 32.

19. Hegel, *Phenomenology*, p. 271.

20. Sophocles, *Antigone*, ll. 1030, 1288–92.

21. Ibid., l. 497, translation by Steiner, *Antigones*, p. 265.

22. Steiner understands Antigone to be expressing fear of bodily suffering in this line: "To choose death freely, to choose it early, is to retain mastery and self-mastery in the face of the only phenomenon against which man knows no remedy (l. 361). We are not far here from the heroic absolutism which we find in the world of Corneille or in the Hegelian allegory of Master and Slave. It is this declaration of ontological liberty which generates the momentarily anguished, if also contemptuous, query in line 497: 'Would you now do more than seize and slay me?' Confronting Creon's vainglorious fury, Antigone wonders whether it is in his power somehow to demean, to trivialize by arbitrary pain, the death which is *hers*, which she has freely chosen" (ll. 264–65). She does not fear physical pain, as I will argue in Chapter 5, but rather she fears the loss of the ownness of her own death. This is another indication of the profoundly Heideggerian skew to Steiner's understanding of death. But this passage in particular seems to be a very German romantic reading of the play. The language about "the only phenomenon against which man knows no remedy" echoes Friedrich Schiller, who described death as that "single terror, *which he* [i.e., the human individual] *simply must do and does not will*" (*On the Sublime*, trans. Julius A. Elias [New York: Frederick Ungar, 1966], p. 194). To be freely, and therefore genuinely human, according to Schiller, one must assume that death through a sort of "moral" suicide (p. 208). For both Heidegger and Schiller, Dasein's authenticity comes through the conscious appropriation of an already inalienable death. For Antigone, however, the relation between subject and death is tremendously fragile and cannot be secured through consciousness or will alone. To misunderstand that fragility is to blind oneself to the power of the

material world and of the corpse that represents it in this play. The dead body exposes the self to danger. It is not exactly the ancestral miasma, but it is a pollution in its own right, and as such it must be managed if it is to serve as a guarantee of individuality, for (*pace* Steiner and Heidegger) death alone cannot offer any such surety.

23. On the notion of the "beautiful corpse" see Vernant, "La belle mort et le cadavre outragé," in *Individu*, pp. 41–79.

24. See Garland, *Greek Way of Death*, chap. 1, e.g.: "Certainly the dead retained the use of their sense enough to be able to perceive when a friendly or hostile presence approached their graves" (p. 4). See also Rehm, *Marriage to Death*, p. 64, and Emily Vermeule, *Aspects of Death in Early Greek Art and Poetry* (Berkeley: University of California Press, 1979), pp. 27, 31–32.

25. See Butler, *Antigone's Claim*, esp. pp. 23–24, 45–55, 76.

26. See *The Seminar of Jacques Lacan, Book VII: The Ethics of Psychoanalysis, 1959–1960*, trans. Dennis Porter (New York: W. W. Norton, 1992), pp. 248, 268, 272, and my discussion of Lacan in Chapter 7, below. For Derrida, however, it is Polyneices's corpse that represents the ambiguous zone between life and death, which functions, in turn, as a figure for the return of the repressed: "'The dead, whose right is injured, knows therefore how to find instruments of vengeance, which are equally effective, actual, and violent as the power that has wounded it.' So the deceased continues to act; the *deceased is wounded*, returns to the charge from the mute and unconscious substance in which one wanted to repulse, reduce, curb, restrain him. The return of the dead, the vengeance of the suppressed" (*Glas*, p. 189).

27. In his reading of these pages from the *Phenomenology*, Jacques Derrida remarks also on the intermediary nature of the cadaver: "This pure singularity, stripped but incapable of passing to universality, is the dead—more precisely the name of the dead—is the corpse, the impotent shadow, the negation of the living being-there inasmuch as that singularity has *not yet* given rise to the life of the citizen. Already dead (as empiric existence), not yet living (as ideal universality)" (*Glas*, p. 143). Derrida understands the forces acting on the dead as unconscious anthropophagic desires on the part of the living: "The feminine operation of burial does not oppose itself to the exteriority of a nonconscious matter; it suppresses an unconscious desire. The family wants to prevent the dead one from being 'destroyed' and the burial violated *by this desire*. Such a remark forms the systematic opening of this analysis on subsequent problematics concerning the work of mourning, anthropophagy, cannibalism, all the processes [*processus*] of incorporation and introjection. Hegel does not determine the unconscious desires against which the dead one must be guarded. The (consanguine) family interrupts the abstract material work of nature and 'takes on itself (*über sich nimmt*)' destruction" (*Glas*, p. 144). What Hegel leaves

undetermined is given name by Derrida, but that indetermination is itself important, because the object of concern here is precisely that which lies outside the laws of meaning. The idea that the family's *Übernahme* of destruction represents an unconscious desire to devour raises, nonetheless, a host of intriguing questions, such as the meaning of eating in Hegel (a topic that Werner Hamacher addressed at length in *Pleroma—Reading in Hegel*, trans. Nicholas Walker and Simon Jarvis [Stanford: Stanford University Press, 1998]). Derrida understands the ravening of natural forces, and the anthropophagic desire that they figure, within the terms used by psychoanalytic studies of mourning and melancholy (see especially Nicolas Abraham and Maria Torok, "New Perspectives in Metapsychology: Cryptic Mourning and Secret Love," in *The Shell and the Kernel: Renewals of Psychoanalysis*, ed. and trans. Nicholas Rand [Chicago: University of Chicago Press, 1994], pp. 107–64, and Derrida's own "Fors: The Anglish Words of Nicolas Abraham and Maria Torok," in *The Wolf Man's Magic Word: A Cryptonymy*, by Abraham and Torok, trans. Barbara Johnson [Minneapolis: University of Minnesota Press, 1986], pp. xi–xlviii). Although such a psychoanalytic reading is undoubtedly valid on certain "ulterior" levels, it does mask another, possibly more fundamental anxiety. Because it concerns a preverbal, presymbolic, and presubjective state, this other anxiety would predate both the Oedipus plays and complex. Such an anxiety also gives a significance to Hegel's animals and processes of putrefaction different from the one Derrida finds in them. In its light, those processes do not represent the unconscious in a Freudian sense, that is, as a nonawareness within consciousness itself. Instead, they figure thought in the nonpsychic or material world. They are not a lack of awareness, but an excess of it. Viewed in this way, Hegel's unconscious is something like the opposite of Freud's. And to follow the mirror symmetry into its Lacanian ramifications: This other unconconscious is probably not structured like a language, is probably, in fact, nameless, *agrapta*.

28. Steiner, *Antigones*, p. 287.

29. Sophocles, *Antigone*, ll. 925–28. Hegel quotes only line 926 (*Phenomenology*, p. 284).

30. Gabriela Basterra has argued that tragic guilt is a means of distracting from the fear of a cosmic guilt. To accept the criminality of the hero is to confirm the justice of the gods, and one does accept, because it is better to be a criminal personally than to believe that the gods are fallible or worse. See *Seductions of Fate: Tragic Subjectivity, Ethics, Politics* (New York: Palgrave Macmillan, 2004), pp. 38–66.

31. Plato, *Phaedo* 80b, in *Collected Dialogues*, p. 63. The relation between meaning and the city's walls will be discussed in the following chapter.

32. In his Jena writings, Hegel described the city as the final shape of the absolute. See Jean Hyppolite, *Genesis and Structure of Hegel's* Phenomenology of

Spirit, trans. Samuel Cherniak and John Heckman (Evanston, Ill.: Northwestern University Press, 1974), pp. 331, 337.

33. Hegel, *Phenomenology*, p. 287.

34. The lines in question read: "Then know well that you shall not accomplish many racing courses of the sun, and in that lapse of time you shall give in exchange for corpses the corpse of one from your own loins, in return for having hurled below one of those above, blasphemously lodging a living person in a tomb, and you have kept here something belonging to the gods below, a corpse deprived, unburied, unholy. Neither you nor the gods above have any part in this, but you have inflicted it upon them! On account of this there lie in wait for you the doers of outrage who in the end destroy, the Erinyes of Hades and the gods, so that you will be caught up in these same evils. . . . For after no long lapse of time there shall be lamentations of men and women in your house; and all the cities are stirred up by enmity . . . (corpses) of which fragments have been consecrated by dogs or beasts, or some winged bird, carrying the unholy scent to the city with its hearths" (Sophocles, *Antigone*, trans. Lloyd-Jones, ll. 1064–83). The reference to altars comes in an earlier speech by Tiresias (ll. 998–1022).

35. Hegel, *Philosophy of History*, trans. J. Sibree, quoted in Hyppolite, *Genesis and Structure*, p. 338.

36. Sophocles, *Antigone*, ll. 847–52.

37. Hegel, *Phenomenology*, pp. 287–88.

38. In a particularly brilliant passage, Vermeule interprets the relation between light and life as a matter of wit and intelligence for the ancient Greeks (*Aspects of Death*, pp. 23–31). Light, she argues, is related to sentience, intellection. "The most familiar Greek virtue, *sophrosyne*," she writes, "began as that quality of mind which would keep you safe and draw you back from the stupidity of the sleeping and the dead" (p. 24). Fear of darkness is, according to this reasoning, a fear of stupidity: "The fear, then, is that the dead have lost what we most admire in ourselves, our intelligence and wit" (p. 27). I have argued in this chapter that a similar fear is unconsciously at work in Hegel's interpretation and that this fear takes the unspoken, phantasmatic form of a mineral sentience among the dead.

4. STATES OF EXCLUSION

1. Kelly Oliver in "Antigone's Ghost" has argued that another figure of the undead runs through Hegel's *Phenomenology*: It is, according to her, haunted by the ghost of female unconsciousness. She seems to be picking up on Irigaray's comment that women are the "*bloodless shadows*— . . . unconscious fantasms" of the Hegelian system (*Speculum*, p. 225). They are, for Irigaray, a "reserve" in the

Hegelian system, a nonparticipant in history (p. 224, trans. modified), whereas for Oliver, their unconscious presence represents a contradiction in the very principle of history, which is, precisely, the making conscious of the unconscious. In both cases, the choice of words for the undead seems strange, since it is precisely the history of *Geist* that Hegel is recounting in the *Phenomenology*. It would seem, instead, to be the corpse that more accurately figures that persistent excess of the system that is woman.

2. On the soul and the notion of individual afterlife in ancient Greece, see Chapter 2, above.

3. Plato, *Alcibiades 1* 129b–133c, in *Plato*, vol. 8, trans. W. R. M. Lamb, Loeb Classical Library 201 (1927; Cambridge, Mass.: Harvard University Press, 1955), pp. 194–213. See also Vernant, "L'individu dans la cité," in *Individu*, p. 227.

4. Plato, *Phaedo* 80b, in *Collected Dialogues*, p. 63.

5. Ibid., 115c, p. 95.

6. Plato, *Laws*, 959a–c, trans. A. E. Taylor, in *Collected Dialogues*, p. 1503.

7. Ibid., 959c–960a, p. 1504. This careful legislation of funerary rites represents a change in attitude from Plato's *Republic*, where codifying "the burial of the dead and the services we must render to the dwellers in the world beyond to keep them gracious" is left to the oracle at Delphi, since "of such matters we [i.e., the lawgivers] neither know anything nor in the founding of our city if we are wise shall we entrust them to any other or make use of any other interpreter than the god of our fathers" (*Republic*, 4.427b–c, trans. Paul Shorey, in *Collected Dialogues*, pp. 668–69). In both the *Republic* and the *Laws*, however, the effect is to limit the role of the corpse in the city, in the first case by placing it under another authority and in the second by minimizing the attention that it may receive.

8. For an overview of legislation concerning funerals, see Introduction, above.

9. Plato, *Phaedo*, 116e–117a, pp. 96–97. *kai pheidomenos oudenos eti enontos* = literally "husbanding the nothing that is left." Peter Rose, of Miami University, has pointed out to me that Socrates's figure of speech alludes to Hesiod's *Works and Days*, l. 369, which holds that it is craven to spare the wine when the cask is almost empty (*deilē d'eni puthmeni pheidō*).

10. In *Alcibiades 1*, Plato does, in fact, use the term "nothing" to distinguish the reality of the soul from the unreality of the body: "But since neither the body nor the combination [of the body and the soul] is man, we are reduced, I suppose, to this: either man is nothing [*mēden*] at all, or if something, he turns out to be nothing [*mēden*] else than the soul" (130c, pp. 200–201). Since man is the soul or he is nothing, all that pertains to the physical world has the value of nothing in the constitution of the individual.

11. Plato, *Laws*, 960b, p. 1504. Cf. the punishment for interfamilial homicide in *Laws*, 873b–c: after the criminal's execution, "all the magistrates, in the name of the state, shall take each man his stone and cast it on the head of the corpse as in expiation for the state. The corpse shall then be carried to the frontier and cast out by legal sentence without sepulture" (p. 1432). Similar punishments are enjoined against the bodies of suicides (873d, p. 1432).

12. Pomeroy has, however, effectively refuted this argument (*Families in Classical and Hellenistic Greece*, pp. 100–105).

13. Note that this is the approach that Plato takes with the *thumos*, part of the mortal and individuating aspect of the soul. The legislator (and the immortal soul) harnesses it against the more unruly impulses of the appetitive drive. See Chapter 6, below on Leontius.

14. Plato, *Phaedrus* 246b–c, trans. R. Hackforth, in *Collected Dialogues*, p. 493.

15. Plato, *Timaeus* 90e–91d, trans. Benjamin Jowett, in *Collected Dialogues*, p. 1210. Cf. another discussion of metempsychosis in *Phaedo* 81d–82b, pp. 64–65.

16. Plato, *Timaeus* 91d–92c, pp. 1210–11.

17. In his analysis of the viscous in *Being and Nothingness*, Sartre writes, "It is not a matter of indifference whether we like oysters or clams, snails or shrimp, if only we know how to unravel the existential significance of these foods. Generally speaking there is no irreducible taste or inclination. They all represent a certain appropriative choice of being. It is up to existential psychoanalysis to compare and classify them" (p. 784). Probably the only animal that Westerners commonly eat while it is still alive, the oyster is put to death at the moment of the eater's pleasure, a pleasure that mingles with the killing, even if the latter is only, putatively, incidental. One wonders what it can feel, at what point it dies and what that death means, how long its sentience—already borderline, already at the limit of nonsentience, but for that reason all the stronger, all the more persistent—continues. In the crushed and viscous fragments? On the palate? Down the throat? Deeper?

18. Plato, *Phaedrus* 250c, p. 497.

19. See Sigmund Freud, "The Uncanny," in *The Standard Edition of the Complete Psychological Writings of Sigmund Freud*, ed. and trans. James Strachey and Anna Freud (London: Hogarth Press, 1966), 17:217–56.

20. Plato was not, of course, the only one to advocate the punishment of the nonhuman. Mosaic law also included such sanctions (Exodus 21). As absurd as it might seem, the question was still relevant in France as late as 1887, when the French translation of Cesare Lombroso's *L'homme criminel* appeared. After a detailed description of carnivorous plants, Lombroso finally concluded that despite arguments to the contrary by several legal theorists, plants cannot be

held responsible for their actions, because of their "absolute dependence on histological conditions" (*L'homme criminel, criminel-né, fou moral, épileptique: Etude anthropologique et médico-légale*, trans. Regnier and Bournet [Paris: Félix Alcan, 1887], p. 4). For Lombroso, too, the attempt to extend human legal concepts to animals and plants represented the desire for a universal judicial system, whereas, conversely, the demonstrable impossibility of applying human legal categories to the nonhuman evidenced "the vanity of the absolute idea of justice" (p. 7).

21. Plato, *Laws*, 9.873e–874a, p. 1433.

22. Carcopino, *Ostracisme athénien*, pp. 78–82.

23. Ibid., pp. 190, 196, 250–51. Ostracism was used as a technique to resolve factional disputes, for example in the case of Alcibiades and Nicias. See Plutarch, "Nicias," chap. 11 (3:247–51), "Alcibiades," chap. 13 (4:29–31), and "Aristides," chap. 7 (2:231–35) in *Plutarch's Lives*, trans. Bernadotte Perrin, Loeb Classical Library 47, 65, 80 (1914; Cambridge, Mass.: Harvard University Press, 1967).

24. See, for example, Carcopino, *Ostracisme athénien*, pp. 31–32, 39.

25. Ibid., p. 31.

26. According to the laws laid down by Solon, the exile "was punished not only in his own person, but through all who were related to him. His race must be destroyed unto dust, Solon said, *kapitetriphthai génos*. Let his family be banished with him—*atimon einai kaì génos—apóllosthai kaì autòn kaì génos tò kéno*; and, like him, his kindred could escape massacre only by flight. The hatred that he had incited toward himself and his family extended to his property . . . , to his mortal remains and those of his children, to which the city refused the right of sepulture within its terrritory—*hyperopizein*" (ibid., p. 39).

27. Jacques Derrida, *Dissemination* (Paris: Seuil, 1972), trans. Barbara Johnson (Chicago: University of Chicago Press, 1981), pp. 130–34. Perhaps because of Derrida's influential essay, the *pharmakos* has recently attracted much interest among philosophers. See Giorgio Agamben, *Homo Sacer: Sovereign Power and Bare Life*, trans. Daniel Heller-Roazen (Stanford: Stanford University Press, 1998), and Julia Kristeva, *La révolution du langage poétique: L'avant-garde à la fin du XIXe siècle: Lautréamont et Mallarmé* (Paris: Seuil, 1974), p. 76. See also *Revolution in Poetic Language*, trans. Margaret Waller (New York: Columbia University Press, 1984), pp. 78–79. Because Waller's excellent translation is heavily abridged and often omits passages or terms that are key to my argument, I have often referred to the French edition while citing the pages from the translation nearest to the missing original section.

28. René Girard, *Le bouc émissaire* (Paris: Grasset, 1982), p. 37.

29. Derrida, *Dissemination*, p. 133.

30. "For the sacrifice represented only the legislative aspect of the thetic phase: the sacred murder indicated only the violence that had been *localized* in

the sacrifice in order to found the social order. The sacrifice represented the thetic only as the foundational *exclusion* from a symbolic order, *setting* the violence into the one who was the 'scapegoat.' The sacrifice marked the punctual, apprehended violence that was contained both in the murder and in the inaugural split [*coupure inaugurale*]" (*Révolution*, p. 76; *Revolution*, pp. 78–79). Plutarch observed that through ostracism the Athenians "cripple and banish whatever man from time to time may have too much reputation and influence in the city to please them, assuaging thus their envy rather than their fear" ("Alcibiades," chap. 13, in *Lives*, 4:31).

31. Jean-Pierre Vernant, "Ambiguïté et renversement, sur la structure énigmatique d'Oedipe-Roi," in *Echanges et Communications: Mélanges offerts à Claude Lévi-Strauss*, ed. Jean Pouillon and Pierre Maranda, vol. 2 (The Hague: Mouton, 1970), p. 1275.

32. Carcopino, *Ostracisme athénien*, p. 33. See also pp. 250–51.

33. This need to redress the defectiveness of the origin, the need to efface its historicity, helps explain the paradox that Gabriela Basterra observes at the very core of tragedy. Basterra points out that while tragedy is the first form of fiction that openly passes for an imaginative creation rather than a reflection of historical events, the notion of tragic fate central to it as an art form denies the very possibility of human agency and creation—which would include the fictionality of tragedy itself. See *Seductions of Fate*, pp. 106–30. Similarly, I am arguing, insofar as tragedy is itself a supplement to the founding of the city, insofar as it corrects and replaces the origin, its originary status must be hidden: To recognize it would be immediately to undo supplementarity, would be to admit that the origin is unfinished. So tragedy must pretend to represent an already existing state of things or, rather, a state that was predestined but as yet unrevealed. For tragedy to acknowledge its own creativity would mean revealing that the origin of the city is still open, that the city must still be founded, and that the dead, with all the chaos they embody, have not been excluded from the state.

34. Carcopino, *Ostracisme athénien*, pp. 10–15.

35. Plato, *Parmenides*, 130c-d, trans. F. M. Cornford, in *Collected Dialogues*, pp. 924–25.

36. Plato, *Menexenus*, 245c-d, trans. Bury, p. 369.

37. Loraux, *Né de la terre*, pp. 169–89.

38. Ibid., pp. 169–70. Loraux's reading is influenced by Derrida's work on the function of the *chōra* in Platonic philosophy. See Jacques Derrida, "Chôra," in *Poikilia: Etudes offertes à Jean-Pierre Vernant*, ed. Marcel Detienne, Nicole Loraux et al. (Paris: Ecole des Hautes Etudes en Sciences Sociales, 1987), pp. 265–96, e.g.: "The thought of the *chôra* would disturb the very order of polarity, of polarity in general, whether or not it is dialectical. Since *chôra*

gives rise to oppositions, it can undergo no reversal itself. And this—as a further consequence—is not because it is unalterably *itself* but because in reaching beyond the polarity of meaning (metaphoric or literal) it would no longer belong to the horizon of meaning, nor of meaning as the meaning of being" (p. 268). Globally, Derrida's project in this and other writings is to demonstrate how the genealogies of certain terms undermine the stability and intelligibility not only of given texts, but of Greek thought in general (which is to say, not only a corpus of texts but the desire to make coherent sense of those texts). In another article, he situates his analyses of the *chōra* within a more comprehensive reading of alterity and indeterminability in Greek thought: "This resistance was especially interesting to me at the point where it limits the possibility of a system or of a corpus, of the complete, controllable, and formalizable self-identity of a set, whether that set be a system, the body of works (*oeuvre*) of Plato (as would be determined by a unifiable meaning), the Greek language, or Greek society (and very concretely it is also an issue of the place—*including exclusion*, if I may put it that way—of the *pharmakos* in that society) and, therefore, the Greek identity in general" ("Nous autres Grecs," pp. 261–62).

39. Loraux, *Né de la terre*, p. 170.

40. Anatole Bailly, *Dictionnaire grec-français* (Paris: Hachette, 2000), cites the *Iliad*, 23.520-21: *ti pollē chōrē messēgus*.

41. Plato, *Timaeus* 51a–b in *Timaeus, Critias, Cleitophon, Menexenus, Epistles*, trans. R. G. Bury, Loeb Classical Library 234 (1929; Cambridge, Mass.: Harvard University Press, 1989), p. 119.

42. Plato, *Timaeus* 51e–52a, trans. Bury, p. 123.

43. Plato, *Timaeus* 52b–c, trans. Bury, p. 123.

44. See Plato, *Timaeus* 49a: "It should be the receptacle, and as it were the nurse [*tithenēn*], of all becoming" (trans. Bury, p. 113), and 50d: "It is proper to liken the Recipient to the Mother [*mētri*], the Source to the Father [*patri*], and what is engendered between these two to the Offspring" (pp. 117–19).

45. Peter Stallybrass and Allon White have pointed out a similar confusion of hired nurse and biological mother in Freud's formulation of the Oedipus complex. See *The Politics and Poetics of Transgression* (Ithaca, N.Y.: Cornell University Press, 1986), pp. 149–70.

46. Both Derrida and Kristeva argue that *chōra* designates a place of thinking in which legitimate paternal authority is disrupted or absent. See Derrida, "Chôra" (291), where he links the latter to mythic, rather than philosophical, modes of expression: "The mythical tale thus resembles a discourse without a legitimate father"; and Kristeva's *Révolution*, pp. 25, 26 (*Revolution*, pp. 25–28).

47. Plato, *Menexenus* 237b–c, trans. Bury, p. 237.

48. Kristeva, *Revolution*, p. 25.

49. Fränkel's notion of a presubjective "field of energy [*Kraftfeld*]" can be compared to the semiotic aspect of language that Kristeva describes throughout her work. See Fränkel, *Early Greek Poetry*, p. 80, and the Introduction, above.

50. Julia Kristeva, "Le sujet en procès," in *Polylogue* (Paris: Seuil, 1977), pp. 55–106.

51. Kristeva, *Revolution*, p. 79.

52. Ibid. Simon Goldhill has expressed some reservations about ritualistic interpretations of tragedy—especially in relation to the figure of the scape-goat—but he refers more to anthropological approaches such as René Girard's than linguistic ones such as Kristeva's (see "Modern Critical Approaches," pp. 332–33).

53. Plato, *Menexenus*, 245d, trans. Bury, p. 369.

54. Or what the phenomenologists call the *conatus in su esse perseverandi* (see Jean-Luc Marion, *Le phénomène érotique: Six méditations* [Paris: Bernard Grasset, 2003], pp. 80–85).

55. To this list one might add what Michel Serres terms "parasite." According to one's semiotic training, "the same series of waves is sign or din, the same matter is stench or perfume, the same food revolting or delicious. All of this defines a reticulated space, that one could term Pascalian, where each, for a period of time, is master of his own segment, where any center is dispersed and produces its local power through an identification with the interior and an expulsion toward the border, where each group finds itself in its own place, where the unstable equilibrium among the relations of force fluctuates. It is a knitted space in which anything that flips from 'for' to 'against' as one crosses any of the network's threads is not only a moral precept or truth value but anything that delights the body or produces repugnance in it. Speech this side of the Pyrenees, noise [*parasite*] on the other. Sound on this side, ruckus on the other. Their language is nothing but noise, a barbarous gurgling of the intestines" (*The Parasite*, trans. Lawrence Schehr [Minneapolis: University of Minnesota Press, 1982], p. 142 [trans. modified]).

56. See especially Agamben's discussions of the included/excluded condition of the *pharmakos* (*Homo Sacer*, pp. 82, 83, 99–100, 131).

5. INVENTING LIFE

1. Nussbaum, *Fragility of Goodness*, pp. 354–72, esp. p. 358.

2. Euripides, *Suppliant Women*, l. 881. See also ll. 836–917: *The Suppliant Women*, trans. Frank Jones in *Euripides IV*, ed. David Grene and Richmond Lattimore (Chicago: University of Chicago Press, 1958), pp. 89–91. See Loraux, *Invention*, pp. 107–8.

3. Loraux, *Invention*, p. 108.

4. Holst-Warhaft relies on a similar reasoning when she observes that Hecuba appears somehow impersonal when she laments Hector as "the dearest of her sons" (*Dangerous Voices*, p. 112).

5. Oddly, given how important a role war plays in Hegel's reading of *Antigone*, I have found no scholarship critiquing this aspect of his analysis.

6. Both Lacan and Mark Griffith analyze the character of Antigone as a figure—and object—of desire for the play's audience. See Lacan, *Ethics*, p. 247 (trans. modified): "*Antigone* shows us the target that defines desire. . . . For we are well aware that beyond the dialogues, beyond the family and the fatherland, beyond the moralizing developments, she is the one who fascinates us in her unbearable splendor [*éclat*]," and Mark Griffith, "Subject of Desire," pp. 116–21.

7. Hegel, *Phenomenology*, p. 275.

8. On biology and contingency in Hegel's readings of *Antigone*, see Mills, "Hegel's *Antigone*," pp. 244, 260.

9. Hegel, *Phenomenology*, p. 288.

10. Hegel, *Phenomenology*, p. 288. Hegel, who related the idea of ornamentation to the subjective aspects of Greek art, seems to have felt some ambivalence about its value. On the one hand, the vanity of bodily decorations turned the individual away from higher responsibilities, such as those to the state. On the other, it expressed an unreflected joy in one's own existence: "The exhilarating sense of personality, in contrast with sensuous subjection to nature, and the need, not of mere pleasure, but of the display of individual powers, in order thereby to gain special distinction and consequent enjoyment, constitute therefore the chief characteristic and principal occupation of the Greeks. Free as the bird singing in the sky, the individual only expresses what lies in his untrammelled human nature—[to give the world 'assurance of a man']—to have his importance recognized" (*Philosophy of History*, trans. J. Sibree [1899; New York: Cosimo Classics, 2007], p. 242).

11. Hegel, *Phenomenology*, p. 289.

12. Loraux, *Invention*, pp. 105–6.

13. Hegel, *Phenomenology*, p. 275.

14. Ibid. This passage ends in one of the rare footnotes to the *Phenomenology*, which cites *Antigone*. On contingency and desire in Hegel, see Mills, "Hegel's *Antigone*," p. 260 and Oliver, "Antigone's Ghost," p. 71. In the *Philosophy of Right*, published some fourteen years after the *Phenomenology*, Hegel will resituate the ethical relationship, moving it from the love between a brother and his sister to the contractual bond between man and wife, but here too, he is careful to subordinate desire to an impersonal law.

15. See Butler, *Antigone's Claim*, pp. 45–55.

16. Mills argues that in the reading of *Antigone* from the *Phenomenology*, "man is necessarily a member of a family and the family is the sphere of the

particularity of the pagan male's existence. Within the family, man is *this* particular father, *this* husband, *this* son, and not simply *a* father, *a* husband, *a* son" ("Hegel's *Antigone*," p. 244). Since Mills does not specify otherwise, this would suggest that for Hegel the family can produce a true and ethically legitimate particularization of its members *as living beings*. This seems to me overly generous. I would argue instead that for Hegel the family bestows an ethically legitimate individuality on its members only through their death (see Chapter 1, above) or through the impersonal notion of "blood," described here. In the first instance, the individual is not living, and, in the second, not really individual.

17. Judith Butler reminds her readers that Antigone "hardly represents the normative principles of kinship, steeped as she is in incestuous legacies that confound her position within kinship" (*Antigone's Claim*, p. 2).

18. Ibid., esp. pp. 23–24, 76.

19. Derrida, *Glas*, pp. 167–87, 199–209

20. See Chanter, *Ethics of Eros*, pp. 120–21.

21. Irigaray, *Speculum*, 214–26.

22. For an analysis of kinship as a vertiginous linguistic construct in *Oedipus Rex*, see Pucci, "Reading the Riddles," p. 142.

23. Pomeroy, *Families in Classical and Hellenistic Greece*, p. 19.

24. Ibid., p. 35. See also pp. 34, 36.

25. For a detailed discussion of the term *philos* and its cognates in fifth-century Greece, see Goldhill, *Reading Greek Tragedy*, pp. 79–106.

26. E.g., *Iliad* 2.261: "phila heimata dusō." This interpretation of the term *philos* has been challenged by Emile Benveniste. See Goldhill, *Reading Greek Tragedy*, p. 82, n. 9.

27. Warren J. Lane and Ann M. Lane, "The Politics of *Antigone*," in *Greek Tragedy and Political Theory*, ed. J. Peter Euben (Berkeley: University of California Press, 1986), p. 171.

28. See Nussbaum, *Fragility of Goodness*, pp. 354–72, and Chapter 7, below.

29. Lane and Lane, "Politics of *Antigone*," p. 174.

30. Mark Griffith, "Subject of Desire," p. 96.

31. Lane and Lane, "Politics of *Antigone*," p. 174.

32. Ibid.

33. Sophocles, *Oedipus at Colonus*, ll. 1103, 1108 (twice), and 1110 in the first instance; ll. 607, 608, and 615 in the second.

34. Ibid., ll. 1615–19.

35. *Philos* and its various cognates have, of course, a broad range of meanings that include rather weak senses that simply seem to indicate ownership (e.g., *philos* = "my own"). It seems clear, however, that in the passages under discussion from *Oedipus at Colonus* the word has a much stronger meaning and

that this stronger meaning resonates through other uses of the word and its cognates. To capture that effect, I have generally translated *philein* as "love."

36. See, for example, Jean-Luc Nancy's interpretation of suffering in Hegel: "The separation that manifestation is in itself is always a singular ordeal. As such, it is pain. Pain—or misfortune—is not universal separation; it is not the pain of a great cosmic drama that sweeps every being up into it, and in which, ultimately, a universal subject would get enjoyment from universal misfortune. Pain is precisely the element of the singularity of separation, for it is to singularity and as singularity that separation occurs. It occurs as the alteration of its subsistence and, thus, as its own self awakened into its alterity" (*Hegel: The Restlessness of the Negative*, trans. Jason Smith and Steven Miller [Minneapolis: University of Minnesota Press, 2002], pp. 40–41 [trans. modified]). Similarly, in *The Body in Pain: The Making and Unmaking of the World* (Oxford: Oxford University Press, 1985), Elaine Scarry observes that pain operates a foundational distinction between self and others through its immediate self-evidence to the former and mediate doubtfulness to the latter. See especially page 4: "So, for the person in pain, so incontestably and unnegotiably present is it that 'having pain' may come to be thought of as the most vibrant example of what it is to 'have certainty,' while for the other person it is so elusive that 'hearing about pain' may exist as the primary model of what it is 'to have doubt.' . . . Whatever pain achieves, it achieves in part through its unsharability."

37. Sophocles, *Oedipus at Colonus*, ll. 184–87.

38. This is an attitude characteristic of fifth-century Greeks. As Simon Goldhill writes: "Perhaps the most basic and generally agreed position with regard to correct behaviour in the ancient world was 'to love one's friend and to hate one's enemy', that is, *philein philous ekhthairein ekhthrous*. The principle is seen throughout the range of Greek writing" (*Reading Greek Tragedy*, p. 83). According to Goldhill, however, Sophocles's plays place that attitude into question (see p. 85). In *Love among the Ruins: The Erotics of Democracy in Classical Athens* (Princeton: Princeton University Press, 2002), Victoria Wohl "attempts to illuminate the erotic imaginary that underlay—supported and subverted—the Athenian political imaginary" (p. 2). Although Wohl discusses the role of love in the conceptualization of the state, she concentrates on erotic love rather than philia.

39. Sophocles, *Oedipus at Colonus*, ll. 944–46.

40. Ibid., ll. 969–73.

41. Ibid., ll. 772–82.

42. Ibid., l. 1552.

43. See also Vernant and Vidal-Naquet, *Myth and Tragedy*: "Just as the tragic character comes into being within the space between *daimon* and *ethos*, so tragic culpability is positioned, on the one hand, between the ancient religious

concept of crime-defilement, *hamartia*, sickness of the mind, the delirium sent by gods that necessarily engenders crime, and, on the other, the new concept in which the guilty one, *hamarton*, above all, *adikon*, is defined as one who, under no compulsion, has deliberately chosen to commit a crime" (pp. 45–46); and "This experience, still wavering and indecisive, of what was subsequently in the psychological history of Western man to become the category of the will (*volonté*)—as is well known, in ancient Greece there was no true vocabulary of the will (*vouloir*)—is expressed in tragedy in the form of an anxious questioning concerning the relation of the agent to his actions: To what extent is man really the source of his actions?" (p. 46). As has already been observed above, however, Aristotle does discuss the difference between voluntary and involuntary actions at length in the *Nicomachean Ethics* (book 3).

44. Sophocles, *Antigone*, l. 523. Ivana Petrovic offers a somewhat different interpretation of the line, even more appropriate to my argument: "Just as in *Ajax* 1316, Sophocles has used *syn-* in *Antigone* 523 in a perfective sense, and the translation of verse 523 must be rendered as follows: I was not born endlessly to hate but to love without limits" ("Die Bedeutung des Verses 523 in der "Antigone" des Sophokles Outoi sunekhthein, alla sunphilein ephun: Ein neuer Deutungsversuch," *Acta Antiqua Academiae scientiarum Hungaricae* 41, no. 2–3 [2001]: 362). For a commentary of this line within a larger reading of *philia* in fifth-century tragedy, see Goldhill, *Reading Greek Tragedy*, p. 98.

45. Sophocles, *Antigone*, ll. 524–25.

46. Ibid., ll. 536–47.

47. The first lines of the play already signal this tension between knowing agency and familial community. Antigone asks: "My own sister Ismene, linked to myself, are you aware . . . ? . . . And now what is this proclamation that they say the general [i.e., Creon] has lately made to the whole city? Have you any knowledge?" (ll. 1–9). The term *koinon* appears in the first line to describe the relation between Ismene and Antigone. It is the same word for communality that Antigone will subsequently reject in line 546, when she refuses Ismene's offer to die with her.

48. On the untransferable nature of death in *Being and Time* and Sartre's response to Heidegger's argument, see Strauss, "After Death." Bonnie Honig has offered a very different reading of this scene, which derives from her interpretation of Ismene's larger role in the play (see "Ismene's Forced Choice: Sacrifice and Sorority in Sophocle's *Antigone*," *Arethusa* 44, no. 1 [2011]: 29–68). Honig proposes that we understand Ismene to have performed the first burial of Polyneices and Antigone only the second. Of this particular scene (ll. 536–47), Honig writes: "Then out loud [Antigone] accuses her sister of being all words, no actions. But methinks she doth protest too much. Why the harsh charge? She is desperate to neutralize Ismene's response to Creon,

and perhaps Antigone suspects that there *was* an act and not just words—in fact a wordless act, the first burial of Polynices, yet to be explained. Ismene did it" (p. 48). Antigone is a difficult choice as a feminist model, given that she sacrifices her life for her brother and repudiates her sister, and Honig's article seems an attempt to salvage the character's feminist credentials. As she writes: "If Ismene did [the first burial], and if Antigone sacrificed herself for her sister, then we have here the story of two women partnered in their difference . . . both acting in resistance to overreaching sovereign power but acting also in love or loyalty for each other. . . . Relinquishing our habitual reading of Antigone as heroic (solitary, autonomous) opens the play up. What we see, however, when we do so is not, contra Goldhill, a really unkind and unheroic Antigone who should discomfit feminists, but something else that has remained undetected for even longer: an agonistic sorority that is solidaristic" (pp. 50–51). Although it is easy to sympathize with Honig's motivations, there are many problems with her approach—e.g., it depends on two unexplained changes of heart on Ismene's part, imagining that Antigone is in a persistent state of bafflement, violence against the narrative arc of the play, etc. The most serious problem, however, is that her interpretation relies on speculations about the unspoken psychological states and motivations of characters (e.g., "she might be silently wondering" [p. 38]; "when Antigone says, "I cannot deny it,' is she wondering: "did someone else bury Polynices before I got there? But who?" [p. 39]; and "perhaps Antigone suspects" [p. 48], etc.) who are, after all, the fictional creations of a male author. Honig herself seems to acknowledge the speculative nature of her interpretation (see pp. 31, 60). Even if we imagine that Antigone did not perform the first burial, however, that does not undermine my interpretation of this scene, which sees it as a concern about the continuity over time created by responsibility—Ismene is not responsible if she just did the deed. She is only responsible if she also pays for it, for only then can identity over time be established. The motivation for the "harsh charge" that puzzles Honig is, from this perspective, quite understandable: Antigone is fighting for her identity.

49. In her analysis of Hegel's reading of Antigone, Anna Mudde argues that a deed cannot in itself establish identity, which arises only through the actor's negotiation of others' reactions to that deed. But her argument ultimately and, I think, unintentionally becomes an issue of the representation and misrepresentation of an already established identity, and it is, precisely, the establishment of that identity that is of concern for Antigone in this passage, at least as I understand it. See "Risky Subjectivity: Antigone, Action, and Universal Trespass." *Human Studies* 32, no. 2 (2009): esp. 198–99.

50. Sophocles, *Antigone*, ll. 454–55. Antigone's stance, in this passage, would represent a defiance, as well, of Lacan's notion of the "other" death that is the

subject's entry into the symbolic register (or language). See the discussion of Lacan in Chapter 7, below.

51. This understanding of individuality as emerging from a deed to which the individual then remains faithful is disturbingly similar to Alain Badiou's notion of subjectivity as fidelity toward an event. See *Ethics*, pp. 40–57. The resemblance is disturbing because it suggests an anachronistic projection on my part.

52. Sophocles, *Antigone*, ll. 891–920.

53. Ibid., ll. 897–99. Scholars have often remarked on the striking similarities between the Greek rituals for weddings and funerals, as if the Greek imagination confused the two events. See, notably, Rehm, *Marriage to Death*, and Beer, *Sophocles*, 76.

54. Sophocles, *Antigone*, ll. 902–14.

55. On the controversy about these lines, see Beer, *Sophocles*, pp. 76–77; Nussbaum, *Fragility of Goodness*, pp. 64–65; Honig, "Antigone's Laments," pp. 15–17; and Karl Reinhardt, *Sophocles*, trans. Hazel Harvey and David Harvey, intro. Hugh Lloyd-Jones (Oxford: Basil Blackwell, 1979), p. 83.

56. See Steiner, *Antigones*, pp. 49–50.

57. Sophocles, *Oedipus at Colonus*, l. 1698.

58. In *Antigone, Hors-la-loi*, which played from January 17 to February 9 2007 at the Théâtre de la Commune in Paris, Anne Théron imagined an Antigone who chooses to kill herself rather than transmit a familial miasma to another generation.

59. Lacan, *Ethics*, pp. 255–56.

6. MOURNING, LONGING, LOVING

1. Derrida, for one, has questioned the possibility of such coherence among Plato's writings by describing the interference, in any such system, of an undecidable remnant. For Derrida, the coherence of the Platonic corpus is undermined by its own form of *pharmakos*, a corpse-like remainder that resists both inclusion and exclusion from the overall system: "This resistance was especially interesting to me at the point where it limits the possibility of a system or of a corpus, of the complete, controllable, and formalizable self-identity of a set, whether that set be a system, the body of works (*oeuvre*) of Plato (as would be determined by a unifiable meaning [*vouloir dire*]), the Greek language, or Greek society (and very concretely it is also an issue of the place—*including exclusion*, if I may put it that way—of the *pharmakos* in that society) and, therefore, the Greek identity in general" ("Nous autres Grecs," pp. 261–62). What Derrida calls a unifying "vouloir dire" ("meaning") in Plato, I would call "vouloir lire"— a desire on the reader's part to find a comprehensible and coherent body of work.

2. Vernant, "L'individu dans la cité," in *Individu*, p. 229.

3. See, for example, Plato, *Republic* 548c, 550b, and 581a–d.

4. Ibid., 439e–440a, in *Collected Dialogues*, p. 682.

5. See ibid., 441d–442b, p. 684.

6. Ibid., 358 d and 369a, pp. 606 and 615.

7. Ibid., 441c, p. 683.

8. The one mention of allegory in Plato's works comes in book 2 of the *Republic*, where Socrates remarks that "the battles of the gods in Homer's verse are things that we must not admit into our city either wrought in allegory or without allegory. For the young are not able to distinguish what is and what is not allegory" (378d, p. 625). The relation of the state to the individual is, however, based on precisely such an inability.

9. Plato, *Republic*, 249d–257a, pp. 496–502.

10. Similarly, Victoria Wohl has argued that in Athenian political discourse of the fifth and fourth centuries B.C.E., "we find political fantasies that contradict or complicate the simple declarations of love of the good Athenian citizen. Within such fantasies, the despised and repudiated (tyrants, effeminates, whores) become objects of desire. Illicit modes of being (excess, passivity, slavishness) become indistinguishable from legitimate masculinity" (*Love among the Ruins*, p. 3). One example of this would be the desire that Creon used to gain power: "Thucydides and Aristophanes both represent this desire as perverted and sick, the insatiable and humiliating 'itch' of a *kinaidos*, a passion that will pollute political discourse, corrupt the relationship between demos and demagogue and, as it runs its violent course in pursuit of satisfaction, destroy the democracy. But this eros is not the ruination of democracy. It is democracy's very essence" (p. 123). I would argue, however, that in the political erotics of the abject I am discussing here, the difference *from* the abject is crucial to its desirability. Even if it is ineradicable from the structure of the city, it is necessarily fantasized as *other* to that city.

11. Marie Delcourt cites another tradition in which the importance of self-knowledge for solving the sphinx's riddle was even more explicit. According to this variant, "Oedipus would have guessed the answer without meaning to. He would have touched his forehead and the Sphinx would have believed that he was pointing to himself in answer to the question. Sure that she had been defeated, she would have asked no more and would have killed herself on the spot" (*Oedipe*, p. 144). That the hero would understand the answer to the riddle only through his victory makes of the encounter with the sphinx not only an account of the mastery of forces hostile to the state but also of the advent of self-knowledge. According to this variant, the birth of philosophical thought is simultaneous to and indissociable from the mythic conquest of the monster. According to Sophocles's version, however, philosophical knowledge would somehow precede the conquest of the city's monstrous enemy.

12. See Jean-Joseph Goux, *Oedipus Philosopher*, trans. Catherine Porter (Stanford: Stanford University Press, 1993), p. 150: "There is a familial relation between Socrates and Oedipus. They are both situated at that moment of de-projection that brings back to the subject what had originally been attributed to external reality or expected from the performance of rituals. The world is no longer laden with cryptophoric signs attesting to the multiple presence of gods, for it is in man himself and only in man that the basis of all significations can be found. It is this familial relation between Socrates and Oedipus that Hegel revealed so magisterially when he identified Oedipus's mythical answer to the Sphinx with the 'know thyself' that gave birth to philosophy in its Socratic origins."

13. Delcourt, *Oedipe*, pp. 108–9. This association with the dead was reinforced, according to Delcourt, by another curious aspect of the iconography associated with the monster, the column almost invariably shown supporting her. "One might wonder," Delcourt wrote, "if this does not result from that fact that an unornamented column was placed over tombs. It would have served as a seat for the *soul* that haunted the body's place of repose. If the painters seated the Sphinx on a column, it is probably because they still sensed in her a spirit of the dead" (p. 137).

14. Ibid., pp. 110–11. On the oppressive nightmares and noon-day demons, see also Vermeule, *Aspects of Death*, pp. 152–55.

15. Delcourt, *Oedipe*, p. 119.

16. Ibid., pp. 110–11.

17. For an analysis of the erotic iconography of the sphinx, see ibid., pp. 119–26, and Vermeule, *Aspects of Death*, pp. 171–75. For the mythical and folkloric material, see pp. 109–40.

18. I speculate that in the earlier, mythopoetic materials, the incest theme was linked to the gynophobia embodied by the sphinx through a fear of the destructive aspects of sexual desire. Although incest is an element in Homer's reference to Oedipus's mother, whom he calls Epikastē (*Odyssey* 11.271–80), Delcourt observes that "the ritual core of the myth seems to me to be *a joust for the right to exercise power*" (*Oedipe*, p. 102), and she argues that this emphasis on the father-son rivalry continues even in *Oedipus Rex*, so that "the entire play is oriented around the idea of parricide. The incest is discovered only incidentally and, religiously speaking, it plays no role in the drama" (p. 73). Still, according to Delcourt, in the mythopoetic source material for Sophocles's version, "the *marriage with the princess* and the *union with the mother* are two separate themes which are brought together nowhere beside the story of Oedipus, whose peculiar tone and painful epilogue derive from their conjuncture" (p. 153). Even if the incest theme is subordinated to the father-son rivalry, it nonetheless constitutes, for Delcourt, both the uniqueness of the Oedipus myth and the source of the misfortunes that characterize his offspring. As the overt sexuality of the

sphinx faded, its deeper significance remained in the persistence of the incest theme.

19. Delcourt, *Oedipe*, p. 117.

20. Ibid., p. 134. See also p. 119, where the sphinx is described as "seductive and capable of song." More recently, Piero Pucci has described the deconstructive aspects of polysemy in the sphinx's riddle—and in *Oedipus Rex* as a whole (see Pucci, "Reading the Riddles," esp. pp. 144–45). Following his reading, one could say that the games encoded in her riddle are a form of singing—in the sense that they open up unmasterable, nonreferential aspects of language.

21. Delcourt, *Oedipe*, p. 135.

22. Fränkel, *Early Greek Poetry and Philosophy*, p. 76.

23. R. Drew Griffith, "Corporality," pp. 232–33. Jan N. Bremmer argues the opposite, contending that the soul of the dead derives from the soul of the living ("Soul, Death and the Afterlife," p. 100), but his argument is based on a questionable analogy to the beliefs of the Siberian tribe of Mordvins. He seems, moreover, to contradict himself later by asserting, "We have already seen that in the course of Greek history the *psyche* becomes more and more the focus of the living person" (p. 101), which would suggest that the *psyche* was originally related to the *dead* person, as Fränkel argues.

24. Loraux, *Invention*, p. 106. As one other indicator of the change in status of the individual between the fifth and fourth centuries B.C.E., see Jean Roberts's analysis of the concept of justice in Aristotle's political writings. In contradistinction to Socrates's notion of justice as subordination to an impersonal state, according to Roberts, "the justice of a political structure has become, in Aristotle, a matter of fairness to individual citizens" ("Justice and the Polis," in *The Cambridge History of Greek and Roman Political Thought*, ed. Christopher Rowe and Malcolm Schofield [Cambridge, U.K.: Cambridge University Press, 2000], pp. 364–65).

25. See Humphreys, *Family, Women, and Death*, pp. 108, 119. J. M. Bremer has argued that the use of grave poems in this period represents a higher level of individuation and intimacy than before in funeral practices ("Death and Immortality," p. 112). It has been suggested that some of the fifth-century *lēkythoi* came from private funerals, but more recent archaeological findings refute that thesis (see Oakley, *Picturing Death*, p. 215). For a general history of grave stelae in classical Greece, see Kurtz and Boardman, *Greek Burial Customs*, pp. 121–41.

26. Scholars frequently remark on this difficulty. See Humphreys, *Family, Women, and Death*, 106; Kurtz and Boardman, *Greek Burial Customs*, pp. 104–5, 139; Pomeroy, *Families in Classical and Hellenistic Greece*, 128; and Rehm, *Marriage to Death*, p. 28.

27. See Kurtz and Boardman, *Greek Burial Customs*, p. 137.

28. There are other stelai that closely resemble the one shown in figure 1. See, for example, the memorial to Mnesagora and her brother Nikochares, shown in Garland, *Greek Way of Death*, p. 85; GR 1894.6-16.1 (Cat. Sculpture 2232) in the British Museum; and Olga Hirsch-Dyczek, *Les représentations des enfants sur les stèles funéraires attiques* (Warsaw: Nakladem Uniwersytetu Jagiellonskiego, 1983). Marilyn Katz of Wesleyan University has graciously helped me with information about funerary stelai and the representation of women in them.

29. In the case of those who drowned at sea, the Greeks tried to palliate this loss of a loss by burying the dead person's clothes in place of their body (see R. Drew Griffith, "Corporality," p. 241).

30. As Michel Foucault has observed, the significance of the married couple changed radically between the fourth century Athens of Xenophon and the first century c.e. Rome of Pliny and Plutarch. Foucault explicitly rejects the possibility that the conception of marriage in Xenophon, Plato, and Isocrates could be considered "the first outlines of an ethics of reciprocal conjugal fidelity" (*The Use of Pleasure*, vol. 2 of *The History of Sexuality*, trans. Robert Hurley [New York: Pantheon Books, 1985], p. 181). By the time of Pliny, however, documents show significant evidence of just such an ethic, and "they reveal, albeit in fragments, the outlines of a 'strong model' of conjugal existence. In this model, the relationship to the other that appears as the most fundamental of all is neither the blood relationship nor that of friendship; it is the relationship between a man and a woman when it is organized in the institutional form of marriage and in the common life that is superimposed on the latter. . . . The art of conjugality is an integral part of the cultivation of the self" (*The Care of the Self*, vol. 3 of *The History of Sexuality*, trans. Robert Hurley [New York: Vintage Books, 1988], p. 163). Ovid, who died some thirty-two years before Plutarch was born, would clearly belong more closely to the new Roman tradition of marriage than to that of the Greeks who provided the source material for his *Metamorphoses*. The idea that an art of conjugality would be integral to the care of one's self would, undoubtedly, have been entirely foreign, if not incomprehensible to the earlier Greeks. Certainly, the extant Greek versions of the myth bear little or no trace of the powerful love that will become the defining principle of Ovid's retelling. Instead, the schematic account in Apollodorus, for example, emphasizes a fatal hubris: "Alcyone was married by Ceyx, son of Lucifer. These perished by reason of their pride; for he said that his wife was Hera, and she said that her husband was Zeus. But Zeus turned them into birds; her he made a kingfisher (alcyon) and him a gannet (ceyx)" (1.7.4, in *Library and Epitome*, vol. 1, trans. Sir James George Frazier [Cambridge, Mass.: Harvard University Press, 1921], 58). The scholiast on Aristophanes's *Birds* 250 gives a similar version of the story (see Douwe Holwerda, ed., *Scholia*

in Aristophanem, part 2, sec. 3 [Groningen: Egbert Forsten, 1991], pp. 44–45). Still, the idea that one's identity might derive from affective bonds with others was not foreign to the ancient Greeks—it is present in *Antigone* and *Oedipus at Colonus*, and it is so strong in Plato that the care of the immortal, impersonal self must be purchased through the violent rejection of sociability and friendship, as when in *Phaedo* 116e–117a Socrates refuses a final dinner with his intimates and turns instead to face his death. Ovid, in short, is continuing an argument against the rejection of life that had previously been hidden, in condensed form, in the figure of the corpse. His version of the Alcyone myth reworks it to subordinate the meaning of death (and any death-based identity) to the love between spouses, but the more general principle that the significance of death derives from affective relations among the living is already present in the drowned body that moves through his retelling of the myth. His version, in this respect, is as much a commentary on the meaning of the corpse as it is on that of the married couple; in fact, it can be understood as the application of a new social/affective order to an old story in order to explain the persistent pathos of the dead body.

31. Ovid, *Metamorphoses*, 11.657–62, trans. Rolfe Humphries (Bloomington: Indiana University Press, 1964), p. 279. Since the translation, though powerful, is somewhat loose, it is worth considering a few of the complexities of the original Latin. In Alcyone's dream, the god Morpheus appears "in faciem Ceycis . . . exanimi similis," or "in Ceyx's form . . . like to a dead man." He then leans over her bed and asks: "Agnoscis Ceyca, miserrima coniunx? / an mea mutata est facies nece? respice: nosces / inveniesque tuo pro coniuge coniugis umbram! / nil opis, Alcyone, nobis tua vota tulerunt! / occidimus!" (11.658–62 in *Metamorphoses*, vol. 2, trans. Frank Justus Miller [New York: G. P. Putnam's Sons, 1916], p. 166). "Agnosco" differs from the similar verb "nosco" in that it indicates a lived familiarity with the object of knowledge. When Ceyx's likeness asks whether his wife recognizes him, he does so, therefore, on the grounds of a shared history that is implicit in the verb itself. His question is not "can you identify me," but something closer to "do you know me?" He explicitly tells Alcyone, moreover, that her gestures of aid toward him have become futile. The verb that is at the crux of this parable, "occidimus," is more complicated than Humphries's—essentially accurate—translation of "I am dead" would suggest. "Occido" means to perish, and it is here given in the perfect and the first person plural. Ceyx would seem to be saying, "We have perished," but Ovid uses the perfect of the verb occido elsewhere to indicate a simple past (see *Metamorphoses* 10.10).

32. Cf. Andrzej Warminski's analysis of the proposition "I die" in "Dreadful Reading: Blanchot on Hegel" (in *Readings in Interpretation: Hölderlin, Hegel, Heidegger* [Minneapolis: University of Minnesota Press, 1987], pp. 189–91). Warminski argues that the statement can be accurate only in the impersonality

of writing but that it expresses the general relation between subject and text. This would seem to make of writing a form of the corpse, something that I will argue below.

33. "Corpus tamen esse liquebat,/qui foret, ignorans, quia naufragus, omine mota est/et, tamquam ignoto lacrimam daret, 'heu! miser' inquit/'quisquis es, et siqua est coniunx tibi!'" *Metamorphoses*, xi, ll. 720–23 (ed. Hugo Magnus). Trans. Rolfe Humphries, p. 281.

34. See Derrida, "Nous autres Grecs," p. 260.

7. EXIT TRAGEDY

1. Mills, "Hegel's *Antigone*," pp. 262–64, details some of the inconsistencies and paradoxes that ensue from this transposition of Sophocles's drama into a Christian context.

2. Hegel, *Phenomenology*, p. 270.

3. Hegel, *Philosophy of Religion*, 2:665.

4. "Love, the ethical moment in marriage, is by its very nature a feeling for actual living individuals, not for an abstraction" (*Philosophy of Right*, p. 122).

5. Hegel, *Phenomenology*, p. 288.

6. See Mills, "Hegel's *Antigone*," pp. 261–65.

7. See §§368–69 and their *Zusätze* (additional commentary taken from notes to Hegel's lectures) in *Hegel's Philosophy of Nature*, vol. 2 of *Encyclopedia of the Philosophical Sciences*, trans. A. V. Miller (Oxford: Oxford University Press, 1970), pp. 411–14. Among Hegel scholars, however, *The Philosophy of Nature* enjoys nowhere near the same importance as the *Phenomenology*.

8. See Chanter, *Ethics of Eros*, pp. 1–12.

9. Mills, "Hegel's *Antigone*," p. 244.

10. Hegel, *Phenomenology*, p. 19.

11. Irigaray, *Speculum*, p. 225 (trans. modified). Kelly Oliver picks up on the general structure of Irigaray's argument about the role of woman in Hegel's larger project and her image, in particular, of bloodless phantoms.

12. "This would be the final meaning of the obedience required of woman. She is merely the passage that serves to transform the inessential whims of a still sensible and material nature into universal will" (ibid., p. 225). Woman is, moreover, "that substance common to all, repressed, unconscious, and dumb" (p. 225).

13. "In this process some substance is lost: blood in its constitution of a living, autonomous subjectivity" (ibid., p. 222).

14. Ibid., p. 224 (trans. modified).

15. Luce Irigaray, *Sexes et parentés* (Paris: Minuit, 1987), p. 154. Translated by Lisa Walsh in "Her Mother Her Self: The Ethics of the Antigone Family Romance," *Hypatia* 14, no. 3 (1999): 116.

16. Walsh, "Her Mother Her Self," p. 116.

17. Ibid. (quoting Irigaray, *Sexes et parentés*, p. 291).

18. Irigaray, *Sexes et parentés*, p. 159. Quoted and translated by Walsh, "Her Mother Her Self," p. 117.

19. Walsh, "Her Mother Her Self," pp. 119–20.

20. "It is in any case true that Hegel nowhere appears to me to be weaker than he is in the sphere of poetics, and this is especially true of what he has to say about *Antigone*" (Lacan, *Ethics*, p. 249).

21. For a fuller discussion of the Lacanian symbolic as the "cancellation" of what it signifies, see Strauss, *Subjects of Terror*, pp. 259–65.

22. "Antigone takes right to the limit the fulfillment of what one could call pure desire, the pure and simple desire for death as such. She embodies this desire" (Lacan, *Ethics*, p. 282, trans. modified). See also page 248 ("The central third of the play consists in the detailed apophany given us of the significance of the position, or the fate, of a life that will blend with certain death, with a death lived in an anticipatory manner, a death that oversteps onto the domain of life, a life that steps over into death" [trans. modified]); page 268 ("After Antigone's song . . . the chorus returns to the mythological song, in which it successively shows three particularly dramatic destinies, all orchestrated at that limit of life and death, of the still animate cadaver" [trans. modified]), and page 317 ("If there is a distinguishing characteristic to everything we ascribe to Sophocles, with the exception of *Oedipus Rex*, it is that for all his heroes the race is run. They are at a limit that is not accounted for by their solitude relative to others. There is something more; they are characters who find themselves right away in a limit zone, find themselves between life and death. The theme of between-life-and-death is moreover formulated as such in the text, but it is also manifest in the situations").

23. Lacan, *Ethics*, p. 281 (trans. modified).

24. See also: "Antigone appears as *autónomos*, as the pure and simple relation between the human being and that which he finds himself miraculously to be the bearer of, i.e. the signifying split [*coupure signifiante*], which confers upon him the indomitable power to be, in face and in defiance of all, what he is" (ibid., p. 282, trans. modified).

25. Ibid., p. 279.

26. Ibid., p. 179 (trans. modified).

27. Ibid., p. 278 (trans. modified).

28. "A concept that moreover represents the disqualification of all concepts, that is, the concept of *ex nihilo*" (ibid., p. 262).

29. Lacan's approach to character is similar to the one Hegel advances in his reading of *Antigone* in the *Phenomenology*: "The [individual] ethical consciousness, because it is *decisively* for one of the two powers, is essentially character"

(*Phenomenology*, 280). Character, for Hegel, is opposed to essence and as such must be superseded.

30. Lacan, *Ethics*, p. 283.

31. Ibid., pp. 262–63.

32. Ibid., p. 277 (trans. modified).

33. Ibid., pp. 282–83 (trans. modified).

34. Jacques Lacan, "Le désir de l'Autre," in *Le séminaire livre V: Les formations de l'inconscient* (Paris: Seuil, 1998), pp. 387–403, and "Pour une logique du fantasme," *Scilicet*, no. 2/3 (1970): 223–73.

35. J.-D. Nasio summarizes the relation between death and the desire of the Other in Lacan's theory of the phantasm, which is central to his understanding of sexual difference. The phantasm, he explains, is a protection against the desire of the other, but it protects by negating that other. "In summary," he writes, "the phantasm thus consists of a staging in which the Other is annihilated, in which it is a pure object at the mercy of the subject, abolished insofar as it speaks and negated insofar as it desires. In short, the phantasmatic structure stages the putting to death of the Other" (*Le fantasme: Le plaisir de lire Lacan* [Paris: Payot, 1992], p. 92). Conversely, when the self allows the phantasm to drop and recognizes the Other as a living being, the self itself is negated (see p. 81). This irreconciliation between two desires led Lacan to state, infamously, that there is "no such thing as a sexual relation" (see *Encore: Le séminaire livre XX* [Paris: Seuil (Essais), 1975], pp. 9–19, 58–60, and 67–82; "Radiophonie" in *Scilicet*, no. 2/3 [1970]: 65).

36. Nussbaum, *Fragility of Goodness*, pp. 51–84. According to Nussbaum, *Antigone* represents the move from two noncompossible, reductive (i.e., partial) notions of the ethical (on the one hand, Creon, for whom the only good is the state and, on the other, Antigone, for whom the only good is the family) to a conception of the ethical in which multiplicities and contradictions interfere with each other. This latter understanding of the ethical is represented by Haemon, the chorus, and Tiresias. Goodness is "fragile" in this sense. Cf. Beer, *Sophocles*, p. 75, and Meier, *Political Art of Greek Tragedy*, p. 201.

37. On Antigone's preference for the dead over the living, see Nussbaum, *Fragility of Goodness*, pp. 64–66. Nussbaum summarizes Antigone's ethical program in the following terms: "The safely dutiful human life requires, or is, life's annihilation" (p. 65).

38. Ibid., p. 81.

39. Sophocles, *Antigone*, ll. 568–69, trans. Lloyd-Jones, p. 57. Cf. Foley, *Female Acts*, p. 184.

40. On the densely complicated relations in the *epitaphioi logoi* between autochthony, gender, sexuality, and plowing see Loraux, *Né de la terre*, pp. 145–68, where a deconstructive reading of primary and secondary texts leads her to

conclude that "*it is the earth that imitates woman*, never the contrary" (p. 168). On the currency of Creon's metaphor in ancient Greece and especially its inclusion in the Athenian marriage contract, see ibid., p. 146, and Nussbaum, *Fragility of Goodness*, pp. 57–58. It appears, also, in Plato's *Timaeus*, 91c–d.

41. In a sustained analysis of the concept in Aristotle's works, Nussbaum has argued that the philosopher theorized a *philia* that values the other in his irreplaceable uniqueness as an end in himself (*Fragility of Goodness*, pp. 352–72). By emphasizing the importance of "living together," moreover, he seems to have premised his notion of friendship on that of life, so that *philia* would establish the value of a specific and *living* individual (see p. 358). *Antigone*, I am arguing, represents an attempt to reach such a living, mutual individuation. Unlike Aristotle's notion of *philia*, however, Sophocles gives a central role to sex difference and desire.

42. Nussbaum, *Fragility of Goodness*, p. 81.

43. Hegel, *Phenomenology*, p. 19. Piera Aulagnier describes in convincing terms how a couple constitute a language. She is describing the relation between a child's experience and the linguistic subject that represents and alienates that experience. The relation between the child's two parents instantiates the communality of language for the child, according to Aulagnier, but her paradigm can be applied to the subjects within the couple itself. Their relation, in other words, makes each of them a person in language—and therefore *meaningful*—but keeps them nonetheless embedded in the affectively charged idiolect that is their mutual invention. See Piera Aulagnier, *La violence de l'interprétation: Du pictogramme à l'énoncé* (Paris: Presses Universitaires de France, 1975), pp. 217–32.

APPENDIX B: TIMELINE OF RELEVANT EVENTS IN ANCIENT GREECE

1. Morris, *Burial and Ancient Society*, p. 111.
2. Vernant, *Individu*, p. 222.
3. Petrucci, *Writing the Dead*, p. 6.
4. Humphreys, *Family, Women, and Death*, p. 121.
5. Vernant, *Individu*, p. 219; Carcopino, *L'ostracisme athénien*, p. 17.
6. Morris, *Burial and Ancient Society*, pp. 100–101.
7. Garland, *Greek Way of Death*, p. 125; cf. Kurtz and Boardman, *Greek Burial Customs*, p. 79.
8. Kurtz and Boardman, *Greek Burial Customs*, pp. 89–90, 121–25.
9. Humphreys, *Family, Women, and Death*, p. 102.
10. Petrucci, *Writing the Dead*, pp. 11–12.
11. Loraux, *Invention*, pp. 288–89.
12. Petrucci, *Writing the Dead*, p. 12.

13. Vernant, *Individu*, pp. 219–20.
14. Loraux, *Invention*, p. 113.
15. Humphreys, *Family, Women, and Death*, p. 119.
16. Joubaud, *Corps humain*, pp. 262–63. Cf. Vernant, *Individu*, p. 221.
17. Vernant, *Individu*, p. 222.

Abraham, Nicolas, and Maria Torok. *The Shell and the Kernel: Renewals of Psychoanalysis*. Edited and translated by Nicholas Rand. Chicago: University of Chicago Press, 1994.

Aeschylus. *Aeschylus*. 2 vols. Edited by David Grene and Richmond Lattimore. Translated by David Grene, Richmond Lattimore, and S. G. Benardete. Chicago: University of Chicago Press, 1953–1956.

———. *Agamemnon, Libation-Bearers, Eumenides, Fragments*. Translated by Herbert Weir Smith. Loeb Classical Library 146. Cambridge, Mass.: Harvard University Press, 1926.

Agamben, Giorgio. *Homo Sacer: Sovereign Power and Bare Life*. Translated by Daniel Heller-Roazen. Stanford: Stanford University Press, 1998.

Alexiou, Margaret. *The Ritual Lament in Greek Tradition*. 1974. Revised by Dimitrios Yatromanolakis and Panagiotis Roilos. Cambridge, U.K.: Cambridge University Press, 2002.

Althusser, Louis. *Positions (1964–1975)*. Paris: Editions Sociales, 1976.

Antonaccio, Carla M. *An Archaeology of Ancestors: Tomb Cult and Hero Cult in Early Greece*. Lanham, Md.: Rowman and Littlefield, 1995.

Apollodorus. *Library and Epitome*. Vol. 1. Translated by Sir James George Frazier. Loeb Classical Library 121. Cambridge, Mass.: Harvard University Press, 1921.

Aristotle. *The Complete Works of Aristotle: The Revised Oxford Translation*. 2 vols. Edited by Jonathan Barnes. Princeton: Princeton University Press, 1984.

———. *Nicomachean Ethics*. Translated by Christopher Rowe. Oxford: Oxford University Press, 2002.

Aulagnier, Piera. *La violence de l'interprétation: Du pictogramme à l'énoncé*. Paris: Presses Universitaires de France, 1975.

Badiou, Alain. *Ethics: An Essay on the Understanding of Evil*. Translated by Peter Hallward. New York: Verso, 2001.

Bailly, Anatole. *Dictionnaire grec-français*. Paris: Hachette, 2000.

Basterra, Gabriela S. *Seductions of Fate: Tragic Subjectivity, Ethics, Politics*. New York: Palgrave Macmillan, 2004.

Beer, Josh. *Sophocles and the Tragedy of Athenian Democracy*. Westport, Conn.: Praeger, 2004.

Bernstein, Alan E. *The Formation of Hell: Death and Retribution in the Ancient and Early Christian Worlds*. Ithaca, N.Y.: Cornell University Press, 1993.

Bremer, Jan Maarten. "Death and Immortality in Some Greek Poems." In *Hidden Futures: Death and Immortality in Ancient Egypt, Anatolia, the Classical, Biblical and Arabic-Islamic World*, edited by J. M. Bremer, Th. P. J. van den Hout, and R. Peters, pp. 109–24. Amsterdam: Amsterdam University Press, 1994.

Bremer, Jan Maarten, Th. P. J. van den Hout, and R. Peters, eds. *Hidden Futures: Death and Immortality in Ancient Egypt, Anatolia, the Classical, Biblical and Arabic-Islamic World*. Amsterdam: Amsterdam University Press, 1994.

Bremmer, Jan N. "The Soul, Death and the Afterlife in Early and Classical Greece." In *Hidden Futures: Death and Immortality in Ancient Egypt, Anatolia, the Classical, Biblical and Arabic-Islamic World*, edited by J. M. Bremer, Th. P. J. van den Hout, and R. Peters, pp. 91–106. Amsterdam: Amsterdam University Press, 1994.

Brunschwig, Jacques. "Aristote et l'effet Perrichon." In *La Passion de la Raison: Hommage à Fernand Alquié*, edited by Jean-Luc Marion and Jean Deprun, pp. 361–77. Paris: Presses Universitaires de France, 1983.

Butler, Judith. *Antigone's Claim: Kinship between Life and Death*. New York: Columbia University Press, 2000.

Calame, Claude. "Performative Aspects of the Choral Voice in Greek Tragedy: Civic Identity in Performance." Translated by Robin Osborne. In *Performance Culture and Athenian Democracy*, edited by Simon Goldhill and Robin Osborne, pp. 125–53. Cambridge, U.K.: Cambridge University Press, 1999.

Canfora, Luciano. *Histoire de la littérature grecque d'Homère à Aristote*. Translated by Denise Fourgous. Paris: Editions Desjonquères, 1994.

Canterella, Eva. *Les peines de mort en Grèce et à Rome: Origines et fonctions des supplices capitaux dans l'Antiquité classique*. Translated by Nadine Gallet. Paris: Albin Michel, 2000.

Carcopino, Jérôme. *L'ostracisme athénien*. Paris: Presses Universitaires de France, 1954.

Chanter, Tina. *Ethics of Eros: Irigaray's Rewriting of the Philosophers*. New York: Routledge, 1995.

———. "Looking at Hegel's Antigone through Irigaray's Speculum." In *Between Ethics and Aesthetics: Crossing the Boundaries*, edited by Dorota Glowacka and Stephen Boos, pp. 29–48. Albany: State University of New York Press, 2002.

Cicero, Marcus Tullius. *Brutus, Orator*. Translated by G. L. Hendrickson and H. M. Hubbell. Loeb Classical Library 342. Cambridge, Mass.: Harvard University Press, 1939.

Delcourt, Marie. *Oedipe ou la légende du conquérant*. Paris: Droz, 1944.

Demosthenes. *Funeral Speech, Erotic Essay LX, LXI, Exordia and Letters*. Translated by Norman W. DeWitt and Norman J. DeWitt. Loeb Classical Library 374. Cambridge, Mass.: Harvard University Press, 1949.

Derrida, Jacques. "Chôra." In *Poikilia: Etudes offertes à Jean-Pierre Vernant*, edited by Marcel Detienne, Nicole Loraux, et al., pp. 265–96. Paris: Ecole des Hautes Etudes en Sciences Sociales, 1987.

———. *Dissemination*. Translated by Barbara Johnson. Chicago: University of Chicago Press, 1981.

———. "Fors: The Anglish Words of Nicolas Abraham and Maria Torok." Translated by Barbara Johnson. In *The Wolf Man's Magic Word: A Cryptonymy*, by Abraham and Torok, pp. xi–xlviii. Minneapolis: University of Minnesota Press, 1986.

———. *Glas*. Translated by John P. Leavey Jr. and Richard Rand. Lincoln: University of Nebraska Press, 1986.

———. "Nous autres Grecs." In *Nos Grecs et leurs modernes: Les stratégies contemporaines d'appropriation de l'antiquité*, edited by Barbara Cassin, pp. 251–76. Paris: Seuil, 1992.

Dherbey, Gilbert Romeyer. "L'âme est en quelque façon tous les êtres (Aristote, *De anima*, T 8, 431 *b* 21)." *Elenchos: Revista di studi sul pensiero antico* 8, no. 2 (1987): 364–80.

Dionysius of Halicarnassus. *Critical Essays*. 2 vols. Translated by Stephen Usher. Loeb Classical Library 465. Cambridge, Mass.: Harvard University Press, 1974.

Douglas, Mary. *Purity and Danger: An Analysis of the Concepts of Pollution and Taboo*. New York: Routledge, 1996.

Eckhart, Meister. *Meister Eckhart: The Essential Sermons, Commentaries, Treatises, and Defense*. Translated by Edmund Colledge and Bernard McGinn. New York: Paulist Press, 1981.

Edwards, Paul. "Existentialism and Death: A Survey of Some Confusions and Absurdities." In *Language, Metaphysics, and Death*, edited by John Donnelly, pp. 32–61. New York: Fordham University Press, 1978.

Euripides. *The Suppliant Women*. Translated by Frank Jones in *Euripides*, Vol. 4, edited by David Grene and Richmond Lattimore, pp. 55–104. Chicago: University of Chicago Press, 1958.

Farenga, Vincent. *Citizen and Self in Ancient Greece: Individuals Performing Justice and the Law*. Cambridge, U.K.: Cambridge University Press, 2006.

Ferrario, Sarah Brown. "Replaying *Antigone*: Changing Patterns of Public and Private Commemoration at Athens c. 440–350." *Helios* 33, supp. (2006): 79–117.

Foley, Helene P. *Female Acts in Greek Tragedy*. Princeton: Princeton University Press, 2001.

Foucault, Michel. *The Care of the Self*. Vol. 3 of *The History of Sexuality*. Translated by Robert Hurley. New York: Vintage Books, 1988.

———. *The Use of Pleasure*. Vol. 2 of *The History of Sexuality*. Translated by Robert Hurley. New York: Pantheon Books, 1985.

Fränkel, Hermann. *Early Greek Poetry and Philosophy: A History of Greek Epic, Lyric, and Prose to the Middle of the Fifth Century*. Translated by Moses Hadas and James Willis. New York: Harcourt Brace Jovanovich, 1973.

Freud, Sigmund. "The Uncanny." In *The Standard Edition of the Complete Psychological Writings of Sigmund Freud*, translated and edited by James Strachey and Anna Freud, 17:217–56. London: Hogarth Press, 1966.

Froriep, Siegfried. *Frühzeit der Städte: Entstehung und Entwicklung im Abendland bis zum Ende der Antike*. Frankfurt: R. G. Fischer, 1989.

Gagarin, Michael. *Writing Greek Law*. Cambridge, U.K.: Cambridge University Press, 2008.

Gagarin, Michael, and David Cohen, eds. *The Cambridge Companion to Ancient Greek Law*. Cambridge, U.K.: Cambridge University Press, 2005.

Garland, Robert. *The Greek Way of Death*. Ithaca, N.Y.: Cornell University Press, 1985.

Girard, René. *Le bouc émissaire*. Paris: Grasset, 1982.

Glotz, Gustave. *La solidarité de la famille et le droit criminel en Grèce*. Paris: A Fontemoing, 1904.

Goldhill, Simon. *Aeschylus: The Oresteia*. Cambridge, U.K.: Cambridge University Press, 1992.

———. "The Audience of Athenian Tragedy." In *The Cambridge Companion to Greek Tragedy*, edited by P. E. Easterling, pp. 54–68. Cambridge, U.K.: Cambridge University Press, 1997.

———. "The Failure of Exemplarity." In *Modern Critical Theory and Classical Literature*, edited by Irene J. F. De Jong and J. P. Sullivan, pp. 51–73. Leiden: E. J. Brill, 1994.

———. "Greek Drama and Political Theory." In *The Cambridge History of Greek and Roman Political Thought*, edited by Christopher Rowe and Malcolm Schofield, pp. 60–88. Cambridge, U.K.: Cambridge University Press, 2000.

———. *Language, Sexuality, Narrative: The* Oresteia. Cambridge, U.K.: Cambridge University Press, 1984.

———. "Modern Critical Approaches to Greek Tragedy." In *The Cambridge Companion to Greek Tragedy*, edited by P. E. Easterling, pp. 324–47. Cambridge, U.K.: Cambridge University Press, 1997.

————. *Reading Greek Tragedy*. Cambridge, U.K.: Cambridge University Press, 1986.

Goux, Jean-Joseph. *Oedipus Philosopher*. Translated by Catherine Porter. Stanford: Stanford University Press, 1993.

Griffith, Mark. "The Subject of Desire in Sophocles's *Antigone*." In *The Soul of Tragedy: Essays on Athenian Drama*, edited by Victoria Pedrick and Steven M. Oberhelman, pp. 91–135. Chicago: University of Chicago Press, 2005.

Griffith, R. Drew. "Corporality in the Ancient Greek Theater." *Phoenix* 52, no. 3–4 (1998): 230–56.

Guthrie, W. K. C. *The Fifth-Century Enlightenment*. Vol. 3 of *A History of Greek Philosophy*. Cambridge, U.K.: Cambridge University Press, 1969.

Hamacher, Werner. *Pleroma – Reading in Hegel*. Translated by Nicholas Walker and Simon Jarvis. Stanford: Stanford University Press, 1998.

Hegel, G. W. F. *Frühe Schriften*. In *Gesammelte Werke*, vol. 1, edited by Friedhelm Nicolin and Gisela Schüler. Hamburg: Felix Meiner, 1989.

————. *Hegel: The Letters*. Translated by Clark Butler and Christiane Seiler. Commentary by Clark Butler. Bloomington: Indiana University Press, 1984.

————. *Hegel and the Human Spirit: A Translation of the Jena Lectures on the Philosophy of Spirit (1805–6) with Commentary*. Edited and translated by Leo Rauch. Detroit: Wayne State University Press, 1983.

————. *Lectures on The Philosophy of Religion*. 3 vols. Edited by Peter C. Hodgson. Translated by R. F. Brown et al. Berkeley: University of California Press, 1984–1998.

————. *Hegel's Philosophy of Nature*. Vol. 2 of *Encyclopedia of the Philosophical Sciences*. Translated by A. V. Miller. Oxford: Oxford University Press, 1970.

————. *Phenomenology of Spirit*. Translated by A. V. Miller. Oxford: Oxford University Press, 1981.

————. *The Philosophy of History*. Translated by J. Sibree. 1899. New York: Cosimo Classics, 2007.

————. *Philosophy of Right*. Translated by T. M. Knox. Oxford: Oxford University Press, 1952.

Heidegger, Martin. *Being and Time*. Translated by John Macquarrie and Edward Robinson. New York: Harper and Row, 1962.

————. *Introduction to Metaphysics*. Translated by Gregory Fried and Richard Polt. New Haven: Yale University Press, 2000.

Hirsch-Dyczek, Olga. *Les représentations des enfants sur les stèles funéraires attiques*. Warsaw: Nakladem Uniwersytetu Jagiellonskiego, 1983.

Holst-Warhaft, Gail. *Dangerous Voices: Women's Laments and Greek Tragedy*. London: Routledge, 1992.

Holwerda, Douwe, ed. *Scholia in Aristophanem*. Part 2, sec. 3. Groningen: Egbert Forsten, 1991.

Honig, Bonnie. "Antigone's Laments, Creon's Grief: Mourning, Membership, and the Politics of Exception." *Political Theory* 37, no. 1 (2009): 5–43.

———. "Ismene's Forced Choice: Sacrifice and Sorority in Sophocles' *Antigone*." *Arethusa* 44, no. 1 (2011): 29–68.

Humphreys, S[arah]. C. *The Family, Women, and Death: Comparative Studies*. Ann Arbor: University of Michigan Press, 1993.

Hyppolite, Jean. *Genesis and Structure of Hegel's* Phenomenology of Spirit. Translated by Samuel Cherniak and John Heckman. Evanston, Ill.: Northwestern University Press, 1974.

Irigaray, Luce. *Sexes et parentés*. Paris: Minuit, 1987.

———. *Speculum of the Other Woman*. Translated by Gillian C. Gill. Ithaca, N.Y.: Cornell University Press, 1985.

Joubaud, Catherine. *Le corps humain dans la philosophie platonicienne: Etude à partir du "Timée."* Preface by Luc Brisson. Paris: J. Vrin, 1991.

Kaufmann, Walter. *Goethe, Kant, and Hegel*. Vol. 1 of *Discovering the Mind*. New Brunswick, N.J.: Transaction, 1991.

Kierkegaard, Søren. *Either/Or: A Fragment of Life*. 2 vols. Translated by David F. Swenson, Lillian Marvin Swenson, and Walter Lowrie. Princeton: Princeton University Press, 1944.

Kojève, Alexandre. *Introduction à la lecture de Hegel: Leçons sur la* Phénoménologie de l'esprit *professées de 1933 à 1939 à l'Ecole des Hautes Etudes*. Edited by Raymond Queneau. Paris: Gallimard, 1947.

Kristeva, Julia. *Polylogue*. Paris: Seuil, 1977.

———. *La révolution du langage poétique: L'avant-garde à la fin du XIXe siècle: Lautréamont et Mallarmé*. Paris: Seuil, 1974.

———. *Revolution in Poetic Language*. Translated by Margaret Waller. New York: Columbia University Press, 1984.

Kurtz, Donna C., and John Boardman. *Greek Burial Customs*. Ithaca, N.Y.: Cornell University Press, 1971.

Lacan, Jacques. *Encore: Le séminaire livre XX*. Paris: Seuil, 1975.

———. "Pour une logique du fantasme." *Scilicet*, no. 2/3 (1970): 223–73.

———. "Radiophonie." *Scilicet*, no. 2/3 (1970): 55–99.

———. *Le séminaire livre V: Les formations de l'inconscient*. Paris: Seuil, 1998.

———. *The Seminar of Jacques Lacan Book VII: The Ethics of Psychoanalysis 1959–1960*. Translated by Dennis Porter. New York: W. W. Norton, 1992.

Lane, Warren J., and Ann M. Lane. "The Politics of *Antigone*." In *Greek Tragedy and Political Theory*, edited by J. Peter Euben, 162–82. Berkeley: University of California Press, 1986.

Liddell, Henry George, and Robert Scott. *An Intermediate Greek-English Lexicon*. 1889. Oxford: Clarendon Press, 1978.

Lombroso, Cesare. *L'homme criminel, criminel-né, fou moral, épileptique: Etude anthropologique et médico-légale.* Translated by Regnier and Bournet. Paris: Félix Alcan, 1887.

Loraux, Nicole. *La cité divisée: L'oubli dans la mémoire d'Athènes.* Paris: Payot [Petite Bibliothèque], 1997.

———. *L'invention d'Athènes: Histoire de l'oraison funèbre dans la "cité classique."* Paris: Payot, 1981.

———. *The Invention of Athens: The Funeral Oration in the Classical City.* Translated by Alan Sheridan. New York: Zone Books, 2006.

———. *Né de la terre: Mythe et politique à Athènes.* Paris: Seuil, 1996.

Lukács, Georg. *The Theory of the Novel: A Historico-Philosophical Essay on the Forms of Great Epic Literature.* Translated by Anna Bostock. Cambridge, Mass.: MIT Press, 1971.

———. *The Young Hegel: Studies in the Relations between Dialectics and Economics.* Translated by Rodney Livingstone. Cambridge: MIT Press, 1976.

Lysias. *Lysias.* Translated by W. R. M. Lamb. 1930. Loeb Classical Library 244. Cambridge, Mass.: Harvard University Press, 1967.

MacDowell, Douglas. *The Law in Classical Athens.* Ithaca, N.Y.: Cornell University Press, 1986.

Marion, Jean-Luc. *Le phénomène érotique: Six méditations.* Paris: Bernard Grasset, 2003.

Meier, Christian. *The Political Art of Greek Tragedy.* Translated by Andrew Webber. Baltimore: Johns Hopkins University Press, 1993.

Merleau-Ponty, Maurice. *Phenomenology of Perception.* Translated by Colin Smith. London: Routledge and Kegan Paul, 1962.

Mills, Patricia Jagentowicz. "Hegel's *Antigone.*" In *The* Phenomenology of Spirit *Reader: Critical and Interpretive Essays*, edited by Jon Stewart, pp. 243–71. Albany: State University of New York Press, 1998.

Montaigne, Michel de. *Essais.* In *Oeuvres complètes*, edited by Albert Thibaudet and Maurice Rat, pp. 1–1097. Paris: Gallimard [Pléiade], 1962.

Morris, Ian. *Burial and Ancient Society: The Rise of the Greek City-State.* Cambridge, U.K.: Cambridge University Press, 1987.

Mudde, Anna. "Risky Subjectivity: Antigone, Action, and Universal Trespass." *Human Studies* 32, no. 2 (2009): 183–200.

Nancy, Jean-Luc. *Hegel: The Restlessness of the Negative.* Translated by Jason Smith and Steven Miller. Minneapolis: University of Minnesota Press, 2002.

Nasio, J.-D. *Le fantasme: Le plaisir de lire Lacan.* Paris: Payot, 1992.

Nussbaum, Martha C. *The Fragility of Goodness: Luck and Ethics in Greek Tragedy and Philosophy.* 1986. Cambridge, U.K.: Cambridge University Press, 2001.

Oakley, John H. *Picturing Death in Classical Athens: The Evidence of the White Lekythoi.* Cambridge, U.K.: Cambridge University Press, 2004.

Oliver, Kelly. "Antigone's Ghost: Undoing Hegel's Phenomenology of Spirit." Family and Feminist Theory, *Hypatia* 11, no. 1 (1996): 67–90.

Ovid. *Metamorphoses*. Translated by Rolfe Humphries. Bloomington: Indiana University Press, 1964.

———. *Metamorphoses*. 2 vols. Translated by Frank Justus Miller. New York: G. P. Putnam's Sons, 1916.

Petrovic, Ivana. "Die Bedeutung des Verses 523 in der 'Antigone' des Sophokles Outoi sunekhthein, alla sunphilein ephun: Ein neuer Deutungsversuch." *Acta Antiqua Academiae scientarium Hungaricae* 41, no. 1 2–3 (2001): 359–62.

Petrucci, Armando. *Writing the Dead: Death and Writing Strategies in the Western Tradition*. Translated by Michael Sullivan. Stanford: Stanford University Press, 1998.

Plato. *Alcibiades* 1. In *Plato*, translated by W. R. M. Lamb, 8:93–223. 1927. Loeb Classical Library 201. Cambridge, Mass.: Harvard University Press, 1955.

———. *The Collected Dialogues of Plato*. Edited by Edith Hamilton and Huntington Cairns. Translated by Lane Cooper et al. Princeton: Princeton University Press, 1961.

———. *Timaeus, Critias, Cleitophon, Menexenus, Epistles*. Translated by R. G. Bury. 1929. Loeb Classical Library 234. Cambridge, Mass.: Harvard University Press, 1989.

Plutarch. *Plutarch's Lives*. 11 vols. Translated by Bernadotte Perrin. 1914. Loeb Classical Library 47, 65, 80. Cambridge, Mass.: Harvard University Press, 1967.

Pomeroy, Sarah B. *Families in Classical and Hellenistic Greece: Representations and Realities*. Oxford: Clarendon Press, 1997.

Poortman, Bartel. "Death and Immortality in Greek Philosophy: From the Presocratics to the Hellenistic Era." In *Hidden Futures: Death and Immortality in Ancient Egypt, Anatolia, the Classical, Biblical and Arabic-Islamic World*, edited by J. M. Bremer, Th. P. J. van den Hout, and R. Peters, pp. 197–220. Amsterdam: Amsterdam University Press, 1994.

Pucci, Piero. "Reading the Riddles of *Oedipus Rex*." In *Language and the Tragic Hero: Essays on Greek Tragedy in Honor of Gordon M. Kirkwood*, edited by Pietro Pucci, pp. 131–34. Atlanta: Scholars Press, 1988.

Redfield, James. "Le sentiment homérique du Moi." *Les Usages de la nature: Le genre humain* 12 (1985): 93–111.

Rehm, Rush. *Marriage to Death: The Conflation of Wedding and Funeral Rituals in Greek Tragedy*. Princeton: Princeton University Press, 1994.

Reinhardt, Karl. *Sophocles*. Translated by Hazel Harvey and David Harvey. Introduction by Hugh Lloyd-Jones. Oxford: Basil Blackwell, 1979.

Roberts, Jean. "Justice and the Polis." In *The Cambridge History of Greek and Roman Political Thought*, edited by Christopher Rowe and Malcolm Schofield, pp. 344–65. Cambridge, U.K.: Cambridge University Press, 2000.

Rose, Gillian. *Mourning Becomes the Law: Philosophy and Representation*. Cambridge, U.K.: Cambridge University Press, 1996.

Sartre, Jean-Paul. *Being and Nothingness: An Essay on Phenomenological Ontology*. Translated by Hazel E. Barnes. New York: Philosophical Library, 1956.

Saunders, Trevor J. *Plato's Penal Code: Tradition, Controversy, and Reform in Greek Penology*. Oxford: Clarendon Press, 1991.

Scarry, Elaine. *The Body in Pain: The Making and Unmaking of the World*. Oxford: Oxford University Press, 1985.

Schiller, Friedrich. *On the Sublime*. Translated by Julius A. Elias. New York: Frederick Ungar, 1966.

Serres, Michel. *Le Parasite*. Paris: Grasset, 1980.

———. *The Parasite*. Translated by Lawrence Schehr. Minneapolis: University of Minnesota Press, 1982.

Snell, Bruno. *The Discovery of Mind: The Greek Origins of European Thought*. Translated by T. G. Rosenmeyer. Oxford: Blackwell, 1953.

Sophocles. *Antigone, The Women of Trachis, Philoctetes, Oedipus at Colonus*. Edited and translated by Hugh Lloyd-Jones. Cambridge, Mass.: Harvard University Press, 1994.

Stallybrass, Peter, and Allon White. *The Politics and Poetics of Transgression*. Ithaca, N.Y.: Cornell University Press, 1986.

Steiner, George. *Antigones*. Oxford: Oxford University Press, 1984.

Strauss, Jonathan. "After Death." In "Post-Mortem: The State of Death as a Modern Construct," special issue, *Diacritics* 30, no. 3 (2000): 90–104.

———. *Subjects of Terror: Nerval, Hegel, and the Modern Self*. Stanford: Stanford University Press, 1998.

Taxidou, Olga. *Tragedy, Modernity and Mourning*. Edinburgh: Edinburgh University Press, 2004.

Taylor, Charles. *Hegel*. Cambridge, U.K.: Cambridge University Press, 1975.

Vermeule, Emily. *Aspects of Death in Early Greek Art and Poetry*. Berkeley: University of California Press, 1979.

Vernant, Jean-Pierre. "Ambiguïté et renversement, sur la structure énigmatique d'Oedipe-Roi." In *Echanges et communications: Mélanges offerts à Claude Lévi-Strauss*, edited by Jean Pouillon and Pierre Maranda, 2:1253–79. The Hague: Mouton, 1970.

———. *L'individu, la mort, l'amour: Soi-même et l'autre en Grèce ancienne*. Paris: Gallimard, 1989.

Vernant, Jean-Pierre, and Pierre Vidal-Naquet. *Myth and Tragedy in Ancient Greece*. Translated by Janet Lloyd. New York: Zone Books, 1990.

Walsh, Lisa. "Her Mother Her Self: The Ethics of the Antigone Family Romance." *Hypatia* 14, no. 3 (1999): 96–125.

Warminski, Andrzej. *Readings in Interpretation: Hölderlin, Hegel, Heidegger.* Minneapolis: University of Minnesota Press, 1987.

Wohl, Victoria. *Love among the Ruins: The Erotics of Democracy in Classical Athens.* Princeton: Princeton University Press, 2002.

Young, R. S. "Sepulturae intra urbem." *Hesperia* 20, no. 2 (1951): 67–134.